Profiles of
Great Black
Americans

❦

PROFILES OF GREAT BLACK AMERICANS

❦

Edited by Richard Rennert

Introduction by Coretta Scott King

The Varsity Company
P.O. Box 14100
Nashville, TN 37214

Published by Thomas Nelson, Inc., Nashville, TN
37214

Printed and bound in the United States of America.

1 2 3 4 5 — 97 96 95

ISBN   0-7852-7967-9

CONTENTS

PIONEERS OF DISCOVERY

FEMALE WRITERS

MALE WRITERS

JAZZ STARS

PERFORMING ARTISTS

SPORTS HEROES

❧ INTRODUCTION ❧

by Coretta Scott King

This book is about black Americans who served society through the excellence of their achievements. It forms a part of the rich history of black men and women in America—a history of stunning accomplishments in every field of human endeavor, from literature and art to science, industry, education, diplomacy, athletics, jurisprudence, even polar exploration.

Not all of the people in this history had the same ideals, but I think you will find something that all of them had in common. Like Martin Luther King, Jr., they all decided to become "drum majors" and serve humanity. In that principle—whether it was expressed in books, inventions, or song—they found something outside themselves to use as a goal and a guide. Something that showed them a way to serve others instead of only living for themselves.

Reading the stories of these courageous men and women not only helps us discover the principles that we will use to guide our own lives but also teaches us about our black heritage and about America itself. It is crucial for us to know the heroes and heroines of our history and to realize that the price we paid in our struggle for equality in America was dear. But we must also understand that we have gotten as far as we have partly because America's democratic system and ideals made it possible.

We are still struggling with racism and prejudice. But the great men and women in this series are a tribute to the spirit of our democratic ideals and the system in which they have flourished. And that makes their stories special and worth knowing.

SHAPERS OF AMERICA

RICHARD ALLEN

Religious leader and social activist Richard Allen was born into slavery on February 14, 1760, in Philadelphia. His master was Benjamin Chew, a lawyer in what was then the colony of Pennsylvania. Allen, his siblings, and his parents were household slaves who took care of the home, did kitchen work, and helped look after Chew's children.

When Allen was seven, Chew sold the entire Allen family to a farmer named Stokeley who lived in Delaware. The Allens became farmhands and spent long hours toiling in the fields. After a decade, Stokeley sold Allen's mother and three of her children, and Allen never saw them again.

Not long after the sale, Allen came upon a Methodist revival meeting in the woods near his master's home. The minister convinced Allen to see himself not as a lowly slave but as a human being who was loved by God. Allen promptly became a Methodist, and at the gatherings in the woods he often heard the institution of slavery being denounced.

One day, after his older brother and sister joined him in converting to Christianity, the teenaged Allen asked his master if Methodist preachers could visit the farm. Stokeley said yes, and several preachers began making the farm a regular stop in their travels. One of them was the Reverend Freeborn Garrettson, a former slaveholder who had become a tireless opponent of slavery. After hearing the reverend argue that slavery was a terrible sin, Stokeley decided to free his slaves.

Stokeley could not afford to release his slaves at once, so he let them buy their freedom. Allen managed to put aside some money by taking on odd jobs. Finally, when he was 20 years old, he handed Stokeley the agreed-upon sum and obtained his liberty.

Allen became an itinerant laborer in rural Pennsylvania and also began to preach. His reputation as a powerful speaker spread quickly, and several leading

Methodist evangelists soon invited him to travel with them.

In 1784, Methodism established itself as a separate denomination, the Methodist Episcopal church. Rigorous preaching, along with a spontaneous, joyous worship service, was at the heart of Methodism, and Allen believed that the combination made the Methodist church a more suitable Christian denomination for blacks than any other.

In early 1786, Allen began preaching at St. George's Methodist Episcopal Church in Philadelphia, a city where two-thirds of the blacks were free. His sermons attracted many converts; but as the number of black churchgoers rose, the white church leaders forced them to stand at the back and sides. Allen and several colleagues tried to form a separate black parish, but they were denied official permission. In response, he helped found the Free African Society, a charitable organization to address the needs of the local black community.

Meanwhile, a new seating gallery was constructed at St. George's. In November 1787, Allen and the other black parishioners went to worship for the first time in the renovated church and sat in the upstairs gallery. While they were praying, a church official told them that blacks were not allowed in the gallery. Outraged, Allen and the others stormed out of the church, vowing never to return.

For a while, the Free African Society served as a gathering place for the displaced black Methodists. But the society soon became affiliated with the Protestant Episcopal church, and many black Methodists, including Allen, did not want to abandon their denomination.

In 1793, in the midst of the struggle to establish a black Methodist church, a severe epidemic of yellow fever broke out in Philadelphia. Allen and a longtime associate, Absalom Jones, who had cofounded the Free African Society, were asked by the city's mayor to help combat the epidemic. Both men organized their black followers to minister to the sick and dying, and were commended for their efforts by the mayor and other government officials.

The following year, a black Methodist church in Philadelphia was finally established. On July 29, 1794, Allen was among the small group that gathered in a converted blacksmith shop on Lombard Street, in the heart of the city's black community, for the dedication of a new church, named Bethel.

The church's focus was to "build each other up," with Allen handling most of the pastoral responsibilities. In 1799, he became the first black to be ordained a deacon in the Methodist church. All the while, he remained eager to have Bethel be recognized as a new denomination.

In 1800, Allen married Sarah, a former slave, with whom he had six children. Now the responsibility of raising a family was added to his obligations of pastoring his flock at Bethel and earning a living as a shoemaker. But for the 40-year-old Allen, nothing was more important than lifting up his race and helping blacks gain their freedom. When a St. George's elder attempted to gain control of Bethel in 1805, Allen had his congregation pass a set of amendments, known as the African Supplement, that gave control of the church to Bethel's trustees.

Finally, in 1816, after much jockeying with St. George's for control over Bethel, the Pennsylvania Supreme Court declared that because Bethel was run by and for the black community, it should be independent. With that, Allen decided that the time had arrived for Bethel to join forces with similar black Methodist churches. On April 9, 1816, at an organizing conference at Bethel, the African Methodist Episcopal (AME) church was officially born. Allen was consecrated as the church's first bishop, thereby becoming the first black bishop in U.S. history. Moral reform, expansion of membership, and political activism to promote the civil rights of blacks became his three stated goals.

Allen promptly injected the AME church in a crisis that was affecting the black community. The American Colonization Society (ACS), an organization that sought to solve the nation's race relations problem by encouraging the return of the United States' free black population to Africa, had recently been formed. In January 1817, Allen convened a protest meeting of more than 3,000 blacks at Bethel. "Whereas our ancestors (not of choice) were the first successful cultivators of the wilds of America," the delegates declared, "we their descendants feel ourselves entitled to participate in the blessings of her soil, which their blood and sweat manured." Thus began Allen's lengthy battle with the ACS.

Among the people who fought alongside Allen were John Russwurm and Samuel Cornish, who founded

Freedom's Journal, the first newspaper in America to be owned and published by blacks. Allen contributed a number of articles to the paper, calling for the abolition of slavery and attacking the ACS's colonization efforts. *Freedom's Journal*, in turn, helped publicize the activities of the AME church among the nation's black population.

In 1819, Congress granted a large sum of money to the ACS to build a settlement on Africa's west coast. Three years later, the first black American settlers crossed the Atlantic and established the West African colony of Liberia. Allen remained an outspoken opponent of the ACS, however, and by 1830 fewer than 2,000 people were lured into sailing for Africa.

And so Allen molded the AME church into a political force. He added to its clout by establishing branches in Massachusetts, New York, Ohio, western Pennsylvania, and South Carolina. America's black communities needed a mouthpiece for making their views known to the world, and the AME church provided it.

In 1830, Allen invited black community leaders across the country to come to Bethel for the first national convention of black Americans. The gathering took place on the night of September 15, with 40 persons from seven states in attendance. Travel restrictions on free blacks kept the number of attendees on the low side. Nevertheless, they organized a national network of black support and cooperation, calling their association the American Society of Free Persons of Colour.

Allen, who was elected the society's president, worked tirelessly on behalf of the new association, urging blacks to become more politically and economically organized and to step up the fight against slavery. Later in 1830, he formed the Free Produce Society and its affiliate, the Free Cotton Society, in an effort to strike a blow against the South's slave economy. Members of these two groups pledged to buy only goods made and raised by nonslaveholders.

Allen's efforts to serve his people were cut short by illness, and on March 26, 1831, he died at his Philadelphia home at the age of 71. Today, Bethel Church still stands in Philadelphia, the mother church of African Methodism and a memorial to Richard Allen's dedication to the cause of black Americans.

MARY MCLEOD BETHUNE

An inspirational educator and adviser to America's leaders, Mary McLeod Bethune was born Mary Jane McLeod in Mayesville, South Carolina, on July 10, 1875. She was the 15th of 17 children born to Samuel and Patsy McIntosh McLeod, who were former slaves. Most of the McLeod children had been sold into slavery on nearby plantations, but the entire family was reunited shortly after the Civil War ended in 1865.

Handed their freedom, the McLeods built their own cabin on a piece of land near Mayesville, and Mary was born and raised there. From an early age, she was expected to work all day in the cotton fields with the rest of the family, then do chores back at the cabin. At the time, there were few schools for blacks in the South; many southerners opposed educating blacks because they wanted them to remain subservient to whites.

But in 1882, Emma Wilson, a black educator, founded a mission school for black children in Mayesville, five miles away from Mary's home. The youngster walked to the school each day to study reading, writing, arithmetic, and the Bible. She graduated in 1886, and a year later Wilson offered her a scholarship to Scotia Seminary (now Barber-Scotia College), a school for black women in Concord, North Carolina.

The blacks and whites who made up Scotia's faculty provided Mary with her first example of interracial cooperation. She trained to become a teacher and, she hoped, a missionary in Africa. When she graduated from Scotia in 1894, she applied for admission to the Moody Bible Institute in Chicago, which trained missionaries. Moody awarded her a scholarship, and that summer 19-year-old Mary McLeod moved to Chicago to begin her Bible studies as the school's only black student. In her free time, she visited prisoners at police stations, went to the slums and offered counseling to the needy, and traveled in the Midwest with Moody students to establish Sunday schools.

After graduating from Moody, McLeod learned that there were no openings in Africa for black missionaries. So she returned to Mayesville, became

Emma Wilson's teaching assistant, and was hired a year later to teach at the Haines Normal and Industrial Institute, a school for black children in Augusta, Georgia.

There McLeod organized an unusual Sunday school program for her pupils. They visited children in nearby shacks and gave them baths and distributed clothing, soap, toothbrushes, and other personal hygiene items. "Africans in America needed Christ and school just as much as Negroes in Africa," McLeod realized. "My life work lay not in Africa but in my own country."

After a year at Haines, McLeod moved to the Kindell Institute in Sumter, South Carolina, where she met her future husband, Albertus Bethune, who was also a teacher. They were married in May 1898 and moved to Savannah, Georgia. Their only child, Albertus McLeod Bethune, was born on February 3, 1899.

Half a year later, Mary McLeod Bethune was asked to join the staff of a Presbyterian church school in Palatka, Florida. Her husband encouraged her to go to Palatka, where she organized a Sunday school program, sang to prisoners in the jails, and began what would be a part-time occupation for the rest of her life: selling insurance policies for the Afro-American Life Insurance Company.

As the Palatka school expanded, Bethune began to think about forming her own school. In 1904, she learned that the Florida East Coast Railway was being built. Black laborers were gathering from all over the South in Daytona Beach, 50 miles from Palatka, to begin work on the railroad, and their children would need an education.

Sensing that she might be able to muster support for a school from wealthy winter residents, Bethune moved to Daytona Beach. She succeeded in getting the backing to open a school, and on the morning of October 4, 1904, the Daytona Normal and Industrial Institute for Negro Girls held its first classes. The schoolhouse was a two-story cottage near the railroad tracks that she rented with a down payment of $1.50, which was all the money she had.

Students were charged 50 cents a week for tuition. They were taught basic skills and crafts and were instructed in the three R's. Bethune also spoke to them about the contributions that blacks had made to African and American cultures. At the heart of her curriculum was black pride, self-respect, and faith in God.

Before long, Bethune was reaching out to the area's entire black community. The school, which had already started to accept boarders, began to offer evening courses for adults and counseling for married couples. Within several years, the Daytona Institute had 250 pupils and needed more space and supplies.

Bethune found it hard to make ends meet. "I saw that our only solution was to stop renting space," she said, "and build our own college." She promptly sought donations from her adult students' wealthy employers.

On land that had formerly been a city dump and that Bethune had purchased with a down payment of $5, she oversaw the construction of a brick building to house her school. In October 1907, the school finally moved to its new home, Faith Hall, even though the building was not yet finished.

Meanwhile, Bethune continued to improve the school. She taught her students how to grow crops and established extensive gardens. Each Sunday, she took some of her students to a nearby migrant labor camp to teach the children and counsel their parents at what became known as the Tomoka Mission. Within five years, she had established a chain of similar missions in the area.

In 1908, the growing male enrollment at Bethune's school prompted her to change its name to the Daytona Educational Industrial Training School. Shortly afterward, her husband left her and returned to South Carolina. He died from tuberculosis in 1919 without ever seeing his wife again.

On her own, Bethune began to tour the North and publicize her school to church groups and charitable organizations. Over the years, these trips attracted the patronage of a number of benefactors, including John D. Rockefeller, Sr., who paid the tuition of Bethune's most promising students, and industrialist Andrew Carnegie, who helped her build a small hospital on the school grounds.

Bethune was in the process of expanding the institute beyond eight grades and having it accredited as a high school when World War I broke out. U.S. vice-president Thomas Marshall invited her to Washington, D.C., to discuss racial segregation as it related to the war effort. Largely through her efforts, the American Red Cross decided to integrate its services and allow blacks to perform the same services as whites.

During these years, the Daytona Institute continued to expand; but Bethune knew she needed to put the school on a firmer financial footing. Finally, in 1923, she agreed to a merger with the Cookman Institute, a school for black males in Jacksonville, Florida. The new school was renamed the Bethune-Cookman Institute.

Bethune was active in several black women's clubs, most notably the National Association of Colored Women (NACW), the country's leading organization for black women; she became president in 1924 and held the post for five years. She also served as vice-president of the National Council of Women, a confederation of women's organizations. Through these groups, she became a nationally known figure. In 1928, she was invited by President Calvin Coolidge to participate in a White House conference on child welfare, and in 1929 President Herbert Hoover named her to the National Commission for Child Welfare.

As the United States became mired in the Great Depression of the 1930s, Bethune decided to form a group that would join together all the black women's clubs and organizations to address national issues affecting black citizens. In December 1935, she founded the National Council of Negro Women.

That year also saw Bethune attain a number of personal honors. She received the Spingarn Medal from the National Association for the Advancement of Colored People (NAACP). And when President Franklin D. Roosevelt named her in 1935 to head the

Division of Negro Affairs within the National Youth Administration (NYA), created to combat unemployment among young Americans, she became the first black woman to head a federal agency. Five years later, she became vice-president of the NAACP.

In the last portion of her life, Bethune helped to establish a pilot training program at the Tuskegee Institute, served as a delegate to the conference that established the United Nations, and was appointed by President Harry S. Truman to a federal committee that helped bring about full racial integration in the armed forces.

Mary McLeod Bethune died in Daytona Beach on May 18, 1955, shortly before her 80th birthday. She was buried on the campus of Bethune-Cookman College, an ongoing monument to her work for black advancement.

FREDERICK DOUGLASS

Abolitionist leader Frederick Douglass was born into slavery as Frederick Bailey in February 1818 on a farm near Easton, on Maryland's Eastern Shore. His mother was a slave named Harriet Bailey. He knew little about his father beyond the fact that he was white, although it was rumored that his mother's master, Captain Aaron Anthony, had sired him.

Bailey began working in the fields at age six. Conditions for slaves were miserable under Captain Anthony, who denied them adequate food, clothing, and shelter, and often beat them. In 1826, Bailey was sent to Baltimore to be a house slave for relatives of the Anthonys. His new masters were Sophia and Hugh Auld, who owned a shipyard. Bailey ran errands for the family and helped look after the Auld's infant son.

Sophia Auld grew fond of the young slave and often read to him from the Bible. She even began to teach him how to read, but her husband ordered her to stop because he believed that slaves should not be taught to read and write. Upon hearing his master's outburst, Bailey concluded that learning to read and write was the pathway to freedom. He immediately set about reading parts of books and newspapers whenever he could and exchanging pieces of bread for lessons from the poor white children he met on his errands. He learned to write at his master's shipyard; he watched workmen label timbers and masts, then furtively copied the letters.

When Bailey was 12, he managed to buy a copy of *The Columbian Orator*, a collection of essays that discussed the evils of slavery. He learned for the first time of the existence of abolitionists—men and women fighting to end slavery—and he began to dream of his own emancipation. "I had penetrated to the secret of all slavery and oppression," he said later. "Slaveholders are only a band of successful robbers."

Three years later, Bailey was sent to work as a field hand on a farm owned by Hugh Auld's brother, Thomas, near the old Anthony plantation. Thomas

Auld was a cruel master who beat and starved his slaves, and Bailey was often whipped for being difficult to control. To break Bailey's spirit of resistance, Auld sent the teenager to Edward Covey, a poor farmer who was often asked by richer farmers to train their slaves to be obedient workers.

Bailey did backbreaking labor for Covey for a year and was often whipped. He was then sent to another farm to work as a field hand. His new master, William Freeland, was relatively kind, but Bailey was now completely determined to gain his freedom. He started a school and began to plot his escape to the North, where slavery was illegal.

In 1836, just before Easter, as Bailey and five other slaves prepared to flee, they were seized and thrown in jail. One of their associates had exposed the plot. When slave traders came to the jail to look him over, Bailey feared he would be sold to a plantation in the Deep South, where life for a slave was said to be unbearably harsh. To his surprise, Thomas Auld appeared at the jail, had him released, and returned him to Hugh and Sophia Auld in Baltimore.

By now, 18-year-old Bailey was 6 feet tall and immensely strong. Auld sent him to the shipyard to learn the trade of caulking the seams of a boat. He was soon skilled enough at sealing these seams to seek employment on his own. Auld, however, kept most of Bailey's earnings.

In his spare time, Bailey met with a group of educated blacks who had formed an association called the East Baltimore Mental Improvement Society. He began to hone his debating skills at the society's meetings, and at one of them he met Anna Murray, a free black who was a servant for a wealthy Baltimore family. They became engaged in 1838.

Meanwhile, Bailey, still longing for freedom, began to plan another escape to the North. On September 3, 1838, disguised as a sailor, carrying money borrowed from Anna, and armed with a friend's document that identified him as a free seaman, he boarded a train going north. He arrived in New York City the next day and found shelter with David Ruggles, who was part of the Underground Railroad, the network of people who harbored runaway slaves and helped them escape to safe areas in the northern United States and Canada.

The 20-year-old runaway slave immediately sent for Murray, and they were married on September 15; they eventually had four children. Ruggles helped them escape farther north, to the port of New Bedford, Massachusetts, where they stayed with Nathan Johnson, a well-to-do black man. Bailey, deciding that a new name might help him avoid being captured, changed his surname to Douglass, after a character in a Sir Walter Scott novel that Johnson was reading.

In New England, Douglass was quickly drawn into the abolitionist movement. He joined the American Anti-Slavery Society, led by William Lloyd Garrison, who edited the popular antislavery newspaper *The Liberator*. "The paper became my meat and drink," Douglass recalled.

In 1841, he met Garrison for the first time, at an abolitionist meeting in New Bedford. A few days later, Douglass addressed the Anti-Slavery Society. Impressed by the former slave's speech, Garrison invited him to travel throughout the North and lecture audiences on the society's behalf.

Douglass's skills as an orator brought him acclaim. Some people doubted, however, that he was telling the truth about his upbringing because he sounded so well educated. To silence these critics, he decided to write his life's story. *Narrative of the Life of Frederick Douglass*, featuring introductions by Garrison and Wendell Phillips, another abolitionist leader, was published in May 1845. The book quickly became a best-seller in the North; European editions also sold well.

Suddenly famous but still a fugitive slave, Douglass decided to seek refuge in England and at the same time win Europe's support for the antislavery movement. He headed overseas in the summer of 1845 and remained abroad for two years, drawing enthusiastic crowds everywhere he spoke. He returned home only after two English friends purchased his freedom for $710.96.

In late 1847, Douglass moved his family to Rochester, New York, and began to issue the *North Star*, a weekly abolitionist newspaper that also supported equal rights for women. It attracted a wide readership and helped him grow in stature. He continued to publish the paper for 16 years.

The abolitionist cause, however, was not making many gains. In 1850, the U.S. Congress passed the Fugitive Slave Act, which strengthened earlier laws requiring that runaway slaves be returned to their owners. Seven years later, the U.S. Supreme Court declared in the Dred Scott decision that slaves "had no rights which the white man was bound to respect."

In response, Douglass became part of the Underground Railroad, and his home in Rochester became an important stop on the line. And when the Civil War erupted in April 1861, he announced that he would fight for the emancipation of all slaves in the Confederacy and the Union border states, and the right of blacks to enlist in the armies of the North. President Abraham Lincoln even held two private meetings with Douglass.

Clearly the nation's leading black spokesman, Douglass vowed after the Civil War ended in 1865 to help his race secure the right to vote. He traveled throughout the North, and the black suffrage movement grew. In 1868, the Fourteenth Amendment, guaranteeing blacks their full rights as citizens, was ratified. Two years later, the Fifteenth Amendment guaranteed all male citizens the right to vote, regardless of race.

Also in 1870, Douglass took over the *New National Era*, a newspaper based in Washington, D.C., and in 1874 he accepted an offer to become president of a bank for black investors. After the Freedmen's Saving and Trust Company failed, he returned to the lecture circuit, giving speeches on a variety of topics, including Scandinavian folklore. Many people described him as one of the world's greatest speakers.

In 1877, Douglass was awarded a political post, U.S. marshal for the District of Columbia. Three years later, he was appointed recorder of deeds for the capital city. Both jobs afforded him ample time for writing and speaking engagements, and in 1881 he published another autobiograpy, *The Life and Times of Frederick Douglass*. Never one to avoid controversy, he married Helen Pitts, a white woman who was 20 years his junior, in 1884, two years after Anna Douglass died.

Douglass's final political appointment came in 1889, when he was named ambassador to Haiti, a position he held for two years. He spent his last years seeking to awaken the nation's conscience to the growing number of violent crimes that were being committed against blacks.

Frederick Douglass was in Washington, D.C., on February 20, 1895, when he died of a heart attack at the age of 77. With his passing, one of America's most eloquent voices for human rights was silenced.

W. E. B. DU BOIS

Scholar and activist William Edward Burghardt Du Bois was born on February 23, 1868, in Great Barrington, Massachusetts. Shortly after William's birth, his father, Alfred Du Bois, abandoned his family. William and his mother, Mary, never heard from the elder Du Bois again.

An excellent, highly motivated student, young Du Bois held odd jobs after school to supplement his mother's income as a domestic servant. He graduated from Great Barrington High School in 1884 with the intention of going to Harvard College, but he lacked the funds. The following year, four towns-people raised enough money for him to attend Fisk University, a black college in Nashville, Tennessee.

Du Bois settled in quickly at Fisk, excelling academically and editing the school newspaper, the *Fisk Herald*. During summer vacations, he taught in a small rural school for blacks in eastern Tennessee. There he experienced the grinding poverty that plagued southern blacks. His work with the rural poor inflamed his social conscience, and "a life that shall be an honor to the Race" became his publicly stated goal.

Du Bois graduated as valedictorian from Fisk in 1888, then enrolled at Harvard. He graduated with honors in philosophy from Harvard in 1890, and two years later he received a master of arts degree from the school. He then was awarded a grant to study for two years at Friedrich Wilhelm University in Berlin.

When Du Bois returned from Germany in 1894, he taught for a year at Wilberforce University, a black institution in Ohio, while he completed his doctoral dissertation on the slave trade. He received a doctorate in philosophy from Harvard the following year. And in 1896, his dissertation became his first published book.

That same year, Du Bois wedded Nina Gomer, a student at Wilberforce. They remained married for 54 years, until Nina's death in 1950. The next year, Du Bois wedded Shirley Graham, one of his former graduate students. He had two children: a son, Burghardt, who died in 1899 at the age of two; and a daughter, Yolande, who was born 16 months later.

In the summer of 1897, Du Bois left Wilberforce to teach at the University of Pennsylvania and to research the social structure of a black neighborhood in Philadelphia. His landmark sociological study, *The Philadelphia Negro* (1899), called on the "black aristocracy" to help its brethren. Blacks would emerge from oppression, he concluded, only after strong black leaders stepped forward.

Du Bois's scholarship continued in the fall of 1897, when he joined the Atlanta University faculty and organized a series of annual conferences that examined the problems facing black Americans. In 1900, he put together an exhibit on black American life at the Paris Exposition. It won the grand prize and added to his growing international reputation as a scholar and a champion of black America. The turn of the century also saw Du Bois devote himself to the cause of a free Africa leading to worldwide unity among blacks; he would eventually become known as the father of this cause, Pan-Africanism.

In 1903, Du Bois published the now-classic *The Souls of Black Folk*, a powerful collection of 14 essays that probed the black American's plight. "One ever feels his twoness—an American, a Negro," Du Bois wrote. "Two souls, two thoughts, two unreconciled strivings, two warring ideals in one dark body, whose dogged strength alone keeps it from being torn asunder."

But of all the points Du Bois made in the book, the one that attracted the most attention was his criticism of educator and racial spokesman Booker T. Washington's accommodationist policies. Washington maintained that blacks should not seek social change until they had raised their economic status—a sticking point that gained him the trust of white leaders. Du Bois countered that blacks should be granted their full civil rights. He called on the educated black elite—the Talented Tenth—to provide strong leadership in the fight for racial justice, declaring, "The problem of the twentieth century is the problem of the color line."

Over the next few years, Du Bois continued to write articles for leading periodicals and published several scholarly books. Meanwhile, he attempted to unify Washington's opponents behind the Niagara Movement, a black protest organization created to promote "aggressive action on the part of men who believe in Negro freedom and growth." Washington successfully withstood Du Bois's challenge for leadership of black America; but this victory did not stand for long.

In 1910, Du Bois left Atlanta University and cofounded the National Association for the Advancement of Colored People (NAACP) in New York City. He became the organization's director of publicity and research, and served as editor of its monthly publication, the *Crisis*, a militant journal that transformed the NAACP into the nation's most powerful civil rights organization. Within a decade, the *Crisis* was boasting a circulation of more than 100,000.

Du Bois was, without any doubt, the driving force behind the *Crisis*. He used its pages to speak bluntly about racial issues and continue his criticism of

Booker T. Washington's accommodationist policies. By the time Washington died, Du Bois was being hailed as the country's foremost black leader.

In the early 1920s, Du Bois turned his attention to a new opponent: Marcus Garvey, the black nationalist leader who won thousands of supporters through spectacular parades and conferences dominated by showmanship and rhetoric. The aim of Garvey and the organization he founded, the Universal Negro Improvement Association (UNIA), was to increase black pride and promote racial separatism instead of the integration that Du Bois and the NAACP favored. The *Crisis* editor, in fact, labeled Garvey "the most dangerous enemy of the Negro race"; and by the mid-1920s, Du Bois's attacks had helped expose the UNIA leader as something of a fraud.

The *Crisis*, with which Du Bois's name will be forever linked, played a leading role in the 1920s in promoting the black cultural movement that became known as the Harlem Renaissance. By the 1930s, however, Du Bois was filling the *Crisis* with a number of his more radical views. When in the January 1934 issue he called for blacks to take advantage of racial segregation by supporting solely black enterprises, his use of the phrase "voluntary segregation" offended many NAACP leaders. Du Bois promptly resigned from his post and returned to Atlanta University to become chairman of the sociology department and resume his wide-ranging scholarly work.

Du Bois reeled off several influential books: *Black Reconstruction* (1935); *Black Folk Then and Now* (1939); and his autobiography *Dusk of Dawn* (1940). Whenever he was not at his writing desk or in the classroom, he was busy championing racial harmony around the globe, especially in Africa. In 1945, for example, he served as a consultant to the U.S. delegation attending the founding conference of the United Nations.

Du Bois's later years were marked by a flurry of activity. He returned to the NAACP for three years as director of special research. He continued his support of Pan-Africanism and attended a number of peace conferences at home and abroad.

In 1950, the 82-year-old Du Bois campaigned unsuccessfully for the U.S. Senate. That same year, his association with alleged Communists resulted in his being indicted by the federal government for failing to register as an agent of the Soviet Union. He was acquitted of all charges in the ensuing trial; yet the government refused to let him travel abroad during much of the 1950s because of his supposed ties with Communist nations. Acquitted of all wrongdoing, Du Bois's name remained tarnished, and his influence on black affairs diminished steadily.

Forced to remain on the sidelines while the civil rights struggle pushed ahead in the late 1950s, Du Bois occupied himself by writing three novels. In 1959, he was finally allowed to leave the country. He went to the Soviet Union, where he held talks with Soviet premier Nikita Khrushchev, received an honorary doctorate from Moscow University, and was awarded the Lenin Peace Prize. He then traveled to China and met with Communist party chairman Mao Tse-tung.

In 1961, shortly after joining the American Communist party, Du Bois moved to the African nation of Ghana. Another skirmish with the U.S. government caused him to renouce his American citizenship and become a Ghanaian citizen. He died in Accra, Ghana, on August 27, 1963, after devoting nearly a century to ending America's racial crisis.

MARCUS GARVEY

Marcus Garvey was born on August 17, 1887, in St. Ann's Bay on the British colony of Jamaica. He was the 11th child of Sarah and Marcus Garvey, a man of tremendous intellect who worked as a stonemason.

Young Marcus received his education in public schools and from private tutors. He especially enjoyed borrowing books from his father's extensive library.

At the age of 15, he left school to work as an apprentice in his godfather's printing shop. Three years later, he moved to Jamaica's capital of Kingston to work as a printer. There he became fully aware of racial divisions in Jamaican society and developed a strong interest in helping the country's poor blacks, who made up 80 percent of the population.

In 1909, Garvey entered Kingston's intellectual circles as a member of the National Club, a group organized to fight the problems created by British rule. He helped publish the club's newspaper, *Our Own*. He then launched his own periodical, *Garvey's Watchman*. He soon realized that if he wanted to improve the lives of his fellow blacks, the effort would take more money than he could raise on Jamaica. Believing that he could earn more money abroad, he sailed to Costa Rica in 1910.

Garvey landed a job on a banana plantation, confident that he could save enough money to return to Jamaica and lead the struggle for black rights. Instead, the poor working conditions on the plantation inspired him to start a newspaper that agitated for the rights of the plantation's many migrant laborers. It met with little success, however, and so he decided to go elsewhere. He traveled to a number of South and Central American nations, where the same scene repeated itself: he found migrant workers performing backbreaking labor. He campaigned to improve the lot of the workers wherever he went but was constantly opposed by government authorities, who viewed him as dangerous.

In 1912, Garvey decided to take his battle to the seat of the British Empire and set sail for England. In

London, he supported himself as a dockworker and attended evening classes at Birkbeck College, a school for working-class people. His studies led him to accounts of Europe's centuries-long domination of Africa and prompted him to seek out other blacks who shared his growing conviction that blacks throughout the world were one people and that Africa was their homeland.

Garvey's thinking was further stirred after he came across a copy of *Up from Slavery*, educator and racial spokesman Booker T. Washington's autobiography. Washington's rags-to-riches story—which included his founding of the black industrial school Tuskegee Institute and his program for racial progress through accommodation—had an electrifying effect on Garvey. After reading the book, he said later, "My doom—if I may so call it—of being a race leader dawned on me."

Garvey returned to Kingston in 1914 and founded the Universal Negro Improvement Association (UNIA). Its purpose was to unite Jamaica's black population with a spirit of racial pride and a program of educational and economic opportunity. The UNIA also vowed to work for the end of colonial rule and the establishment of independent black-led nations in Africa. Garvey, who became the UNIA's president and chief recruiter, intended it to be the standard-bearer of international black protest.

In March 1916, Garvey arrived in New York City and attempted to gain support for the UNIA abroad. He settled in Harlem, the district that had recently become the center of the city's black population, and found work as a printer. In his free time, he spoke on street corners, explaining his program for racial solidarity to anyone who would listen.

Within three months, Garvey saved enough money to embark on a lecture and fundraising tour to major cities in the eastern half of the United States, concentrating on areas with large black populations. There he spoke about conditions in Jamaica and the rest of the Caribbean and met with black community leaders to hear their views on racial relations. After a year, he returned to Harlem and established a New York chapter of the UNIA. This eventually became the organization's international headquarters.

To help spread the UNIA's message, Garvey in 1918 began publishing the newspaper *Negro World*. It covered the UNIA's activities and reported issues and events that were of interest to blacks. Garvey wrote many of the articles that focused on important figures in black history. Distributed worldwide, the paper gradually saw its circulation rise to 60,000.

The energetic Garvey managed to make the UNIA grow quickly. By 1919, he claimed that the organization had a membership of 2 million in 30 chapters around the world. He urged black audiences at his Harlem headquarters, a large auditorium called Liberty Hall, and on his speaking tours to take pride in themselves and their appearance and to stop emulating whites. He told them to regard members of their race as heroes and to worship God as a black divine being.

Garvey's message of black pride was just what tens of thousands of black Americans wanted to hear. In an era when racial relations were growing worse by the day, he became a hero to them. Before long, he was bearing the nickname Black Moses.

In 1919, Garvey established the Negro Factories Corporation to encourage black-owned businesses. That same year, he announced the formation of the Black Star Line shipping company. It would be owned and operated exclusively by blacks, he said, and would mark the start of a movement to achieve black economic independence.

As soon as advertisements for the shipping line were placed in *Negro World*, money to finance the business began to pour in. Stock in the Black Star Line cost $5 a share, and within the line's first year more than $600,000 was raised. Much more money would follow.

In late 1919, Garvey took time out from his busy activities to marry his secretary, Amy Ashwood, in a lavish ceremony at Liberty Hall. After the marriage ended in divorce two years later, he married his new secretary, Amy Jacques, with whom he had two children, Marcus, Jr., and Julius.

Garvey, however, was always wedded to the UNIA. To capitalize on the organization's rise, he held a 30-day international convention of black organizations that commenced on August 1, 1920, in New York. Black delegates came from as far as Africa, and they witnessed quite a show in celebration of the opening of the convention. Garvey, dressed in a fancy uniform and a plumed hat, led a spectacular parade of hundreds of uniformed marchers through the streets of Harlem. That night, all of them packed Madison Square Garden to hear Garvey speak.

By the convention's end, Garvey was beginning to form an ambitious plan to establish a black homeland in Africa. It would become known as the Back to Africa movement.

But as Garvey's dreams grew, so did his troubles, for the Black Star Line turned into a humiliating fiasco. His critics demanded to know what had become of the large sums of money that investors had put into his shipping business. Then the U.S. government stepped forward, and in early 1922 Garvey was indicted for using the mail to deceive Black Star Line investors. One year later, a jury found him guilty of mail fraud. He was fined $1,000 and was sentenced to five years in prison. In February 1925, after an appeal to have his conviction overturned was rejected, he surrendered to federal authorities and was taken to the Atlanta Federal Penitentiary.

Garvey was not forgotten by his faithful followers, who held protest rallies and flooded government offices with letters and petitions in their effort to convince the authorities to release him. It was the opinion of many that Garvey had been imprisoned only because he had become a strong black leader who posed a threat to white America. To put an end to the furor, U.S. president Calvin Coolidge ordered Garvey released from prison in late 1927 and had him deported to Jamaica.

Back in his homeland, Garvey attempted to build up the branches of the UNIA outside the United States. He managed to found a chapter in Europe and to organize a successful UNIA convention in Kingston in 1929. But for the most part, his golden touch was gone. The American branches missed his strong presence, and without his leadership, the organization collapsed.

For a few years, Garvey turned to local politics, serving several terms on Kingston's governing council. In the late 1930s, he made one last push to rebuild the UNIA. But there would be no more rallies or parades.

On June 10, 1940—five months after he had suffered a serious stroke while in London—Marcus Garvey died at the age of 53. He was laid to rest in England. But in 1964, in accordance with his last wishes, his body was returned to Jamaica, where he was given the country's highest honor, the title of first national hero.

SOJOURNER TRUTH

Antislavery actvist Sojourner Truth was born into slavery around 1797 in Hurley, New York. Her name was originally Isabella, and she was the ninth child of the slaves Betsey and James. By the time of her birth, her older brothers and sisters had already been sold to other slaveholders.

Home for Isabella was a damp cellar on the Hardenbergh's farm near the Hudson River in upstate

New York. Her mother, being a deeply religious woman, taught Isabella that if she led an upright life, God
would always watch over her. Yet when Isabella was
11, her master separated her from her parents and her
younger brother, Peter. She was sold to John Nealy,
who owned a store and dock in nearby Kingston.

Life at her new home was hard for Isabella. She did
not know how to speak English because her previous
owners, the Hardenberghs, had spoken solely Dutch;
so she was frequently beaten for not being able to
follow her new masters' orders. Nealy and his wife
attempted to teach Isabella English. But their efforts
failed, and they grew frustrated. One Sunday morning, John Nealy beat Isabella severely with metal
rods he had heated in a fire. When her father got
wind of this brutal punishment, he persuaded Martin
Schryver, a local fisherman and tavern owner, to buy
her from the Nealys.

Isabella worked on the Schryvers' farm and helped
them bring in catches of fish. Under her new owners'
guidance, she became relatively fluent in English. She
never learned to read or write, however, and her
speech was always marked by a strong Dutch accent.

In 1810, the Schryvers sold Isabella to John
Dumont, a farmer who lived in nearby New Paltz. He
was not a harsh master, but his wife took an instant
dislike to Isabella and treated her cruelly. Isabella
remembered her mother's advice, however, to repay
evil with good, believing that her hard work would
eventually be rewarded.

In her middle teens, Isabella fell in love with a young
slave named Robert, who lived on a neighboring estate. Their romance was forbidden by Robert's owner,

who beat the boy senseless for visiting her. Not long afterward, she agreed to become the wife of Thomas, one of Dumont's older slaves. Their first child, Diana, was born in 1815; and during the next 12 years, Isabella had four more children: Elizabeth, Hannah, Peter, and Sophie. When they were infants, they usually went with her into the fields, strapped to her back.

Isabella taught each of her children the lessons about hard work and faith that she had learned from her mother. As she continued to labor for the Dumonts, rumors began to spread that slavery would be outlawed in New York State. Finally, in 1824, the state legislature passed an emancipation law. Under its provisions, Isabella would become eligible to receive her freedom in 1827.

Isabella was ecstatic that her prayers had been answered, and she became even more industrious when her master told her that he would free her a year earlier if she worked especially hard. When 1826 came, however, he went back on his promise. Isabella promptly decided to escape.

One day that autumn, without telling her husband or children, Isabella gathered some food and clothes, took hold of baby Sophie, and left the Dumont farm. She found shelter at the home of a Quaker couple, the Van Wageners. And when Dumont came looking for her, the Van Wageners bought her and Sophie for a small sum, then set them free.

The grateful Isabella remained at the Van Wageners' house as a domestic servant. Meanwhile, she turned her attention to freeing her other children. She soon learned that her son, Peter, had been sold to a man named Gedney, who had sent the boy south, violating a New York law that forbade transporting slaves out of state. In the spring of 1828, with the help of antislavery activists, she successfully sued Gedney for Peter's return and became one of the first black women in the country to win a court case.

During the two years that Isabella worked for the Van Wageners, she settled her differences with the Dumonts and was allowed to visit with her three older daughters. Her husband, who had been emancipated in 1827, had chosen to go his own way.

Isabella's strong religious faith prompted her to join the local Methodist church. There she met a schoolteacher who was planning to move to New York City and offered to help Isabella find work. Isabella and Peter moved to New York City in the summer of 1828, joining the swelling number of former slaves who had come to the city in search of jobs. Isabella was hired as a servant, and Peter enrolled in a navigation trade school.

Isabella soon joined the Zion African church, which encouraged its members to talk openly about their religious feelings. She became known for her loud and vigorous testimonials and for her ability to recite biblical passages. As the years passed, she heard voices telling her that she had a mission to help the needy and the oppressed. And in June 1843, she left New York City to become a traveling preacher, bearing the new name she had given herself, Sojourner Truth.

Truth slowly made her way to New England, where she became increasingly involved in the antislavery crusade. When it was suggested to her that a published account of her life as a slave, stressing her profound faith in God, would be uplifting to many people,

Truth agreed to tell her story. In 1850, *The Narrative of Sojourner Truth*, which included an introduction by the noted abolitionist William Lloyd Garrison, was published. The book made Truth widely known, and Garrison promptly persuaded her to become a traveling lecturer for the abolitionist cause throughout New England.

Truth was also interested in another cause: equal political and legal rights for women. In the United States in the 1840s, women could not vote or hold political office, were paid far less than male workers, and had few educational opportunities. A married woman and her property were entirely under her husband's control; in the event of divorce, the husband was always given custody of the children.

Truth readily embraced the women's rights movement, led by Susan B. Anthony, Lucretia Mott, Lucy Stone, and other prominent feminists. Many of them were also active in the Underground Railroad, the network of people who helped runaway slaves escape to the North. Truth was well aware that women and slaves endured similar hardships, and her speeches at abolitionist meetings forcefully pointed out that she continued to be oppressed even after she had become a free woman.

In 1848, feminists held the first national women's rights convention, in Seneca Falls, New York. There they drew up a plan for helping women achieve equality with men. Truth did not attend the convention, but she went to many other women's rights meetings, and in 1850 she addressed that year's national women's rights conference. Two years later, at the national conference in Akron, Ohio, she gave one of her most famous speeches. Stating that the work she had done throughout her life was equal to any man's, she cited a list of accomplishments, punctuating each achievement with the refrain "And ain't I a woman?"

By the mid-1850s, Sojourner Truth's name was known throughout much of America. Her audiences were not always friendly or even courteous, and sometimes she was jeered by opponents of both of her causes. But nothing deterred her from delivering her message. In 1857, Truth moved to Battle Creek, Michigan, a town with strong abolitionist roots that had always given her a favorable reception. Two of her daughters and their families later moved to Battle Creek to be near her.

Following the outbreak of the Civil War in 1861, Truth toured the Midwest to rouse support for the Union war effort. As always, she supported herself by occasionally hiring herself out as a domestic servant. But when the 66-year-old Truth became too ill to work in 1863, friends collected enough money for her to buy a small house in Battle Creek.

The following year, with her health vastly improved, Truth journeyed to Washington, D.C., where she met with President Abraham Lincoln and personally thanked him for all he had done on the behalf of black Americans. She remained in the nation's capital to counsel freed blacks, and after the Civil War ended in 1865, she worked as an administrator at the Freedmen's Hospital, run by the Freedmen's Bureau, the federal agency established to help former slaves.

In 1868, she launched what proved to be an unsuccessful campaign to persuade Congress to grant land in the West to black settlers.

Sojourner Truth returned to Michigan in the early 1870s and spent her remaining years among family and friends. She died in Battle Creek on November 26, 1883.

HARRIET TUBMAN

Antislavery activist Harriet Tubman was born as the slave Harriet Ross around 1820 on a plantation on Maryland's Eastern Shore. Put to work as a household servant at five, she was roughly treated, ill clothed, and always hungry. At the age of seven, she stole a piece of sugar, then fled in terror from her mistress's rage. Starving and fearful, the little girl returned after hiding in a pigpen for five days. Her "lady" gave her a savage whipping.

In 1835, an overseer ordered 15-year-old Harriet to hold a slave he intended to whip. She refused, and the slave ran, prompting the enraged overseer to hurl a lead weight at him. The missile struck Harriet, severely gashed her head, and put her into a coma for weeks. For the rest of her life, she carried a deep scar and suffered from what she called "sleeping fits": without warning, she would fall unconscious for hours at a time.

In 1844, Harriet Ross married John Tubman, a free black man, but she remained a slave. Her greatest fear was being "sold south"—sent to live on an Alabama or Mississippi cotton plantation where slaves' lives were shorter and even more brutal than in Maryland. In 1849, Tubman's worst fears materialized: two of her sisters were led south in irons. She knew she would meet the same fate unless she acted quickly.

During the 1830s, antislavery activists had set up a network of houses where slaves could hide as they fled northward to freedom. Known as the Underground Railroad—its safe houses were "stations"; its guides, "conductors"—the network helped thousands of people escape.

Tubman had heard stories of the Underground Railroad; when she learned that she too had been sold south, she decided to flee. Saying nothing to John Tubman—who had not only forbidden her to escape, but threatened to report her—she packed a bit of cornbread, anxiously glanced at the moonless autumn sky, and headed north. Hiding by day, traveling by night, sometimes stopping at "stations" along the route, Tubman trudged through some 90 miles of swamp and forest. Many painful days after she started, she reached Pennsylvania and stood on free soil at last. "I felt like I was in heaven," she said later. She resolved to bring the rest of her family north as soon as she could.

Tubman made her way to Philadelphia, got a job as a dishwasher, saved her money, and kept her ears open. Learning of the Philadelphia Vigilance Committee, an organization that helped fugitive slaves, she began visiting its office. There, she talked with abolitionists, listened to fugitive slaves' stories, and plotted ways to set her family free. She found such a way in 1850, when a Maryland abolitionist asked the Vigilance Committee to help a black woman and her two children escape from Baltimore. Listening to his description, the astonished Tubman realized that the woman was her sister Mary. Although committee leaders feared for Tubman's life, she insisted on bringing the family out herself. Making the first of at least 19 daring rescue missions, she slipped into Maryland and led her passengers back safely.

On one of her perilous conducting trips to the Eastern Shore, Tubman tried to persuade John Tubman to go north with her, but he had taken a new wife and refused. Tubman never saw her husband again and rarely spoke of him, but for the rest of her life she identified herself as Mrs. Tubman.

After Congress passed the Fugitive Slave Act of 1850, bounty hunters captured more and more runaways in Philadelphia. Aware of the great danger, Tubman's friends persuaded her to move to St. Catharines, Canada, in 1851. She now faced a 500-

mile journey each time she traveled to the Eastern Shore. Her standard procedure was to gather money and supplies, then steal down the coast to Delaware and into Maryland. There she would make contact with slaves who were ready to escape. She usually started them north on a Saturday night, hoping they would not be missed and pursued until Monday. Before heading out, she paid someone to take down the Wanted posters that would be sure to appear across the countryside.

Tubman knew all the places to hide: along with the Underground Railroad's safe houses, there were drainage ditches, hedges, abandoned sheds, and tobacco barns. Merciful and humane, Tubman could also be tough: she always carried a revolver, and if a passenger grew fainthearted, she would hold the gun to his or her head and bark, "Move or die!" Tubman's work earned her the nickname Moses, after the biblical prophet who had brought his people out of bondage and into the Promised Land.

In the course of her crusade, Tubman met many abolitionist leaders, including Frederick Douglass, John Brown, and U.S. senator William Seward. A great admirer of Tubman's, Seward presented her with the deed to a small house in the upstate New York village of Auburn, in 1857. Auburn, a major Underground Railroad station, became Tubman's home for the rest of her life.

Not long after moving there, Tubman learned that her father was to be tried for helping another slave escape. Hurrying south, she "borrowed" a horse and wagon, sped to the plantation, and drove off with her amazed parents, whom she later settled in Auburn. To support them and herself, she worked full-time as a hotel chambermaid when she was not traveling. Whenever she could, she addressed antislavery meetings, where highly educated audiences listened spellbound to speeches by the illiterate former slave.

As thousands of slaves fled their masters, the South called for ever more rigorous enforcement of the Fugitive Slave Law. In 1860, Tubman made what would be her last, and perhaps most dangerous, trip on the Underground Railroad. She returned with seven men and women, then, at the insistence of friends, crossed the Canadian border.

After the Civil War broke out in 1861, Tubman traveled to Beaufort, South Carolina, to care for the thousands of slaves who had been abandoned by their masters and were now flooding Union army camps. Working in a makeshift hospital, she nursed ailing, malnourished blacks as well as wounded white soldiers. From Beaufort, Tubman went to a Florida military hospital, where she treated soldiers and former slaves suffering from dysentery, smallpox, and malaria.

In the spring of 1863, union officers assigned Tubman to a new job: spy. Shifting her base to South Carolina, she guided a small expedition deep into enemy territory and returned with invaluable intelligence on Confederate encampments. That summer, she conducted her most celebrated exploit, leading a raid up the Combahee River to destroy enemy-held railroads and bridges and to cut off Confederate supplies and troops. A phenomenal success, the exploit cost the enemy millions of dollars and 800 slaves.

During the next year, Tubman participated in numerous guerrilla operations for the Union Army. Visiting her parents while on leave in 1864, she suffered an intense bout of the sleeping seizures that had continued to plague her; but by early spring, 1865, she felt well enough to return to the South. This time, she operated out of Washington, D.C., serving as a nurse for the U.S. Sanitary Commission, an early version of the Medical Corps.

The Civil War ended in April, and that summer Tubman returned to Auburn. On the train home, she received her first shocking hint of the new battle that lay ahead for black Americans: when she presented her half-fare military pass to the white northern conductors, they not only refused to honor it, they shoved her into the baggage car, severely injuring her arm. Blacks, they said, rated no special privileges.

Although Tubman had been entitled to military pay for her services as a scout and nurse, she had neither requested nor received it. Now 45 years old, she was penniless, responsible for her aged parents, and in steady pain from her wrenched arm. Presenting Tubman's carefully saved records as evidence, Seward and other influential officials petitioned the government for the money it owed her, but the payment never came through. With the help of well-to-do neighbors, the undaunted Tubman continued to feed, clothe, and nurse the stream of impoverished blacks who appeared at her door.

In 1869, Tubman married Nelson Davis, a 25-year-old former slave and soldier she had met during the war. For many years, she supported her tubercular husband by selling vegetables from her garden. In 1890, two years after Davis's death, the government awarded her $8 per month as a Civil War veteran's widow.

In the 1890s, Tubman vigorously supported Susan B. Anthony and the women's rights movement, and in 1908, she reached a long-held goal by establishing a home for sick and needy black people. On March 10, 1913, the Underground Railroad's most famous conductor, who proudly asserted that she had "never lost a passenger," died in Auburn at the age of 93.

BOOKER T. WASHINGTON

Educator and racial spokesman Booker Taliaferro Washington was born a slave on April 5, 1856, near Hales Ford, Virginia. He received his last name from the slave Washington Ferguson, whom his mother, Jane, married in 1860. Booker never knew who his real father was, although the man was almost certainly white.

Home for Booker was a 200-acre farm, where he handled some of the heavier chores as soon as he was able. He lived in a squalid cabin that had empty cupboards and no stove. His bed was the dirt floor.

The slaves' world changed dramatically—in theory, at least—on April 9, 1865, when the Civil War ended, leaving all blacks free to go their own way. For many of these former slaves, however, there was nowhere to go. Poor and never given the chance to get an education, they had few prospects of finding new employment.

Booker's stepfather was luckier than most. He found work as a salt packer in Malden, West Virginia, where he was joined by Jane and her three children, Booker, John, and Amanda. It was not long before a fourth child came into the family, an orphan boy named James.

Like their stepfather, Booker and John went to work in the mine, shoveling salt into barrels. The work was backbreaking, and it left Booker with only one hope: to get an education and free himself from a life of slavelike labor. Fortunately for him, a school for blacks was established in the nearby community of Tinkersville not long after he arrived in West Virginia. He began to attend classes at night, after his workday was done.

In 1872, 16-year-old Booker T. Washington made a decision that would shape the rest of his life. Determined to make something of himself, he traveled more than 200 miles—most of them on foot—to Hampton, Virginia, the site of Hampton Normal and Agricultural Institute, a large industrial school for blacks. He arrived there with only 50 cents in his pocket and an appetite to learn. In recognition of his drive and desire, he was permitted to pay his way through school by working as a janitor.

Washington remained at Hampton Institute for three years. The school emphasized self-discipline, morality, personal hygiene, and what its founder, General Samuel Armstrong, called the "routine of industrious habits." He believed that the key to racial advancement was the acquisition of practical trade skills, which would help blacks become contributing members of society and enable them to win the respect of whites. It was a theory that Washington would also adopt. Indeed, he learned his lessons so well that in 1875, when he graduated from Hampton, he was asked to deliver the commencement address.

Washington then returned to the Tinkersville school, this time as a teacher, and put into practice what he had learned at Hampton. He left his job in 1878 to enroll at a Baptist seminary in Washington, D.C., but after half a year he was convinced that his future lay in education, not the ministry. When Armstrong invited him to join the Hampton faculty in the fall of 1879, he jumped at the chance.

Washington proved to be such an able and popular educator that Armstrong wholeheartedly recommended him for the post of principal at a new black school in Tuskegee, Alabama. He arrived in the southern town in June 1881 eager to begin work but was dismayed to find that the school had not yet been built. Washington set to work at once getting the school off the ground. To the townpeople's astonishment, he opened the Tuskegee Normal and Industrial Institute on July 4, 1881, just 10 days after his arrival.

Classes for the students were held in a large shack while Washington raised the down payment for a permanent site, an old farm outside of town. As soon as the property was purchased, he and his pupils set to work constructing their own school brick by brick.

At first, Tuskegee Institute's primary goal was to prepare its students to teach in black elementary schools. But Washington gradually broadened the curriculum to include vocational courses, much like those at Hampton. Academic subjects were reinforced with practical learning: math students measured floors for new carpets; English students wrote essays on cabinetry or dressmaking. When deposits of brick clay were discovered on the school's land, brickmaking became part of the curriculum. In time, the Tuskegee kiln became a major industry, selling the bricks that were not used in the construction of new campus buildings to people throughout the county.

Washington had help in making the institute's enrollment grow. Fanny Smith, his longtime sweetheart, married him in 1882 and devoted herself to the school. She gave birth to a daughter, Portia, in 1883 and died the following year. Sadly, Washington was beset by tragedy again a few years later. In 1885, he married Olivia Davidson, Tuskegee's first "lady principal," who bore him two sons, Booker, Jr., and Ernest Davidson. Her health failed after the birth of Ernest, and she died in 1889. Two years later, Washington married for a final time. His third wife was Margaret Murray, who had replaced Olivia as principal.

By the 1890s, Washington had built Tuskegee into the largest and best-endowed black institution in America. He promptly used his reputation for being a successful educator as a springboard to national prominence. Washington had devoted his adult life to working to uplift his race, and at the 1895 Cotton States and International Exposition in Atlanta, Georgia, he gave the speech that marked him as America's leading black spokesman.

Addressing an audience of several thousand with what has become known as the Atlanta Compromise, Washington exhorted blacks to postpone their demands for equal rights and focus on improving themselves through education, industriousness, and racial solidarity. "In all things that are purely social," he said, "we can be as separate as the fingers, yet one as the hand in all things essential to mutual progress." Requiring no change in the existing social order, his program for racial progress for blacks won the support of white society and opened the door to black opportunity. During the next two decades, U.S. presidents Grover Cleveland, William McKinley, and Theodore Roosevelt all sought his advice on black issues.

Washington found many ways to make his views felt. In 1900, he founded the National Negro Business League, which quickly evolved into a highly successful organization that promoted black business. The following year, the story of his life, the now-classic *Up from Slavery*, was published; it inspired Americans of every color and prompted some of the nation's most influential philanthropists to assist the black cause. In fact, his status as the nation's most important black leader enabled him to build the Tuskegee Machine, a powerful group of politicians, businessmen, philanthropists, and educators who helped advance the Tuskegee president's doctrines.

Washington certainly had his opponents, chief among them the highly educated scholar and activist W. E. B. Du Bois. Maintaining that Washington's industrial program stunted the intellectual growth of their race, Du Bois called on the educated black elite to provide strong leadership in the fight for racial justice and demanded that blacks be immediately granted their full civil rights. By the early 1900s, the black community was divided between Washington's camp and Du Bois's.

For the rest of his life, Washington jockeyed with his rivals for control of black America. He continued to stress the importance of accommodation, education, and economic advancement within the black community. But his message fell increasingly on deaf ears. His program was not working; accommodationist polices were not leading to black advancement.

In his last few years, Washington kept up his grueling pace as an educator and leader of his race. But he also began to speak out against racism more forcefully than ever before. Unfortunately, his attempts to expose the ugliness of racism did not have much impact. An accommodationist at heart, he could never attack the system of white supremacy with any real vigor.

By 1915, Washington's health had been failing for some time. In early November, he collapsed in New York City during a fundraising tour. He insisted on returning home to Tuskegee, where he died on November 13, at the age of 59. It was an apt resting place for this latter-day Moses, who achieved the highest position of influence ever held by a black American.

Leaders of America

BLANCHE K. BRUCE

Political leader Blanche K. Bruce was born Branch Kelso Bruce in Farmville, Virginia, on March 1, 1841. He was one of eleven children of Polly, a slave owned by Lemuel Bruce, a prosperous plantation owner. When Branch was still a baby, one of Lemuel Bruce's heirs took Polly and her children, along with the other slaves, to a farm in Missouri. There the older slaves did farm chores and were hired out to work in brick and tobacco factories. Slaves too young to work, including Branch, played with the children of the master and learned to read and write.

During the years of Branch Bruce's childhood he also lived as a slave on plantations owned by the master's family in both Virginia and Mississippi. By the time he was 15, Branch was once again in Missouri, where he was apprenticed for a while to a printer. Later he was allowed to farm a piece of his own land on the family plantation, and also made rails with other slaves. In 1861, when Kansas was admitted to the Union as a free (nonslave) state, Branch Bruce gained his freedom by moving to Lawrence, Kansas, where he soon changed his first name to Blanche.

For several years Blanche Bruce taught black children at an elementary school he had helped establish in Lawrence. One night in August 1863 a group of proslavery raiders from Missouri descended upon the town, maiming and killing both black and white residents as they looted and burned. Bruce narrowly escaped, and memories of the harrowing event remained with him for the rest of his life. As Bruce saw buildings being burned around him, he made a pledge to himself. He knew that if there were ever to be unity between the races, it had to come about with brains, not torches. Bruce believed that one day there would be a need for black people in positions of leadership, and with the desire to gain more education, he promised himself he would be ready.

He continued to teach at his school for another year, returning to Missouri in early 1865 following that state's passage of an emancipation law. Bruce settled in Hannibal, where he founded the first public school for blacks in the state. As his students increasingly challenged Bruce, he realized that he needed further education. An old friend who was attending Oberlin College, an integrated institution near Cleveland, Ohio, encouraged Bruce to apply. Bruce enrolled at Oberlin, where he became the outstanding student in his class and excelled in mathematics. After a year, however, his money had run out, and his requests to the college for financial aid were turned down. He then moved to St. Louis, where he worked at various trades for a year before traveling farther south into Arkansas and Tennessee.

Increasingly, Bruce heard stories of new opportunities for black Americans in the Deep South, who were now guaranteed the right to vote under the newly passed Reconstruction Acts. In several southern states black Americans made up the majority of the population, and they were slowly beginning to exercise political power. In Mississippi in 1868, 17 freed slaves had joined 49 white men to form a group that wrote a new constitution for the state.

In that same year, Bruce visited Mississippi at the invitation of Samuel Ireland, a prominent black leader whom Bruce had met in St. Louis. Ireland introduced Bruce to James L. Alcorn, a former slave owner who was running for governor. Both Ireland and Alcorn encouraged Bruce to move to Mississippi, and in 1869 he settled on a farm in Floreyville, where he became a successful planter and quickly acquired considerable landholdings. Bruce also became active in Republican party politics, and following the inauguration of James Alcorn as governor in 1870 Bruce was appointed to Alcorn's personal staff. Bruce was especially impressed by Alcorn's promise in his inaugural address to gain full equality for black men in the state.

During the next few years Bruce became prominent in state politics. He held appointed offices of increasing importance, including superintendent of schools for Bolivar County, and then sought elective office. He became county sheriff in 1872 and two years later was elected by the state legislature to serve in the U.S. Senate. Bruce's election as a senator attracted public attention throughout the country, and even the *New York Times* praised Bruce's election in an editorial that lauded his intelligence and "irreproachable private character."

Bruce took his Senate seat in March 1875. With the support of influential Republican members, he was appointed to several important Senate committees, including Education and Labor. During his six years in the Senate, Bruce was a strong supporter of minority rights, including those of the American Indian, and he strongly opposed the exclusion of Chinese workers. He also took a special interest in legislation that strengthened navigation of the Mississippi and worked for the implementation of a flood-control program along the river.

One of Bruce's fellow senators was Lewis V. Bogy, who represented Missouri. Many years earlier, when Bruce was still in his teens and visiting St. Louis, Bogy had asked Bruce to carry his heavy valise down to the docks, then refused to pay him as promised for the service. Now both men were serving together in the Senate, and Bogy needed Bruce's support for a bill. Bruce refused to give him automatic support, reminding him of the incident many years earlier. Bogy quickly apologized and offered payment with interest, but Bruce declined, saying that he would support the bill only if Bogy could convince him of its merits. The two men became close friends and their relationship continued until Bogy's death some years later.

By 1880 the Democratic party controlled the Mississippi state legislature, and Bruce, who was the first black to serve a full term as senator, was not reelected to a second term. Two years earlier he had married Josephine Wilson, a schoolteacher from Cleveland, and the couple had an infant son. They now decided to remain in Washington rather than returning to Bruce's home state. Bruce hoped that the newly elected Republican president, James Garfield, whom he had strongly supported, would name him to an important government post.

Garfield tried to persuade Bruce to accept an appointment as ambassador to Brazil, but Bruce declined on the grounds that slavery was still legal in that country. Bruce also refused an appointment as an assistant to the postmaster general and requested instead that the president name him register of the treasury. His wish was granted and in May 1881 Blanche Bruce was confirmed by the Senate for this position. It was the highest political appointment that a black American had ever received.

At that time the U.S. Treasury Department employed more blacks than all other government departments combined, and Bruce is believed to have chosen this position because of the opportunity it offered to serve other members of his race. The position of register was also prestigious in its own right: Bruce's signature now became one of three that appeared on every piece of paper money printed in the country.

Bruce held the position of register for four years, until the inauguration of a Democrat, Grover Cleveland, in 1885. During the next four years, Bruce became a popular lecturer on a variety of topics, including race relations and education, and toured the country giving speeches that were widely praised. Following the election of the Republican Benjamin Harrison in 1888, Bruce received another political appointment, this time as recorder of deeds for the District of Columbia, which lasted until Cleveland's reelection in 1892. During the early 1890s Bruce also served as a member of the Washington, D.C., school board and in 1894 became a member of the board of trustees of Howard University, which had awarded him an honorary degree a year earlier.

In March 1897, following the inauguration of Republican president William McKinley, Bruce asked the president for his old job as register of the treasury.

However, it took months for McKinley to respond, and Bruce was not sworn in until December 1897. He died three months later, on March 17, 1898, as a result of chronic diabetes and kidney disease.

The black race and all of Washington mourned the passing of Blanche Bruce with his family and friends. The *Boston Herald* reported: "The death of Blanche K. Bruce, Register of the Treasury, removes one of the strong men of the colored race in this country. He was not so popular among his own people as he deserved to be, but he enjoyed the confidence of those who knew him without regard to color." Bruce once said, "I have diligently sought to be advised of the will and wants of the people of my state, that I might faithfully represent one and effectually meet the others. . . . Appreciating my obligation to my race, I have sought impartially and justly to ascertain and subserve the interests of all classes of the citizens of Mississippi."

RALPH BUNCHE

Diplomat and Nobel Peace Prize winner Ralph Bunche was born in Detroit, Michigan, on August 7, 1904. He was the descendant of slaves and also had several Native American ancestors. Bunche's father was a barber and his mother a musician. When Ralph was 10 years old, the family moved to Albuquerque, New Mexico, because Mrs. Bunche, who was ill, needed to live in a dry climate.

However, in 1916 both of Ralph's parents died, and he was sent to Los Angeles to be raised by his maternal grandmother.

When Ralph Bunche was attending school, his grandmother received a note on his report card that he was unruly in class. She went to see the principal and asked if her grandson was being given courses that would prepare him for college. The principal said no; like all black children, Ralph was enrolled in practical commercial courses which would prepare him for a job after finishing school. Bunche's grandmother insisted that he was going to college no matter what the cost and the school should prepare him for it. Although the principal argued that few white children, let alone blacks, attended college, he changed Bunche's curriculum to academic courses and he graduated in 1922 with highest honors from Jefferson High School, where he was class valedictorian.

The school principal congratulated Bunche's grandmother on his achievements. He commented that he did very well in academics and athletics and that the school had never thought of him as a Negro. To this, his grandmother said, "Why not? He *is* a Negro and proud of it. So am I. What you have just said is an insult to Ralph, to me, to his parents, and the whole race. . . ." Ralph later said, "success, I must confess, had a sweeter taste because of color."

Bunche received several scholarships to the University of California at Los Angeles (UCLA), where he majored in international relations. He supported himself by working as a janitor and doing other odd jobs.

At UCLA Bunche distinguished himself as both a student and an athlete. He was the star guard on three championship basketball teams and also played baseball and football. In addition, he became a skilled debater and orator. During his undergraduate years, Bunche developed an interest in race relations, a field in which he would later become an expert.

Bunche graduated with highest honors from UCLA in 1927 and was elected to Phi Beta Kappa, the national honor society. Delivering the valedictory address, Bunche spoke of respecting each person's rights. He said our basic dilemma is that "Man *learns* and *knows* but he does not *do* as well as he knows." He told the audience to "Look up, not down, look out, not in, and lend a hand. . . vision is the quality which all men may have in common. It is that 'bigness' of soul and heart which enables man to understand—to understand and love his fellows."

Residents of his neighborhood raised $1,000 so that Bunche could continue his education, and that fall he enrolled at Harvard University. In 1928, after receiving a master of arts degree in government from Harvard, Bunche began teaching political science at Howard University in Washington, D.C. While there he married Ruth Harris, one of his students, and they eventually had three children. Bunche became a full professor at Howard and chairman of the political science department.

After four years at Howard, Bunche returned to Harvard in 1932 to earn his Ph.D. in government. A fellowship from the university allowed him to do research in Africa for his dissertation, a comparative study of the governments of French Togoland (now the Republic of Togo) and Dahomey (now Benin). Instead of using official government reports for his research, Bunche traveled with natives into the interiors of both countries and personally observed conditions there. Bunche's dissertation received a prize from the Harvard faculty and earned him the Ph.D. in 1934.

Bunche returned to Howard to teach for several years. Then, in 1936–37, on a fellowship from the Social Science Research Council, he did further study at the London School of Economics and at the University of Capetown in South Africa. He also traveled extensively in East Africa and lived for three months with the Kikuyu tribe in Kenya as an honorary tribal citizen. Returning to the United States, Bunche traveled around the world via Malaya, the Philippines, China, Japan, and Hawaii.

Bunche's first long publication on race relations, a booklet entitled *A World View of Race*, was issued in 1937 by the Progressive Education Association. He also published a number of articles on the subject in several periodicals. From 1938 to 1940 Bunche was on leave from Howard University to serve on the staff of the Carnegie Corporation in New York City. During these years, he worked as chief assistant to Gunnar Myrdal, a prominent Swedish sociologist who was studying the conditions of black Americans. The two often traveled together, and several times they were driven out of towns in the South by angry residents who accused them of "stirring up trouble." Myrdal later published the results of his research in a book called *An American Dilemma* (1944), long considered a classic study of race relations in the United States.

In 1941, as World War II raged in Europe and Asia, Bunche again obtained a leave from Howard University so that he could work as a policy analyst for the U.S. government. He served in the Office of Strategic Services (OSS) as an expert on Africa and the Far East and advised the Joint Chiefs of Staff on colonial areas around the world. After several years with the OSS, Bunche joined the U.S. Department of State as a specialist on colonial affairs. He received several promotions and for a time served as acting chief of the Division of Dependent Area Affairs—the first African American to hold the post of acting chief in any State Department office.

In 1945 Bunche was an adviser to the U.S. delegation attending the Conference on International Organization in San Francisco. This was the meeting that led to the formation of the United Nations. Earlier, Bunche had written sections for the organization's charter on the governing of former colonies. After the war he served as a U.S. representative to the UN General Assembly, which met in London, and also represented his country at major conferences in Europe and America.

Bunche joined the Secretariat of the United Nations in 1946 as director of the Trusteeship Division, which he had helped to organize. A year later he was sent to the Middle East as a representative of the United Nations Special Committee on Palestine. In December 1947 he became principal secretary of the UN Palestine Commission. Bunche would have preferred to continue in the Trusteeship Division, which oversaw lands that had been colonies prior to World War II. However, he realized that the resolution of conflict in Palestine was an important issue that he could not ignore.

At the heart of the Palestine conflict was warfare between Jews and Arabs, both of whom lived in the region. For many years the region of Palestine had been ruled by Great Britain. After World War II Britain agreed to let the United Nations decide Palestine's future. In 1947 the UN voted to divide the region into separate Arab and Jewish states. Civil war broke out as Jews and Arabs fought over territory.

In his role with the UN Palestine Commission, Bunche became a major figure in resolving the Arab-Jewish dispute. When the UN–appointed mediator, Count Folke Bernadotte, was assassinated in September 1948, Bunche (who had also been targeted in the assassination but, thanks to a passport dispute, had been prevented from accompanying Bernadotte as planned) became acting mediator in the conflict. Bunche's primary challenge during the weeks of often-tense negotiations was getting delegates from the new Jewish state of Israel and the surrounding Arab states to sit down together. He used every means possible to get the two sides to think of each other as humans rather than enemies, including three-way billiard games between himself and the Israeli and Arab delegates. Eventually his persistence paid off, and he brought about an armistice between Israel and its Arab neighbors.

Bunche returned home to a flood of acclaim and prestigious job offers, including an offer from President Truman to become the first black assistant secretary of state. (Mindful of the Jim Crow laws existing in Washington, D.C., Bunche refused the offer.) The greatest honor of all came from the Norwegian Parliament—Bunche was awarded the 1950 Nobel Peace Prize in recognition of his efforts to bring peace to the Middle East. In his acceptance speech, Bunche, the first African American to be so honored, stated, "If today we speak of peace, we also speak of the United Nations, for in this era, peace and the United Nations have become inseparable," and claimed that the UN must work toward an end to colonialism if it wished to promote peace. Bunche's words proved prophetic: he returned to the UN as an expert on trustee and colonial affairs and spent five years attempting to mediate peaceful paths toward nationhood for African colonies agitating for independence.

In 1955, Bunche was named an under secretary of the UN, and in 1956 was asked to turn his attention to the Suez Canal conflict, which was escalating rapidly from a military dispute between Israel and Egypt into an international incident involving Great Britain, France, and the Soviet Union. Bunche and UN Secretary General Dag Hammarskjöld drafted a resolution establishing the United Nations Emergency Force, impartial UN troops that would keep the peace. These troops proved essential in upholding the UN–mandated cease-fire in the Suez conflict, and their presence has played a crucial part in the UN's efforts to be an effective peacekeeping organization.

Bunche was named under secretary for special affairs in 1957, a post he held for 10 years. During this period, he directed successful peacekeeping operations in Yemen (1963), the Congo (1964), Cyprus (1964), and Kashmir (1965). For this work, President John F. Kennedy named Bunche a winner of the Presidential Medal of Freedom, the highest award that can be bestowed upon an American civilian.

In 1967, Bunche, in failing health, tendered his resignation but was called out of retirement at the outbreak of the Six Day War between Israel and the Arab countries of the Middle East. In 1970, he played an essential role in negotiating the independence of Bahrain, a small island located in the Persian Gulf that was simultaneously gaining its independence from Great Britain and attempting to defend that independence from the territorial claims of Iran. A year later, Bunche was hospitalized, and on December 9, 1971, he died in New York City, leaving behind an unparalleled legacy of dedication to the cause of world peace.

BENJAMIN O. DAVIS, SR., and
BENJAMIN O. DAVIS, JR.

Military leader Benjamin O. Davis, Sr., was born on June 1, 1877, in Washington, D.C. One of his grandfathers was a slave who bought his freedom in 1800. Davis's father worked as a messenger for the Department of the Interior. Benjamin Davis attended public schools in Washington, and as a teenager he often visited Fort Myer, the U.S. Army post across the Potomac River near Arlington, Virginia.

After attending Howard University in Washington, D.C., Davis joined the 8th U.S. Infantry as a first lieutenant in July 1898, during the Spanish-American War. He was mustered out of the infantry the following March, and three months later enlisted in the cavalry of the regular army as a private. Davis was sent to the Philippine Islands, where he served for two years. He was promoted to corporal and then to squadron sergeant major. In February 1901 Davis was commissioned a second lieutenant of cavalry and later that year became adjutant at Fort Washakie, Wyoming.

Following his promotion to first lieutenant in March 1905, Davis became a professor of military science and tactics at Wilberforce University, a black institution in Wilberforce, Ohio. He remained there for four years. In 1909 Davis was sent by the army to Monrovia, Liberia, where he served as military attaché until 1912. He was then assigned to the 9th Cavalry at Fort Russell, Wyoming. The 9th Cavalry later moved to Douglas, Arizona, where it patrolled the U.S.–Mexico border.

In 1915 Davis returned to Wilberforce to teach military science. That same year he was promoted to captain and two years later became an acting major. In the summer of 1917 Davis was again sent to the Philippines, where he served as supply officer of the 9th Cavalry at Camp Stotsenburg. In 1918 Davis was named a temporary lieutenant colonel; two years later the rank became permanent.

From 1920 to 1924 Davis served as a professor of military science and tactics at the Tuskegee Institute, the world-famous educational institution for blacks founded in the late 19th century by Booker T. Washington. In 1924 Davis was sent to Cleveland, Ohio, where he became an instructor in the Ohio National Guard for five years.

In 1929 Davis was ordered to accompany a delegation of mothers and widows of U.S. soldiers to Europe. The soldiers had been killed during World War I, and the women were making a pilgrimage to the cemeteries where they were buried. Upon his return to the United States, Davis was highly commended for his role in this assignment by both the secretary of war and the army's quartermaster general. In 1930 Davis was promoted to colonel.

During the next eight years, Davis taught alternately at Wilberforce and Tuskegee. In 1938 he became commanding officer of the 369th Infantry of the New York National Guard. Two years later, in October 1940, Davis was promoted to brigadier general—the first black American general in the U.S. Army. Davis served as brigade commander with the Second Cavalry Division in Fort Riley, Kansas, for six months before his retirement in June 1941.

Davis was recalled to active duty later that month as assistant to the inspector general in Washington, D.C. In October 1942, 10 months after the United States entered World War II, Davis was sent to

England as an adviser to General Dwight D. Eisenhower, then commanding general of the European Front. Throughout the war Davis advised the general on the use of black soldiers. He worked to ease racial tensions and to end discrimination in all of the armed services.

Davis's years of service between 1941 and 1945 seem to be the most important. With his rank of brigadier general, he showed that blacks can attain positions of authority and leadership. During the time that he worked in the inspector general's office, black soldiers and officers felt that they could speak freely to Davis, and he worked privately with other high ranking blacks in trying to end discrimination in the military. It has been said that the eventual change in the military's policy of segregation came about partly due to Davis's contributions.

As Davis approached his 64th birthday, he was often questioned about retirement, to which he replied: "I think I have done my share but if the War Department desires me to continue to serve in the national emergency, I will have an open mind." Davis retired permanently from the army in 1948 after 50 years of service. He died on November 26, 1970. Davis was married for many years and had three children: two daughters and a son, Benjamin O. Davis, Jr., who was born on December 18, 1912, in Washington, D.C.

Like his father, Benjamin O. Davis, Jr., attended public schools in Washington, D.C. In 1929 he graduated from Central High School in Cleveland, Ohio, where he was president of his class and an outstanding student. Davis junior attended Western Reserve University in Cleveland for one year, then studied mathematics for two years at the University of Chicago. He hoped to become a mathematics teacher, but in 1932 his plans changed when he was offered an appointment to the U.S. Military Academy at West Point, New York.

Although he failed the entrance examinations the first time he took them, Davis junior studied hard and succeeded in his second attempt. During his first year at West Point, he was subjected to a rigorous form of hazing known as the silent treatment. No other cadet spoke to him for an entire year, but Davis junior endured this treatment without complaint and was cheered by his classmates when the year had ended.

Davis graduated in 1936, the first black to do so since 1889. Davis junior then attended Infantry School at Fort Benning, Georgia, and then served for several years as an instructor in military science and tactics at Tuskegee Institute—again following in his father's footsteps. During World War II Davis junior trained as a pilot at the Advanced Army Flying School and served with the Army Air Corps in Italy and North Africa. He received regular promotions and in May 1944 became a full colonel. In September of that year he received the Distinguished Flying Cross—which was pinned on his chest by his father, Brigadier General Benjamin O. Davis, Sr.

In April 1945 Davis junior led an air corps bombing attack on railway targets in Austria. For his bravery he won the army's Silver Star—the first time that a black American fighter pilot had been given that award. After the war Davis became field commander of the 477th Composite Group at Godman Field, Kentucky, the first black American to hold such an important position in the Army Air Corps. From 1946 to 1949 Davis was commander of the Lockbourne Army Air Base.

From 1941 to 1949, Davis experienced eight years of a segregated Army Air Force. In June 1949, Secretary Symington and chief of staff Vandenberg imposed integration on the air force, which surprisingly was an immediate success. According to Davis, "These men had correctly determined that the Air Force would be a better military service in a better nation by the elimination of segregation. The courageous performance of black airmen in World War II helped Symington and Vandenberg immeasurably in making their decision."

In the 1940s, the army reported having one general and 10 colonels as top black officers. While the number of blacks enlisting in the military increased over the years, in 1965 blacks made up less than four percent of officers in the army and two percent in the air force.

In 1949 Davis enrolled at the Air War College in Alabama and graduated a year later. He then joined the staff at the headquarters of the U.S. Air Force in Washington, D.C., where he was named chief of the fighter branch in 1951. In early 1954 he became director of operations and training of the Far East Air Forces.

In October 1954 Davis was promoted to the rank of brigadier general in the air force by President Dwight D. Eisenhower—whom his father had advised when Eisenhower commanded American troops in Europe during World War II. Benjamin O. Davis, Jr., thus became the first black American air force general.

In addition to the Distinguished Flying Cross and the Silver Star, Davis was awarded the Air Medal, with four oak-leaf clusters; the Legion of Merit; and the French Croix de Guerre, with palm. He was elevated to the rank of lieutenant general before retiring from the air force.

WILLIAM H. HASTIE

Judge and educator William H. Hastie was born on November 17, 1904, in Knoxville, Tennessee. He was the only child of William and Roberta Childs Hastie. Young Hastie's father had attended Ohio Wesleyan and Howard universities, where he studied mathematics and pharmacy, but as a black man he was unable to find employment as an actuary or a pharmacist. He eventually found a job with the U.S. government, becoming the first African American to be appointed a clerk in the Pension Office. Roberta Childs Hastie was a schoolteacher who had been educated at Fisk University.

Young William Hastie attended public schools in Knoxville and, after the age of 12, in Washington, D.C., where his father had been transferred. He went on to attend Washington's Dunbar High School, one of the country's leading secondary schools for black students. One of his classmates was Charles Drew, who later became a world-renowned doctor who pioneered the preservation of blood plasma. At Dunbar, students were taught that there was nothing they could not do. They would do well in school, go to college, and enter a profession. Parents of many students pushed them to be academically outstanding.

Hastie graduated from Dunbar at the top of his class in 1921, although the occasion was bittersweet; his father had died suddenly a few months earlier. Fortunately, William and Roberta Hastie had carefully saved money for many years so that their talented son could attend a leading college, and that fall he was able to enroll at Amherst College in Massachusetts.

Blacks at Amherst were not treated with the same respect as white students. They were not allowed opportunities such as joining fraternities or the glee club. Hastie, along with fellow blacks, simply wanted to be given the chance to compete equally with other students. Willing to fight for this, he said, "You with brown skins will not make Chi Phi nor even get bids to fraternity dances, not now. But continue sending more and more representatives of your race against whom no negligibility can be found except the color of their skins, and unless human nature is basically rotten, recognition will come in time."

Hastie majored in mathematics at Amherst, but he took a variety of courses in other fields, including German, Greek, and physics, as well as a class in creative writing with the poet Robert Frost. Hastie also found time for athletics at Amherst and starred as a member of the varsity track team. In 1925 he graduated as the top student in his class. He was elected to Phi Beta Kappa, the national honor society, and later served as president of the Amherst chapter of that organization.

Hastie's high academic standing earned him a fellowship for further study at either the University of Paris or Oxford University in England, but he decided to remain in the United States and earn money so that he could eventually attend law school. For two years Hastie taught mathematics and science at the Bordentown Manual Training School, an institution for black youth in New Jersey. Then, in 1927, he entered Harvard Law School where he excelled in his studies and served as an editor of the *Law Review*.

After graduating near the top of his class in 1930, Hastie joined the faculty of the Howard University Law School in Washington, D.C., which he said was "the one institution to which a colored man at present can look for an opportunity to teach law." In 1931 he began practicing law in Washington and a year later earned a doctorate in law from Harvard University.

In 1933 Hastie began his long career of service with the U.S. government when he became assistant solicitor of the Department of the Interior. Four years later he was appointed judge of the U.S. District Court for the Virgin Islands and thus became the first black person ever appointed to a federal judgeship. This position was especially appropriate for a black appointee because the Virgin Islands then had a population that was 90 percent black.

After his two-year term expired, Hastie returned to Howard University as dean and professor of law. In November 1940 he took a leave of absence from Howard to become an aide to Secretary of War Henry L. Stimson. Hastie's job was to advise Stimson on the role of African Americans in the armed forces. Hastie was successful in his efforts to increase the number of blacks in the army and air force. However, he was dismayed to find that there were few black officers, and that the armed services seemed unwilling to train soldiers for these positions.

At that time, the armed forces were segregated, and whites and blacks did not serve in the same unit. Moreover, white troops were given the more prestigious, skilled jobs, while blacks were assigned to menial labor. Hastie protested the continuation of these policies but he was ignored. Finally, in January 1943 Hastie resigned from the War Department in protest.

Hastie returned to Howard University as a professor and dean of the law school. However, he continued to protest the unfair treatment of blacks in the armed forces, including reports of assaults on black soldiers by white civilians and policemen near bases where they were stationed. Hastie's protests had some positive consequences: in March 1944 army officials ordered that black and white soldiers be trained together at officer candidate schools. Four years later President Harry S Truman issued an executive order ending all forms of segregation in the U.S. armed forces.

Hastie battled segregation in other areas besides the military. He was a leading opponent of the poll tax, a fee that was used to keep poor blacks from voting in the South. The poll tax was finally banned in national elections by the Twenty-fourth Amendment to the U.S. Constitution, which was ratified in 1964. Two years later the U.S. Supreme Court also banned the poll tax in state and local elections. Hastie's vigorous opposition to segregation earned him recognition from several organizations, including the National Association for the Advancement of Colored People (NAACP), which awarded him its prestigious Spingarn Medal in 1943.

In 1946 Hastie was appointed governor of the Virgin Islands by President Truman. He accepted the position of governor because he thought of it as an honor to his race. Hastie had been content with his work at Howard University, and the move to the Virgin Islands transferred him out of the middle of the civil rights battle. Hastie did, however, return to the mainland often in order to remain involved with the civil rights movement.

Although Hastie worked hard to improve conditions in the Virgin Islands and encouraged tourism to bolster the country's faltering economy, he was often frustrated in his role as governor. Hastie was hailed by the people at first—Isdor Paiewonsky, a Virgin Island businessman said, "Hastie was such an example of the proper use of political power"—but later was condemned by legislators who believed the governor was not spending his time wisely. The editor of the St. Thomas *Daily News* wrote that although Hastie's first obligation was clearly to the Virgin Islands, "However, there is evidence that he devotes too much of his attention and energy to dealing with racial, educational and political matters on a national scale while his government continues to disintegrate under him."

During the 1948 presidential election, Hastie took a leave of absence to campaign widely for Truman. Following the president's reelection, Hastie was rewarded for his support when Truman named him to a seat on the U.S. Court of Appeals for the Third Circuit. While waiting to be confirmed [by the U.S. Senate] it was said that failure of all members to provide "a prompt, favorable report can only be attributed to the fact that [Hastie] is a Negro." Following his confirmation in July 1950, Hastie became the first black federal judge.

For the rest of his life, Hastie and his family—he had married in 1943 and had a daughter—made their home in Philadelphia, the site of the Third Circuit Court of Appeals. In 1968 Hastie became chief judge of the court and served in that capacity until 1971, when he retired with the title of senior judge. In 1975 he was named that year's recipient of the Philadelphia Award, presented annually to an individual for advancing the "best and largest interest of the community." This unsung pioneer of the civil rights movement died in East Norriton, Pennsylvania, on April 14, 1976.

The United States Supreme
Court justice Thurgood Marshall was born on July
2, 1908, in West Baltimore, Maryland. He was the
second son of William, a waiter, and Norma Marshall,
a schoolteacher. William Marshall, who had little
education but a keen mind, taught young Thurgood
how to debate and encouraged him to pursue a legal
career. From his mother, Thurgood learned tact and

diplomacy. The Marshalls stressed the value of personal dignity and modesty, but they never recommended meekness. "Anyone calls you nigger," said William to Thurgood, "you not only got my permission to fight him—you got my orders to fight him."

Graduating from high school in 1925, Marshall enrolled in Lincoln University, an all-black Philadelphia institution where he became a star debater. In the fall of his senior year, Marshall married University of Pennsylvania student Vivian Burey; the following June, he graduated from Lincoln with honors in the humanities. He entered the law school of Howard University, a black institution in Washington, D.C., in 1930.

At the end of his first year, Howard's professors named Marshall top student in his class. Among the distinguished professors who helped him polish his skills was Charles Hamilton Houston, a brilliant attorney and pioneering civil rights activist. Houston provided legal assistance to the National Association for the Advancement of Colored People (NAACP), an organization founded in 1909 to combat racial discrimination. Marshall often helped him plan strategy for his NAACP cases.

In 1933, Marshall graduated first in his class from Howard Law School. Although Harvard University immediately offered him a postgraduate scholarship, he was eager to begin practicing law and turned it down. After passing the Maryland State law examination, he opened a law office in east Baltimore.

In the grip of the Great Depression (1929–40), few Americans of any race could afford legal representation, and black lawyers had a particularly hard time. In his first year of practice, Marshall had no paying clients, and he often took on the cases of poor people, thereby earning him a reputation as "the little man's lawyer." Preparing for each trial with painstaking care, he won many of his early cases.

Marshall's public service work gained him not only experience but a steadily growing reputation. In 1934, the local chapter of the NAACP named him as its lawyer, an unpaid but exhilarating job. He kicked off his NAACP career by organizing a boycott of white-owned Baltimore stores that sold to blacks in a black neighborhood yet employed only whites. When the shopkeepers responded by suing the NAACP, Marshall teamed up with Charles Houston and successfully defended the organization in federal court.

In 1935, the NAACP began to concentrate on integrating graduate and professional schools. With Houston, Marshall scored his first major court victory when he won a suit against the University of Maryland for refusing to admit blacks to its law school. In 1936, Marshall accepted a job as assistant to Houston, who had become first special counsel at NAACP headquarters in New York City. Defending the rights of black students and teachers in the South, the two men spent the next two years traveling from one southern courthouse to another. Between trips, Marshall continued to help poor clients at his small Baltimore office.

Marshall's first case as assistant special counsel involved the University of Missouri Law School, which had refused to admit a qualified black student. Working with Houston, Marshall used the "separate-but-equal" doctrine in arguing the Missouri case, asserting that the law school had to admit the student unless it could offer "equal" education at an all-black institution. (U.S. courts had been using this doctrine, established by a Supreme Court case known as *Plessy v. Ferguson*, to decide segregation cases since 1896. Basically, *Plessy* allowed racial segregation as long as blacks had access to "equal" or equivalent facilities.)

The Missouri Law School case went all the way to the U.S. Supreme Court, which found in the NAACP's favor by a vote of six to two. The decision meant that Missouri—and other states—now had only two choices: to admit blacks to their all-white, publicly funded schools, or to build and staff brand-new, equal facilities for blacks—an almost impossibly expensive proposition. Elated NAACP officials realized that one day the Supreme Court might extend the doctrine to the nation's public schools at all levels.

In 1939, Marshall, now black America's most prominent attorney, became director-counsel of a new organization: the NAACP Legal Defense and Educational Fund, Inc., a body created to provide free legal aid to blacks who suffered racial injustice. As fund chief, Marshall prepared his first solo Supreme Court brief in 1940. In this case, *Chambers v. Florida*, the NAACP sought to overturn the convictions of a white man. Marshall argued that police officials had wrung confessions from the men after five days of nonstop grilling, and that such "sunrise confessions" violated the U.S. Constitution's guarantee of "due process of law."

Marshall next focused his sights on a notorious device employed to keep southern blacks from voting. In the South, primary winners always won the election. Only party members could vote in the primary, and only whites could belong to the party. Marshall based his 1944 challenge to the "white primary" on the Fifteenth Amendment, which forbids states to deprive citizens of their vote "on account of race, color, or previous condition of servitude." The U.S. Supreme Court upheld Marshall's argument, a decision that sounded the death knell for the South's white primary.

In 1946, the NAACP awarded Marshall its highest award, the Spingarn Medal. By 1948, the 40-year-old lawyer had earned the nickname "Mr. Civil Rights." That same year, he went after unfair housing practices. Arguing before the Supreme Court, Marshall maintained that restrictive covenants—agreements between whites that effectively kept blacks out of white neighborhoods—restricted blacks' rights as Americans. Agreeing, the court struck down the covenants. Two years later Marshall argued and won two major segregation-in-education cases before the Supreme Court. His twin victories led to the admission of black students to the Universities of Oklahoma and Texas, and in 1950 he succeeded in getting a black law student enrolled at Louisiana State University.

In 1952, Marshall and his NAACP team scored one of the organization's most resounding triumphs. After extensive preparation, the lawyers brought *Brown v. Board of Education of Topeka* to the Supreme Court. A combination of five cases from around the country, *Brown* was aimed at a formidable target: public school segregation in America. Marshall argued that segregation was inherently unequal because it implied that government believed "Negroes [to be] inferior to all other human beings," and that it had a permanent, devastating effect on black children. In May 1954, a year and a half after he began his battle for Brown, Marshall had the joy of hearing Chief Justice Earl Warren read the Supreme Court's unanimous verdict: "In the field of public education the doctrine of 'separate but equal' has no place." School segregation had been declared unconstitutional.

Marshall's victory was marred by the news that his wife was fatally ill with cancer. Following her death in 1955, Marshall married a Hawaiian, Cecelia Suyat, with whom he eventually had two sons. During the seven years that followed his marriage, he waged to escape school desegregation, opposing southern attempts to ban the NAACP, lining up his forces to back the Reverend Martin Luther King, Jr., and vigorously defending civil rights demonstrators.

In September 1962, President John F. Kennedy appointed Marshall to the Second Circuit Court of Appeals. During his four years as a judge, Marshall ruled on a variety of cases, including the use of illegally obtained evidence in criminal trials, the deportation of aliens, and the First Amendment right to free expression. Not one of his 98 majority opinions was overturned by the Supreme Court. This remarkable record was in large part responsible for Marshall's 1965 appointment as U.S. solicitor general, a post never before held by a black citizen. During his two years as the nation's top-ranking courtroom advocate, Marshall won 14 of his 19 cases, most of them dealing with civil rights and privacy issues.

In 1967, Thurgood Marshall again made history when President Lyndon B. Johnson named him America's first black Supreme Court justice. In case after case, he defended individual rights and educational and legal equality for all races. After more than two decades of distinguished service as an Associate Justice, Marshall retired from the court in 1991.

Two years later, on January 24, 1993, Marshall died of heart failure at Bethdesda Naval Medical Center in Maryland. He was 84 years old.

At Marshall's funeral service, Chief Justice William H. Rehnquist said in his eulogy: "As a result of his career as a lawyer and as a judge, Thurgood Marshall left an indelible mark not just upon the law but upon his country. Inscribed above the front entrance to the Supreme Court building are the words 'Equal justice under law.' Surely no one individual did more to make these words a reality than Thurgood Marshall."

COLIN POWELL

Military leader Colin Powell was born in New York City on April 5, 1937. His father was a shipping clerk and his mother worked as a seamstress. Both parents, who had emigrated many years earlier from Jamaica, stressed the importance of education to Colin and his older sister, Marilyn.

Powell grew up in the Hunts Point section of the South Bronx and graduated from public high school there in 1954. He then enrolled at the City College of New York, where he majored in geology. The ambitious and energetic Powell also joined the Reserve Officers' Training Corps (ROTC), where he found that he thrived under military discipline. He became commander of the Pershing Rifles, the ROTC precision drill team, and graduated at the top of the college's ROTC class of 1958 with the rank of cadet colonel, the highest rank in the corps.

Upon graduation, Powell was commissioned a second lieutenant in the U.S. Army and went to West Germany after completing the necessary military training. There he helped to maintain a watch on the troops of the Warsaw Pact nations. He rose from platoon leader to commander of a rifle company. By 1960, when he returned to the United States, Powell was a first lieutenant—he had begun to climb the military ranks.

After several years of service, Powell was sent to South Vietnam as a military adviser to an infantry battalion in the early 1960s. Powell returned to South Vietnam for a second tour of duty in the late 1960s as a division operations officer. Wounded twice during his years in Vietnam, he was cited for bravery and received eleven medals for his service, including the Legion of Merit.

After returning to the United States, Powell enrolled in the graduate school of George Washington University in Washington, D.C., where he earned a master's degree in business administration in 1971. The following year Powell, who then held the rank of major, was appointed a White House Fellow. The fellowship sponsored promising military officers the opportunity to serve for a year in a department of the executive branch. This program was important to Powell because it helped officers who desired a career in policy-making. He was assigned to the staff of Frank C. Carlucci, then deputy director of the Office of Management and Budget (OMB). Both Carlucci and OMB director Caspar W. Weinberger were impressed with Powell and years later would hire him as their deputy.

During 1973 Powell served as a battalion commander in Korea. The following year he was appointed to a staff job at the Pentagon. In 1975 Powell, now a colonel, enrolled at the National War College. Before completing the course of study, he was assigned as the commander of the Second Brigade of the 101st Airborne Division at Fort Campbell, Kentucky. He returned to the War College in 1976 to graduate with distinction.

During the late 1970s Powell served as a military aide in the Department of Defense and as an assistant to the Secretary of Energy. After the election of President Ronald Reagan in 1980, Powell, now a major general, worked briefly as an aide to the new deputy secretary of defense, Frank Carlucci. Carlucci described Powell as "extraordinarily bright, articulate, and with excellent judgement." He said, "Nobody could provide you with better guidance . . . in the United States government." In 1981 Powell began two years of service as assistant commander of the Fourth Infantry Division at Fort Carson, Colorado. In the spring of 1983 Powell became deputy commander at Fort Leavenworth, Kansas, but he left this position in July to become senior military assistant to the secretary of defense, Caspar Weinberger.

Powell worked for Weinberger for three years, during which time he acquired a reputation as a skilled assistant who could expedite the flow of information and get along with different groups of people. He played an important role in several major military operations, including the U.S. invasion of Grenada in October 1983 and the 1986 raid on Libya.

In June 1986 Powell left the Department of Defense to assume another infantry command, this time as commanding general of the Fifth Corps, stationed in Frankfurt, Germany. However, six months later Powell was asked by Frank Carlucci, President Reagan's new national security adviser, to be Carlucci's deputy. Powell was reluctant to leave his military post for another civilian job, but President Reagan himself intervened and persuaded Powell to accept the offer.

Carlucci had succeeded Rear Admiral John Poindexter as national security adviser. Poindexter had been forced to resign after public disclosure of a secret arms deal with Iran, later known as the Iran-Contra scandal. General Powell was given the job of reorganizing the operations of the national security staff in line with the recommendations of the Tower Commission, which had been created by the president to investigate the scandal.

Powell proved once again that he was an efficient organizer who could work well with other people. Since he and Carlucci were alike in their approach to security policy, Carlucci often sent Powell to the White House to brief President Reagan. The personal relationship between Powell and Reagan grew, and in November 1987, when Carlucci succeeded Weinberger as secretary of defense, Reagan promoted Powell to national security adviser. Powell thus became the first African American to head the National Security Council.

In his new post Powell successfully coordinated the efforts of various technical advisers during the summit meeting in December 1987 between President Reagan and Russian leader Mikhail Gorbachev that led to the signing of the intermediate-range nuclear forces (INF) treaty. In the following months Powell had the responsibility of setting up an inspection program to make sure that the terms of the treaty were carried out. Despite existing rivalry among the involved government agencies, Powell worked out a cooperative effort with the Pentagon, the State Department, and the Arms Control and Disarmament Agency.

In August 1989 President George Bush nominated Powell to become chairman of the Joint Chiefs of Staff, the highest position of leadership in the nation's armed forces next to the president himself. In October, following his confirmation by the Senate, Powell became both the first African American and the youngest man to hold this important post.

Powell's skills as a military commander were soon needed. President George Bush and other government officials were angered by the international drug smuggling activities of General Manuel Noriega, the dictator of Panama. When Noriega's soldiers killed a U.S. marine in Panama, President Bush consulted with Powell, and both decided that the time had come to remove Noriega from power. As chairman of the Joint Chiefs, Powell had to see that the job was done.

In December 1989 Powell launched Operation Just Cause, an invasion of Panama by 26,000 U.S. troops. The operation was an enormous success: Noriega was quickly captured and brought to Florida for trial. He was later convicted on drug-trafficking charges and given a prison sentence.

In August 1990, when troops from Iraq invaded the neighboring country of Kuwait, Powell was again called upon by President Bush. Powell organized Operation Desert Shield, a deployment of 180,000 U.S. soldiers in Saudi Arabia, near the border that it shares with both Kuwait and Iraq. As both the United States and the United Nations demanded Iraq's withdrawal from Kuwait, Powell quietly made plans for an attack on Iraq, in cooperation with General H. Norman Schwarzkopf, head of U.S. forces in Saudi Arabia. Powell's major task was to coordinate the combined efforts of the United States and 17 other nations who had committed troops to the operation.

The U.N. Security Council ordered Iraqi leader Saddam Hussein to withdraw from Kuwait by January 15, 1991, or face military action. When Hussein ignored the deadline, Operation Desert Shield became Operation Desert Storm as multinational forces launched a massive air assault on Iraq. Following weeks of heavy bombing, a ground offensive began on February 24. Four days later Saddam Hussein, his army in shambles, agreed to withdraw from Kuwait.

Both Powell and Schwarzkopf were hailed as national heroes for leading the allied forces to victory in the Persian Gulf war. Powell was even considered as a likely candidate for vice-president in the 1992 election, but he told President Bush that he was not interested in becoming his running mate, choosing instead to remain as chairman of the Joint Chiefs of Staff, in which capacity he began to serve a new commander-in-chief, President Bill Clinton, in January 1993.

Powell's term as chairman of the Joint Chiefs of Staff ended eight months later, and so did his life in the military. Retiring from the U.S. Army made for a bittersweet time for him. Characteristically, he was looking forward to taking on new challenges. Yet he could not forget that he had been a soldier for more than 30 years and had enjoyed an honor-studded career that had carried him from the streets of the Bronx to the corridors of power in the nation's capital.

L. DOUGLAS WILDER

Politician Lawrence Douglas Wilder was born on January 17, 1931, in Richmond, Virginia, the seventh of eight children. His father was an insurance salesman and his mother worked as a maid. Wilder's grandparents on his father's side had married as slaves and then been separated; they were reunited after the Emancipation Proclamation of 1863.

Both of Wilder's parents paid close attention to his upbringing. His father was a strict disciplinarian, while his mother emphasized the importance of education and made him learn a new word every day. The family was poor but never went without food because they were able to grow and raise it themselves, despite the fact that they lived in the city.

Wilder attended segregated public schools in Richmond and earned spending money by doing various odd jobs, including shining shoes, washing windows, and operating an elevator. As a teenager he worked as a waiter in all-white Richmond hotels and clubs, where he was constantly exposed to racism. Years later he remembered racial jokes being told in his presence by diners, who treated him and other black personnel "like invisible men."

After graduating from high school in 1947, Wilder tried to enlist in the navy. However, he was only 16, and his mother refused to give the necessary permission. Instead he enrolled at Virginia Union College, an all-black institution in Richmond, and majored in chemistry. However, by the time he graduated in 1951 he had decided to become a lawyer.

Wilder's plans to enroll in law school were interrupted when he was drafted into the army to fight in the Korean War. He received the Bronze Star for valor—he braved enemy fire to rescue wounded troops—and later distinguished himself by forcing the surrender of a squad of enemy soldiers. When he and other black servicemen did not receive promotions for their efforts, Wilder filed a formal complaint with the government that led to more rapid recognition of African Americans in the armed services. Wilder ended his army service in 1953 with the rank of sergeant first class.

Wilder then returned to Richmond and was hired as a chemist by the state medical examiner's office. He spent most of his time running tests for alcohol levels in the blood. Wilder was impatient to begin the study of law, which the G.I. Bill would pay for, but he could not continue his studies in Virginia: at that time, blacks were banned from the state's law schools. In 1956 Wilder moved to Washington, D.C., and enrolled at the law school of Howard University, an all-black institution.

After graduating from Howard in 1959, Wilder returned to his old neighborhood in Richmond and set up a law practice. He specialized in criminal law and personal-injury cases, but because his clients were poor he found it difficult to earn a living. Wilder had to work hard to support himself and often took on too many clients. One of them sued Wilder for malpractice, claiming that the attorney had not given him adequate representation. As a consequence, Wilder was reprimanded by the Virginia Supreme Court for unprofessional conduct.

During the 1960s Wilder became involved in state politics as a spokesman for black causes, although he deliberately distanced himself from the national civil rights movement led by Martin Luther King, Jr. Although Wilder did not openly oppose King, privately he made it clear that he did not agree with

King's policy of nonviolence in working to end segregation.

Many blacks were upset by the remarks that Wilder made concerning racial issues. He said that blacks should stop making excuses and control their own destiny. Wilder told young people not to shun menial jobs, because any job is better than none. He said that blacks should accept some of the blame for the plight of their race.

In 1969 Wilder entered the race for a seat from Richmond in the state senate. The white vote was split among several white candidates, and Wilder was declared the winner. He became the first black elected to the Virginia legislature since the days of Reconstruction in the 19th century.

The Reverend Jesse Jackson, who knew Wilder in college, said: "The first time I met Doug, it was quickly apparent to me that he had his sights set on a goal higher than average. . . . We were just in fraternity politics then, but you could determine leadership traits and qualities."

As a state senator, Wilder cultivated a reputation as a confrontational, angry young black and often denounced racism from the senate floor. He became chairman of the important Privileges and Elections Committee and worked for legislation that would guarantee fair housing, labor union rights for public employees, and an increase in minority hiring by private businesses. Wilder also became known as an outspoken opponent of the death penalty, claiming that it was given far more often to blacks than to whites. Later he switched his position and became an advocate of the death penalty because he believed that blacks were being treated more fairly in the courts.

In July 1984 Wilder announced his candidacy for lieutenant governor of Virginia. By this time he had moderated his stand on other issues besides the death penalty and was no longer considered an outspoken liberal. Wilder campaigned throughout the state for the post for more than a year. He won the election in November 1985 with 51 percent of the vote, becoming the first African American to be elected to statewide office in Virginia.

Although the lieutenant governor's office is largely a ceremonial position, Wilder was sometimes called upon to make important decisions. In his official role of presiding over the state senate, he cast the tie-breaking vote that led to the establishment of a sex-education program in the state's schools. Wilder also served as chairman of the Drug Interdiction Task Force and chaired the National Democratic Lieutenant Governors Association.

For some time Wilder had been feuding privately with Charles Robb, the state Democratic leader who had been governor in the early 1980s. By 1986 their disagreements had become publicly known when some of Wilder's supporters accused Robb of secretly opposing the nomination of Wilder as lieutenant governor and offering only lukewarm support to his election campaign. Wilder himself began publicly criticizing the tax policies of the current governor, fellow Democrat Gerald Baliles.

Despite these intraparty wranglings, Baliles, Robb—now a U.S. senator—and Wilder had resolved their differences by the summer of 1989, and Wilder received the Democratic nomination for governor without opposition. His Republican opponent in the November election was J. Marshall Coleman, former state attorney general. Although Coleman was white, race was not discussed openly in the campaign. However, as the November election drew closer, Wilder occasionally drew attention in political speeches to his unique position as the first black candidate for governor of any state since Reconstruction.

The two major issues in the campaign were abortion rights and crime, especially drug-related offenses. Coleman supported a state constitutional amendment banning virtually all abortions, while Wilder was a strong defender of abortion rights. When Coleman accused Wilder of being "soft" on crime, Wilder proposed a tough antidrug program that he claimed he would personally supervise if elected.

On the eve of the election, Wilder appeared to have a comfortable lead. However, when returns were in, they showed Coleman losing by such a thin margin that a recount was ordered—the first statewide recount in Virginia history. The final tally declared Wilder the winner by less than 7,000 votes—one-third of one percent of the total cast.

Wilder immediately became a national political figure. He began making major speeches in other states, including New York, California, and Illinois—states with large numbers of electoral votes. Speculation immediately arose that Wilder was considering running for the U.S. presidency in 1992. In his speeches Wilder urged Democrats to move to the right politically, saying that they would recapture the White House only if they adopted a policy of "fiscal responsibility," stopped calling for tax increases, and reduced federal spending.

Speculation became reality in September 1991, when Wilder announced his candidacy for the Democratic presidential nomination. Meanwhile, he was having difficulty resolving financial problems in his own state. The Virginia economy was in decline, and the state government was faced with a severe loss of revenue that it needed for state services. Critics began referring to Wilder as an "absentee governor." In January 1992, four months after entering the presidential race, Wilder withdrew, saying that he needed to devote his full attention to governing the state of Virginia.

Douglas Wilder has made accomplishments that no other black man has. Speaking of the governor, Jesse Jackson said, "The people who are the first always have got to be overqualified, to be able to survive the double and triple standards, and obviously Doug was prepared to match those standards, to make a breakthrough." In 1993, Wilder announced his intention to pursue another first—becoming the first black man to be elected to the U.S. Senate from Virginia.

FEMALE LEADERS

SHIRLEY CHISHOLM

Shirley Chisholm, America's first black congresswoman, was born Shirley Anita St. Hill on November 20, 1924, in the Bedford-Stuyvesant section of Brooklyn, New York. She was the oldest of Ruby and Charles St. Hill's four daughters. Hoping to save money for the girls' education, their parents sent them to live with their grandmother in Barbados in 1927. Seven years later, Shirley and her sisters returned to the United States, which was by then in the grip of the Great Depression.

Like millions of other Americans of the 1930s, the St. Hills had very little money, but they never considered letting a school-age child work. To Charles St. Hill, a fifth-grade dropout himself, education came first. His girls rewarded his faith by doing well at school; Shirley led the pack by graduating at the top of her high school class and receiving scholarship offers from Vassar and Oberlin. Unable to afford a distant school even on a scholarship, Shirley St. Hill enrolled in Brooklyn College, from which she graduated cum laude in 1946.

Urged by her college professors to consider politics as a career, star pupil St. Hill had demurred: "You forget two things," she said. "I'm black—and I'm a woman." After college, she took a job at a Harlem child-care center, where she worked for seven years while studying for a master's degree in early childhood education at Columbia University night school. She received the degree in 1952. During this period, she met and married a recent immigrant from Jamaica, graduate student Conrad Chisholm.

From 1953 to 1964, Shirley Chisholm served as an educational consultant for the New York City Bureau of Child Welfare. Meanwhile, she had finally entered politics. In 1960, the 36-year-old educator, along with a group of reform-minded neighbors, decided to oust the local Democratic political machine and replace it with a new, liberal party organization. Their group, the Unity Democratic Club, failed in its first bid to take over the district, but their second try, in 1962, fared differently.

That year, the Unity Club managed to place two of its candidates on the slate. Both won election to the New York State Assembly, thereby giving control of the 17th Assembly District to the reformers. Two years later, one of these assemblymen became a judge, leaving a vacant slot. Chisholm decided to fill it herself.

After what she later called "a long, hard summer and fall," Shirley Chisholm swept to a win in a three-way contest, racking up 18,151 votes to her nearest opponent's 1,893. She went to Albany, New York's capital, and from 1964 until 1968 served as assemblywoman for the 17th District. During those four years, the Brooklyn woman proved herself a tough, independent politician. Among her accomplishments was the enactment into law of two of her pet projects: SEEK, a program providing college funds for poor youngsters, and an unemployment insurance fund for domestic employees.

After two terms in Albany, Assemblywoman Chisholm turned her eyes toward the nation's capital. A redistricting of her residential area created the new, predominantly black 12th Congressional District. Nominated by an independent citizens' committee, she defeated the party regular for the nomination, then went on to defeat the Republican candidate, Congress of Racial Equality founder James Farmer.

In early 1969, Congresswoman Shirley Chisholm took her seat in the House of Representatives—the first black woman ever to do so.

As a member of the 91st Congress, Chisholm showed herself as independent minded as she had been in the state legislature. When House leaders assigned her to the Agricultural Committee—a post they had assumed she would appreciate because of the committee's jurisdiction over food stamps—Chisholm astonished her colleagues by protesting vehemently. Showing unusual political skill for a congressional freshman, she managed to get herself reassigned, first to the Veterans Affairs Committee, where she served two years, then to her first choice: the powerful Education and Labor Committee. Demonstrating her sentiments—and her strengths—Chisholm helped engineer passage of a number of major bills. Included were laws that aided the poor, increased minimum wages, and created federal subsidies to support day-care centers for working mothers.

In 1970, voters of the 12th Congressional District enthusiastically returned Chisholm to Washington. But as a congresswoman, she soon felt she had pushed her agenda as far as possible. To accomplish what she believed America needed—among other things, a more equitable share of work and power for minorities and women—she decided to aim for the top. In 1972, she announced her candidacy for the Democratic nomination for president of the United States. Never before in the nation's history had a black or a woman—to say nothing of a *black woman*—sought the presidential nomination of a major party.

Chisholm had acquired a core of dedicated campaign workers and supporters, but with limited funds at their disposal, these loyalists made scant headway against the well-financed, well-organized opposition. When Chisholm went to the Democratic National Convention in 1972, she went with only 24 committed delegates. Candidate Hubert Humphrey, aware that he could not block the candidacy of South Dakota's senator George McGovern, released his delegates to Chisholm, but the battle was not even close. McGovern took the nomination, going on to lose the election (by a landslide) to incumbent Richard Nixon.

Despite her failure to capture the presidential nomination, Chisholm looked on the effort as its own kind of triumph. She spoke to reporters after the election:

> In terms of black politics, I think an effect of my campaign has been to increase the independence and self-reliance of many local elected black officials and black political activists from the domination of the political "superstars." The United States was said not to be ready to elect a Catholic to the presidency when Al Smith [Governor Alfred E. Smith of New York, a Democrat and a Roman Catholic, who lost to Republican Herbert Hoover in 1928] ran in the 1920s. But Smith's nomination may have helped pave the way for the successful campaign John F. Kennedy [a Roman Catholic Massachusetts senator] waged in 1960. Who can tell? What I hope most is that now there will be others who will feel

themselves as capable of running for high political office as any wealthy, good-looking white male.

Undiscouraged by her unsuccessful tilt at the presidency, Chisholm sought and easily won reelection to Congress in 1972. By this time, she had gained a secure national reputation for her undeviating advocacy of minority and women's rights. She once said that although she had been the first black woman elected to the U.S. Congress, she wanted to be remembered instead "as a catalyst for change, a woman who had the determination and a woman who had the perseverance to fight on behalf of the female population and the black population, because I'm a product of both."

As the years passed—Chisholm would eventually win and serve a total of seven terms in Congress—the Brooklyn maverick came somewhat closer to joining ranks with the party she represented. But she still resisted party discipline, sticking to her own route when she saw it as best for her constituents. She voted, for example, against several Democratic-backed bills that aimed at protecting the environment, asserting that their immediate result would be job losses among the poor.

In February 1982, Chisholm announced her retirement; she would finish out her term, but she would not be a candidate in November 1982. Supporters reacted with dismay, but many understood that personal reasons played a large role in the congresswoman's decision. In 1977, soon after a quiet divorce from Conrad Chisholm, 52-year-old Shirley Chisholm married Arthur Hardwick, Jr., a black businessman and former New York State assemblyman. Two years after the wedding, Hardwick had almost died in an automobile accident; Chisholm found the conflict between caring for her recovering husband and serving in Congress more than she wished to face. As one observer put it, "Her husband's accident and the new conservative climate in Washington [right-wing Republican Ronald Reagan had been elected in 1980] prompted Shirley to think about her own goals."

After retiring from politics, Chisholm taught political science and women's studies at Mount Holyoke College; she also gave frequent lectures and, in 1985, accepted the post of honorary scholar at Spelman College. Her husband died in 1986, and she gave up her teaching positions shortly afterward. In 1988, she joined Jesse Jackson's campaign for the presidency, just as she had four years earlier.

In the mid-1980s, Chisholm created a new organization, the National Political Caucus of Black Women, which soon counted thousands of members across the United States. An active member of the League of Women Voters, the National Association for the Advancement of Colored People, and the National Board of Americans for Democratic Action, she has also written two autobiographies: *Unbought and Unbossed* and *The Good Fight*.

MARIAN WRIGHT EDELMAN

Marian Wright Edelman, founding president of the Children's Defense Fund (CDF), was born Marian Wright on June 6, 1939, in Bennettsville, South Carolina. Named for groundbreaking black contralto Marian Anderson, she was the youngest of five children born to clergyman Arthur Jerome Wright and his activist wife, Maggie

Bowen Wright. Arthur Wright, a disciple of educator Booker T. Washington, set high standards for his children: they must not only obtain the best possible education, he said, they must use it to help others. "Working for the community," recalled the adult Marian Wright, "was as much a part of our existence as eating and sleeping and church."

Both Maggie Wright, who operated a home for the elderly in Bennettsville, and her husband, pastor of the town's Shiloh Baptist Church, exerted a strong influence on their youngest daughter. Arthur Wright died in 1954, but Maggie Wright carried on his ideals; when Marian graduated from high school, her mother sent her to Spelman College, a black liberal arts school in Atlanta, Georgia. There Marian racked up such an outstanding record that she won a fellowship to study in Europe during her junior year.

Wright attended the Sorbonne in Paris for one semester, the University of Geneva in Switzerland for another, then spent the summer studying the work of Russian writer Leo Tolstoy in the Soviet Union. After 15 months abroad she returned home in the fall of 1959—and experienced something of a shock. Europeans had seemed virtually color-blind, but in Wright's own country, segregation's grip remained tight, especially in her native South.

As it happened, Wright's return to the United States coincided with the dawn of the 1960s—a decade of antidiscrimination protests that would rock the South and eventually outlaw segregation. In Wright's senior year at Spelman, she took part in a student sit-in at Atlanta's city hall and wound up in the city jail. The arrest triggered a major switch in her career plans: Instead of getting a graduate degree in Russian studies, then entering the nation's diplomatic corps, Wright now decided to go to law school and specialize in civil rights law. A crusader had been born.

Wright graduated from Spelman—as valedictorian of her class—in 1960. That year, she explained her new motives in an article in the college newspaper:

> I realize that I am not fighting just for myself and my people in the South when I fight for freedom and equality. I realize now that I fight for the moral and political health of America as a whole and for her position in the world at large. . . . I know that I, in my individual struggle for improvement, help the world. I am no longer an isolated being—I belong.

Not only accepted by prestigious Yale University Law School but given a scholarship, Wright headed for New Haven, Connecticut, in the fall of 1960. In her last year of law school, she reached another of her life decisions, this one sparked by a visit to Mississippi. After spending spring break helping the Student Nonviolent Coordinating Committee (SNCC) with a voter-registration drive, she vowed that as soon as she received her law degree, she would return to the South and work for civil rights, preferably under the banner of the National Association for the Advancement of Colored People (NAACP).

Those who knew Marian Wright had long understood one essential feature of her personality: what she said she would do, she would do. After graduating from Yale in 1963, she spent a year training in New York City, then went to work as a legal intern with the NAACP Legal Defense and Education Fund in Jackson, Mississippi. Inspiring Wright—who was one of the Legal Defense Fund's first two interns—was the daring and charismatic Thurgood Marshall. The NAACP attorney, who would later become the nation's first black Supreme Court justice, had headed the Defense Fund since 1938. In the 1960s, he spearheaded the NAACP's campaign to wipe out segregation and racism.

Marshall was unswerving in his support for the right to protest, a right by no means taken for granted in the mid–20th-century American South. "Protest is part of our tradition," he said. "It goes back to tea dumped in Boston Harbor. [Blacks] have a right to say they want their rights."

Marian Wright agreed wholeheartedly. In Mississippi, she spent much of her time arranging for the release of protesting students from illegal detention. No more popular with white southern lawmen than was Marshall himself, Wright sometimes wound up in jail along with her clients. Although she was an accredited lawyer, she also found herself refused entry into certain courthouses as well as threatened by snarling police dogs. Did she, someone once asked her at the time, ever doubt the ability of the law to change southern segregationist ways? "Sure, like every morning," she shot back. "But one keeps plugging, trying to make our institutional processes work."

In 1964, the 25-year-old South Carolinian became head of the NAACP Legal Defense Fund in Mississippi, a position she would hold for the next four years. In 1965, she became the first black woman to pass the bar (obtain the right to practice law) in Mississippi. But even as she crusaded tirelessly for civil rights, Wright began to realize that before the situation changed in Mississippi, it would have to change in the nation's capital. Accordingly, she applied for and received a grant from the Field Foundation and, in 1968, moved to Washington, D.C., and established the Washington Research Project, predecessor of the Children's Defense Fund. "It became clear to me that the poor needed a voice in Washington, just like General Motors and other big interests have," she told an interviewer in 1993.

In Washington, D.C., Wright reencountered Peter Edelman, a white fellow civil rights worker she had met in Mississippi. In July 1968, four months after her move to the capital, Wright married Edelman. The couple worked in Washington until 1971, when they both accepted new jobs in Boston, Massachusetts. Marian Wright Edelman became director of the Harvard University Center for Law and Education, a position she held while making twice-weekly flights back to Washington to oversee the Research Project—and while raising her two sons, Joshua and Jonah. (A third son, Ezra, was born to the couple in 1974.)

In 1973, Marian Edelman founded the Children's Defense Fund (CDF), a Washington-based organization that aimed at providing long-range assistance to children and at getting children's issues included in public policy. Six years later, Edelman and her husband returned to the nation's capital, he to teach at the Georgetown University Law Center, she to concentrate on the CDF.

In the years since then, Marian Wright Edelman has dedicated herself to the young, earning herself a national nickname: "the children's crusader." She has zeroed in on a diverse range of related topics, starting with teenage pregnancy. "I saw from our own statistics that 55 ¹/₂ percent of all black babies were born out of wedlock, a great many to teenage girls," she told a reporter in 1983. "It just hit me over the head," she continued, "that that situation ensured black child poverty for the next generation."

Under Edelman's direction, the CDF staged a massive campaign to help prevent unwanted pregnancies among black teenagers. Offering options to pregnancy, CDF messages appeared in buses and subways, on radio and television broadcasts, and on posters in teen gathering places. And in late 1987, the U.S. Senate passed the Act for Better Child Care, legislation designed and sponsored by Edelman's CDF.

As Edelman sees it, the CDF's mission is vast but simple: to improve the lot of America's children. The organization aims to teach the general population about children's needs and to encourage investment in preventive rather than remedial care. In other words, the Fund wants to help children before they become mentally, physically, or emotionally ill, drop out of school, get pregnant, or run afoul of the law. The CDF also concerns itself with young people's employment.

Dynamically energetic, Edelman serves on many boards, including those of the Yale University Corporation, the Carnegie Council on Children, Spelman College, the NAACP, Citizens for Constitutional Concerns, the Joint Center for Political Studies, the U.S. Committee for UNICEF, the Center for Budget and Policy Priorities, and the March of Dimes. She is also a member of the Council on Foreign Relations. In 1985 she became a MacArthur Foundation Prize Fellow.

Among Edelman's many publications are *Children out of School in America*; *Families in Peril: An Agenda for Social Change*; *Portrait of Inequality: Black and White Children in America*; and, in 1992, the best-selling *The Measure of Our Success: A Letter to My Children and Yours*.

Barbara Charlene Jordan, the South's first black U.S. congresswoman, was born in 1936 in a poor black neighborhood of Houston, Texas. She grew up in a small two-bedroom house shared with her parents, Arlyne and Benjamin, her two older sisters, and her grandparents.

Barbara bristled at the rules laid down by her father, warehouse clerk and preacher Benjamin Jordan: no movies, no novels or comic books, no card playing, no dancing, and church all day on Sunday. He also demanded that his daughters gain a first-rate education. ("No man," he told them, "can take away your brain.") With that, however, Barbara had no problem: she sailed through school with a virtually straight-A average.

In high school, Barbara became a formidable debater. By the time she graduated, she had been named "Girl of the Year" by her classmates and had collected more than a dozen medals for "Declamation" and "Outstanding Accomplishments in Speech." Barbara Jordan enrolled in Texas Southern University (TSU), a new, all-black Houston college, in 1952. In college, she continued her triumphal record as a debater. Her voice was commanding and deep, her vocabulary extensive, her wit quick and sometimes biting. "She had a truly God-given talent for speaking," commented one impressed rival.

Soon acknowledged as the university's star debater, Jordan traveled with the TSU debating team, meeting and crushing opposing teams in cities as far off as Chicago, Boston, and New York. Jordan and her friends enjoyed the contests, but their carefree days were darkened by racial discrimination and segregation, then facts of American life. "You had to plan for food and even plan ahead to locate service stations where blacks could use restrooms," recalled one of Jordan's teammates.

In 1954, attorney Thurgood Marshall of the National Association for the Advancement of Colored

People won a spectacular Supreme Court victory—
the school-segregation challenge known as *Brown v.
Board of Education of Topeka*—that began the slow but
eventual desegregation of the nation's public schools
and other public places. Jordan had already been
thinking of law as a career; after Marshall's triumph,
she made up her mind to do it. Graduating from TSU
with honors in 1956, she entered Boston University
Law School. She received her law degree in 1959, then
headed back to Houston, where she opened a law
office in her family's dining room.

Not very busy at first, Jordan decided to try political volunteerism. As a county Democratic Committee
aide, she helped round up voters for the ticket headed
by John F. Kennedy and Texan Lyndon B. Johnson.
The Democrats won, and Jordan made an important
self-discovery: "I had really been bitten," she said
later, "by the political bug."

The 24-year-old lawyer also discovered that her
debater's skills translated handily to the political
stump. In 1961, she became president of the Harris
County Democrats, joined the Houston Council on
Human Relations, and won the presidency of the
all-black, hitherto all-male Houston Lawyers Association. The following year, she ran for a seat in the
Texas House of Representatives. Defeated by a white
male candidate, Jordan received some harsh advice
from a local political expert.

"You're black, you're a woman, and you're large,"
said the pundit, adding, "People don't really like that
image." He recommended that she drop politics.

Characteristically, Jordan listened, then went her own way. In 1964, she ran again—and lost again. "I did not like losing," she said. In 1965, she ran for state senator. After a grueling contest with another white male opponent, she won the election by a margin of two to one. In January 1967, she became Texas's first black state senator since 1883.

Jordan's carefully prepared Senate speeches soon earned respect not only from her colleagues but from the president of the United States. A month into her term, President Lyndon B. Johnson invited her to Washington, D.C., to discuss a fair-housing bill, and over the next two years he invited her back several times and even appointed her to a special economics commission.

In 1968, Jordan easily won a second term in the Texas Senate. Over the next few years, she orchestrated a substantial amount of legislation, including bills dealing with workmen's compensation, unemployment, equal rights for women, low-cost housing, and the establishment of a state department of labor. In October 1971, she began raising funds for another campaign. A newly formed congressional district, established because of a shift in Texas's population, called for a new U.S. representative, and Jordan intended to be it.

Up against a hard-fighting state representative (yet another white male), Jordan now fought the political battle of her life. Among those who aided her was her friend Lyndon Johnson, by then no longer president but still awesomely powerful. (Republican Richard

Nixon had been elected president in 1968.) In May 1972, 80 percent of the 18th Congressional District's voters cast their ballots for Barbara Jordan. On January 3, 1973, the 36-year-old Texan, the first black women ever sent to the House by a southern state, took her seat in the 93rd Congress of the United States. She was soon appointed, at Johnson's suggestion, to the influential House Judiciary Committee.

From the beginning of Jordan's term, Washington had been in a state of turmoil about the Watergate scandal. It had begun in June 1972, when District of Columbia police arrested five men for breaking into Democratic National Committee offices in the Watergate building. Members of President Nixon's reelection committee, the men had been trying to discover how much the Democrats knew about Republican campaign funds. The illegal break-in triggered an avalanche that would rock the nation.

By the fall of 1973, the rumblings had begun. Nixon denied all knowledge of the Watergate break-in, but he did his best—which included a White House–directed cover-up—to cripple the congressional investigation into the episode. At this point, outraged House members introduced articles of impeachment (grounds for a trial that could lead to the president's removal from office). The articles were turned over to the House Judiciary Committee for study.

Jordan, who had an almost mystical faith in constitutional government, found the idea of impeaching the president horrifying. Nevertheless, Nixon's continued stonewalling of the issue at last led her to believe that the country's interest demanded the impeachment, and she explained her views to the American people on national television. Her meticulously reasoned, passionately delivered speech scored a bull's-eye on America's moral compass. After the address, thousands of Americans contacted Jordan's office to praise her speech and her stand. Two weeks after the speech, Nixon escaped the prospect of impeachment by resigning.

At the Democratic presidential convention two years later, Jordan made another speech that electrified the nation. Delivered from Manhattan's Madison Square Garden, her keynote address transfixed millions of Americans and helped elect Democrat Jimmy Carter. "The Democratic Party," observed the *Washington Post* the next day, "never had an opening night like this before, and never will again."

Jordan, who had been reelected to the House in a 1974 landslide, continued her frantic schedule in Washington. To the Judiciary Committee, she added membership in the House Government Operations Committee and the Steering and Policy Committee of the House Democratic Caucus, to which she was the first black women ever assigned. As a legislator, Jordan displayed a careful impartiality; although she felt an intense interest in laws that would further the rights and interests of blacks and women, she believed she had been elected to represent all the people, not just these groups. The many bills she introduced or supported in the House dealt with matters as wide ranging as crime, civil rights, fair trade laws, federal-state revenue sharing, labor, bilingual ballots, abortion, education, and the Equal Rights Amendment.

The legislator, who had been suffering since 1973 from a progressive neurological impairment (about which she refused all public comment), started using a wheelchair in the late 1970s. She never explained if her illness was what led her to leave politics, but leave she did. After six highly visible years in the House, she suddenly announced her retirement from public office in 1978, at the end of her third term.

Stating only that she needed "a new direction," Jordan left Washington and returned to Texas, where she had accepted a professorship at the University of Texas in Austin. In 1982, she was named to the Lyndon Baines Johnson Centennial Chair in National Policy at the university. From the beginning, so many students clamored to take her courses that officials awarded admission to her lectures by lottery.

Jordan has made periodic public appearances at political events such as conventions, each time demonstrating oratorical powers as awesome as ever. Most of her time, however, is spent working as an educator, a job she shows every sign of caring about intensely. Of her students, she has said, "I want them to be premier public servants who have a core of principles to guide them. They are my future, and the future of this country."

CORETTA SCOTT KING

Coretta Scott King—civil rights activist, author, lecturer, columnist, and the widow of the Reverend Martin Luther King, Jr.—was born Coretta Scott in Marion, Alabama, on April 27, 1927. One of the three children of Obadiah and Bernice Murray Scott, she graduated from Lincoln High School in Marion, then won a scholarship to Antioch College in Yellow Springs, Ohio.

The young Alabama woman had sought admission to a northern school with a purpose: she had seen enough of her native South and its whites' idea of justice toward blacks to last her a lifetime. When her father's small but promising sawmill was burned to the ground by envious whites, she made up her mind: she would leave the South and spend her life in the non-violent world of music in the North.

A poor family, the Scotts could ill afford spending money for a daughter in college. At Antioch, from which she would earn a bachelor's degree in music and elementary education, Coretta divided her time between studying and working at a string of odd jobs. After graduation, she moved on to Boston, where she had won another scholarship, this one to study voice at the New England Conservatory of Music. To stretch her scholarship funds, Coretta cleaned her fellow students' rooms.

Studying in Boston at the same time as Coretta Scott was a divinity student from Atlanta, Georgia: Martin Luther King, Jr. The young southerner liked the North, but, he recalled telling a confidante, he missed the "particular charm" of southern women. Claiming she had the perfect solution to that problem, King's friend handed him the phone number of a student from Alabama. That night, King called Coretta Scott and asked her for a date.

"He had quite a line," recalled Coretta Scott King years afterward—but she agreed to have lunch with the smooth-talking divinity student the following day. When she met him in person, Scott saw a disappointingly short, solemn young man, but over a leisurely lunch in a Boston cafeteria, her view began to change. "The young man became increasingly better looking as he talked so strongly and convincingly," she recalled. King, meanwhile, had already decided he had met the right woman, and he told her so. "You have everything I have ever wanted in a wife," he said. "There are only four things—character, intelligence, personality, and beauty—and you have them all."

Coretta Scott had long ago made several important decisions about her life: she would leave the South, she would have a career as a singer, and she would never marry except on a basis of complete equality. King's future as a great preacher might have been predicted by his conversion of the woman he loved. She knew she wanted to marry him, but, she told him, she intended to pursue her singing career. The tradition-minded King said he would be glad to run the household until she earned her master's degree from the conservatory, but after that, he would work, and she would not. "I'm supposed to earn enough to take care of you and the family," he said.

Scott then reminded her husband-to-be that she had no intention of returning to the South. "I'm going to be pastor of a church," he replied. "I'm going to live in the South because that's where I'm needed." Somewhat to her own surprise, Scott acceded to King's wishes. "Martin was such a very strong man," she said later. In June 1953, Scott, 26, and King, 24, were married by King's father, the Reverend Martin Luther King, Sr., in the front yard of the Scotts' modest home in Marion, Alabama.

After the wedding and a summer in Atlanta, the young couple returned to Boston. There Coretta completed her requirements for a master's degree in voice, and Martin polished his doctoral dissertation (which he would complete in 1955). In late 1953, King gave a sermon at the Dexter Avenue Baptist Church in Montgomery, Alabama; soon afterward, the church offered him its pastorate. In September 1955, the Kings moved to Montgomery; there, a year later, their first child, Yolanda, was born. Her arrival would eventually be followed by those of three siblings: Martin III, born in 1957; Dexter in 1962; and Bernice in 1963.

The spring before the Kings settled in Montgomery, the Supreme Court had ruled school segregation illegal. Like Americans of all races, Coretta King saw that the black South was finally on the move. "I remember thinking one day in Montgomery [in 1955], 'This is what I have been preparing for my entire life,' " she said years later. " 'I don't know where it is going to take us, but we are involved in a worldwide struggle.' It was a good thing to know that my life had purpose and meaning."

The struggle Coretta King had anticipated began not much more than a year after the Kings' arrival in Montgomery. It started one December evening in 1955 when a black seamstress, Rosa Parks, refused to give up her bus seat so that a white man could sit down in comfort. Arrested, jailed, and fined, Parks became the center of an epic conflict. Black leaders instantly recognized her case as one upon which they could mount a devastating attack on segregation all over the South.

Deciding to call an all-out black boycott of the Montgomery bus system, which depended on black passengers for 75 percent of its business, the black community selected a boycott leader: the Reverend Martin Luther King, Jr. What followed was a 381-day absence of black riders, a strike that crippled the city's transportation system and ultimately forced it to integrate its buses. During that time, the Kings were subjected to a reign of terror: they received death threats, harassing telephone calls, bricks hurled through their windows. Martin Luther King was arrested and jailed, and his home was bombed.

Through it all, Coretta King stood firmly at her husband's side. "After our home in Montgomery was bombed," she said, "I had to recommit myself and my life. I realized then that I could be killed and that it was important to make this my struggle also." By now wholeheartedly dedicated to the cause her husband would die for, King saw her role as that of supporter and ally, a role she considered as important as that of frontline battler.

Repeatedly questioned about her part in the civil rights revolution, Coretta King patiently gave the same answers: "Martin's needs and the raising of our four children were my primary concern. He knew that I was going to take care of everything at home, and in this way I was able to support him and free him so that he could go and do the work of the movement."

Although she emphasized her domestic contributions, King in fact served as more than loyal helpmate. She gave speeches, participated in marches and rallies, organized concerts, and raised funds for the civil rights and peace movements. She also accompanied her husband on his world travels, acting as his ambassador and as a representative of black America. The couple's first overseas trip was to Ghana, where they helped celebrate the new nation's independence in 1957. Other King destinations included Nigeria, India, and England. In 1964 the couple traveled to Oslo, Norway, where Martin Luther King became history's youngest Nobel Peace Prize recipient.

When her husband fell to an assassin's bullet in 1968, Coretta King kept marching. Four days after his tragic death in Memphis, Tennessee, his widow led a massive rally at the site of the murder, urging Americans to seek not revenge but a "peaceful society." Two months later, Coretta King played a key role in the "Poor People's March" on Washington, D.C., making the event's keynote speech to 50,000 people.

Coretta King went on to raise her children, guard her husband's memory, and carry on his work. She founded and continues to run the Martin Luther King, Jr., Center for Nonviolent Social Change, an organization committed to achieving the slain leader's unrealized goals. In 1983, Coretta King headed the half-million people who converged on the nation's capital for the 20th anniversary of the original March on Washington. As chair of the Martin Luther King Holiday Commission, she has worked to bring all states into the annual celebration of her husband's birthday.

As she approaches the age of 70, Coretta Scott King shows no sign of flagging. She has been showered with awards and honors, including more than 100 doctoral degrees. She has been outspoken in her support for the blacks of South Africa and the leader of the African National Congress, Nelson Mandela. She continues to run the King Center, serves as cochair of the Full Employment Action Council, and maintains active memberships in the Black Leadership Roundtable and the Black Leadership Forum. She also maintains a heavy speaking schedule, addressing women's groups, children, black societies, and others on her favorite subject: the need for commitment to social justice and human rights all over the globe.

CAROL MOSELEY-BRAUN

Although her career in national politics has just begun, U.S. senator Carol Moseley-Braun of Illinois has already had a profound impact on the way politics is understood and conducted in this country. Only the second African American to serve in the Senate since Reconstruction, Moseley-Braun is the first black woman ever to serve in her country's highest legislative office. Her election on November 3, 1992, sent shock waves through an institution that has long been dominated by white males and has renewed the interest of millions of women, African Americans, and other disaffected groups in the promise of national electoral politics.

Born on August 16, 1947, in Chicago, Illinois, Carol Elizabeth Moseley was the oldest daughter of a Chicago police officer and a former hospital technician. She grew up in a segregated, middle-class neighborhood on the city's South Side, where she attended public schools along with her three younger siblings. All of the children were encouraged from an early age to prepare themselves for college and a professional career.

Even as a youngster, Moseley-Braun had little doubt concerning what her chosen profession would be—or what skills she would need to develop in order to pursue it. "I've always felt that my obligation—my calling—is to use my talents on behalf of the public interest," she recently told one reporter. "Elected officials have to be very clear that they are not leaders, but servants of the people."

After finishing high school, Moseley-Braun attended the Chicago campus of the University of Illinois, where she majored in political science. That experience deepened her desire to pursue a political career. Her next step was to return to her old neighborhood on the city's South Side, where she earned a law degree from the University of Chicago Law School.

Following law school, Moseley-Braun worked for three years as a prosecutor in the office of the U.S.

Attorney in Chicago, eventually earning that office's Special Achievement Award. It was during this period that the future politician got her first real taste of electoral politics, working as a campaign volunteer for Chicago's late mayor Harold Washington, who was then serving as a state representative. Moseley-Braun immediately fell in love with the excitement of campaigning and the challenges of public life. In 1978, with the encouragement and support of Congressman Washington and her colleagues in the U.S. Attorney's office, she ran for and was elected to a seat in the Illinois House of Representatives. She was 31 years old.

With her skills in building coalitions and her uncompromising commitment to responsible government, Moseley-Braun compiled a distinguished record during her 10 years in the Illinois state legislature, specializing in the areas of educational reform and antidiscrimination legislation. At the end of her second term, she was selected by her peers to serve as Assistant Majority Leader, making her the first African American in Illinois history to serve in that position. Though her public reputation was still modest at the time, she was already highly regarded by her fellow legislators and other groups who monitored legislative activity in the state. Incredibly, one such group, the Independent Voters of Illinois–Independent Precinct Organization (IVI–IPO), presented her with its Best Legislator Award for each of the 10 years that she served in the state House of Representatives. In 1987, Moseley-Braun was nominated by her party to run for the office of Recorder of Deeds in Cook County, a powerful but low-profile position in one of the most populous regions in the country. In a historic election, the five-term state representative accumulated more than 1 million votes to become both the first woman and the first black politician to hold an executive office in Cook County government.

Following the election, Moseley-Braun applied herself to her new job with the same vigor and tenacity with which she had performed as a legislator. She discovered soon after taking office that the county's old-fashioned, manual record-keeping system was actually costing taxpayers more money than it collected. Within months, she had replaced it with a highly efficient, computerized operation that more than doubled the state's returns by the end of the decade.

For a time, it seemed that Moseley-Braun's skills as a county executive and her commitment to her position might have taken the place of any grander political ambitions. All of that changed in September 1991, when law professor Anita Hill accused Supreme Court nominee Clarence Thomas of sexual harassment before millions of stunned television viewers.

In spite of her undeniable success in the state legislature and county government, Moseley-Braun was virtually a political unknown when she decided to give up her position as Cook County recorder of deeds and challenge fellow Democrat Alan Dixon for his seat in the U.S. Senate. A popular two-term incumbent known as Al the Pal, Dixon had angered many of his constituents in the fall by voting for Thomas's confirmation, in spite of the outspoken disapproval of the majority of women and minorities in his state.

Watching the hearings on television, Moseley-Braun was appalled at the insensitivity with which the Senate Judiciary Committee treated the real concerns of women and black people around the country. "The whole thing was an embarrassment," she would later explain. "It was an embarrassment from the beginning and by the time it got to the sexual harassment issue, it was beyond embarrassing. It was mortifying." Equally distressing was the composition of the Senate committee itself, which Moseley-Braun would later describe as "an elitist club made up of mostly White male millionaires over 50."

As the confirmation spectacle dragged on, Moseley-Braun soon discovered that she was not the only person who was outraged by what she saw. "Women were saying, 'Where are the women?'" she told one reporter. "Minorities said, 'Where are the minorities?' Workers said, 'Who are these millionaires? These aren't regular Joes.'"

With little money, few endorsements, and even less hope of actually winning her party's nomination, Moseley-Braun ran a low-key, grass-roots campaign, slowly winning support from women, blacks, and other disaffected groups throughout the state. But win or lose, her greatest goal in running was to change people's minds about who could, and should, run for national public office.

"We all thought of the Senate as this lofty place where weighty decisions were made by these serious men," she explained to one interviewer. "Instead, we saw that they were just garden variety politicians making bad speeches. We need to open up the Senate to the voices that have been excluded."

As she traveled around the state, however, and saw just how angry and disillusioned many voters had become, Moseley-Braun began to believe that she actually had a chance to win. In the final weeks of the primary, she campaigned relentlessly, overcoming a substantial lead by Dixon and the other challenger, attorney Albert Hofeld, in order to gain the Democratic nomination. Although both of her opponents had outspent her by more than 10 to 1 during the campaign, she had become the first black woman ever to win her party's nomination for the U.S. Senate.

In the general election, she faced a more formidable challenge. Her opponent in the race was Republican candidate Richard Williamson, an assistant secretary of state in the Reagan administration with years of experience in national public service. Moseley-Braun, in contrast, had no previous experience in national politics and had been able to overcome her major opponent in the primary largely on the single issue of the Thomas confirmation. Now it was the young Democratic nominee's qualifications to serve that became the issue, as Williamson and his supporters publicly attacked her inexperience in national politics and her failure to run a more substantive, issue-oriented campaign in the primary.

Moseley-Braun met the challenge, answering Williamson point by point on the issues and stubbornly defending her qualifications and experience. "This candidacy is not a fairy tale," she said to one skeptical interviewer during the campaign. "In the first place, I am qualified for this job. I am more qualified for this job than any of my opponents."

On November 3, 1992, Moseley-Braun prevailed over Williamson in a close race, gathering 53 percent of the vote and becoming the first black woman to serve in the U.S. Senate. As a freshman member of the Senate, Moseley-Braun serves on the Banking, Housing and Urban Affairs Committee; the Small Business Committee; and the powerful Judiciary Committee. Although she is now only at the beginning of her career in national politics, one of her most important goals in public life has already been realized. "To the extent that there will be other women and Black people who will see the possibilities because of my candidacy," she told a reporter during her campaign against Senator Dixon, "then I think that being nominated is a contribution that I can be proud of."

ROSA PARKS

Rosa Parks, the Birmingham seamstress who made civil rights history on a city bus in 1955, was born Rosa Louisa McCauley in Tuskegee, Alabama, on February 4, 1913. Rosa and her younger brother, Sylvester, were the children of James and Leona McCauley, a carpenter and rural school-teacher, respectively. When Rosa was two years old,

James moved north and out of his children's life; Leona then took Rosa and Sylvester to live with her parents in Pine Level, Alabama.

Mr. and Mrs. Edwards, Rosa's grandparents, had been born into slavery, and they often talked to the little girl about the hardships and horrors of plantation life. They were kind, but both they and their daughter Leona were in poor health, which put most of the household burdens on young Rosa. She cooked and cleaned and shopped and sewed for all of them. She received a few years of tutoring from her mother, then, at the age of 11, went to stay with an aunt in Montgomery, Alabama, where she enrolled in the Montgomery Industrial School for Girls.

Too poor to pay tuition at the private institution, Rosa earned it by cleaning classrooms after school. On graduation, she entered high school, but not for long; her mother's by-now-serious illness forced the teenager to stay home and act as nurse. At 19, Rosa met and married Raymond Parks, a Montgomery barber whose greatest sorrow was his lack of education; as a young man, poverty and lack of availability had kept him out of any classroom.

Rosa Parks had been listening to the facts about racial injustice since her early childhood; Raymond's story provided one more chapter. Deeply opposed to segregation and discrimination in all their noxious forms and perhaps inspired by the experiences of her family members, she joined the National Association for the Advancement of Colored People (NAACP) in

1943. Her first NAACP assignment: to encourage local blacks to register and vote, no simple matter in the racist Deep South of the 1940s.

"As far back as I can remember," Parks said many years after reaching adulthood, "being black in Montgomery we were well aware of the inequality of our way of life. I hated it all the time. . . . My mother believed in freedom and equality even though we didn't know it for reality during our life in Alabama. . . . If a woman wanted to go in [a store] and try on a hat, they wouldn't be permitted to try it on unless they knew they were going to buy it, or they put a bag on the inside of it. In the shoe stores they had this long row of seats, and all of those in the front could be vacant, but if one of us would go in to buy, they'd always take you to the last one, to the back of the store. There were no black salespersons."

As time passed, the daily, inescapable presence of segregation grew steadily more grating to Rosa Parks. Whenever she could, she avoided public drinking fountains, movie theaters, beaches, and other facilities that flaunted WHITE and COLORED signs. If she could walk instead of riding a bus or train—with front seats off-limits to blacks—she did. Otherwise, she always faced the prospect of boarding a bus, finding a seat, then jumping up to give it to a white person when the "White" section filled up. Tired as she might be at the end of a day's work, Rosa Parks preferred walking to jumping.

Like most southern blacks, Parks had no doubt heard countless tales from friends of humiliations they

suffered on the Montgomery transit system. One
woman recalled that when she and her blind husband
boarded a bus too slowly to suit the driver, he shut
the door on the man's leg, then stepped on the gas.
Another black passenger told of getting on a bus
without the exact change and, when he hesitated,
being chased off at gunpoint by the driver. A third man
spoke of his pregnant wife, forced by a driver to give
up her seat to a young white woman, and yet another
recalled a driver calling her an "ugly black ape."

Understandably, when Parks had the energy, she
walked home from work. By the 1950s, she was holding a reasonably good job. She had always enjoyed
sewing, and now she worked at Montgomery Fair,
a city department store, doing alterations for customers. The job was pleasant enough, but Parks spent
most of the long workday on her feet.

One late fall day—it was Thursday, December 1,
1955—the 42-year-old Parks finished her work,
boarded a Cleveland Avenue bus, and sank into a seat.
"Coming up to the Christmas holiday," she said later,
"the work was a bit heavy. When I left the store that
evening I was tired." Parks sat next to a black man
in the first row of the back section, which was traditionally reserved for blacks. The first 10 rows of the
bus—always off-limits to blacks—were filled with
white passengers.

A few stops after Parks had taken her seat, a white
man boarded the bus and looked around for a place to
sit. This was the signal, of course, for a "good nigra"—
a white southerner's phrase for a humble, deferential

black person—to give the white passenger his or her seat, then go to the back of the bus and stand. But on this day, there seemed to be a shortage of good nigras. No one moved.

Sighing with exasperation, the driver stopped the bus, walked back to Parks and her seatmate, and said, "Y'all make it light on yourselves and let me have those seats." The black man rose and moved to the back. Parks stayed put. The driver seemed to be trying to keep his voice under control. "If you don't stand up," he told Parks, "I'm going to call the police and have you arrested." By now, Parks had moved too many times, had stood aside too many times, had waited for service too many times. Tense but absolutely determined, she looked straight at the furious driver. "You may do that," she said softly.

Writing of that moment, civil rights activist Eldridge Cleaver said, "Somewhere in the universe a gear in the machinery had shifted."

Called by the bus driver, two policemen boarded at the next stop and said to Parks: "Why don't you stand up?" "I don't think I should have to," she replied. The officers arrested Parks, booked her on a misdemeanor charge, and released her on a $100 bond. The news flashed through the black community, whose members had long been considering some action against the bus company, its arrogant drivers, and segregation in general. Black leaders asked if they could use her case as a test case, and after conferring with her mother and her husband, she agreed. "I just felt resigned to give what I could to protest," she said.

When Parks's case came up for trial a few days later, she was found guilty and fined $10 plus $4 in court costs. She refused to pay and filed an appeal. Now the gears began to move. Inspired by a young Montgomery clergyman named Martin Luther King, Jr., blacks organized a one-day boycott of the city's buses. Its success led to a 381-day strike by the black community, 25,000 people who accounted for 75 percent of the bus company's business.

Meanwhile, the department store fired Rosa Parks; her husband lost his job as well. Parks began to receive threatening telephone calls and letters; she responded by helping to arrange car pools so that people could get to work without riding the buses. At last, on June 2, 1956, the U.S. District Court ruled that segregated seating on buses was unconstitutional; the ruling was upheld by the U.S. Supreme Court, which, in December 1956, ordered Montgomery to integrate its buses. Rosa Parks's gesture of defiance had sparked the civil rights movement of the 1950s and 1960s, tumultuous decades that would change the course of American social history forever.

Unable to find other jobs in the wake of publicity surrounding the boycott, Parks, her husband, and her mother moved to Detroit in 1957. Parks worked as a seamstress for several years, spending her free time volunteering at the Detroit branch of the Southern Christian Leadership Conference (SCLC). In 1965, U.S. congressman John Conyers of Detroit hired her as his staff assistant, a job she held until her retirement in 1988. In 1992, she published *Rosa Parks: My*

Story, an autobiography written with the aid of Jim Haskins. Rosa Parks received the NAACP's coveted Spingarn Medal in 1979 and the Martin Luther King, Jr., Nonviolent Peace Prize in 1980. She has been awarded numerous other awards and honors and holds ten honorary college degrees. Upon reaching her 80th birthday in 1993, Parks said she planned to continue to fight injustice. "I have no choice but to keep on," she said.

MADAM C. J. WALKER

Madam C. J. Walker, America's first black female millionaire, was born Sarah Breedlove on December 23, 1867. She spent her poverty-stricken early years on the Delta, Louisiana, cotton plantation where her parents had worked as field slaves. By the time she was five, Sarah herself was planting seed and hauling water to the sharecroppers.

Owen and Minerva Breedlove dreamed of educating Sarah and her two siblings, but the dream proved elusive. Their former masters had never taught them to read or write, and in the virulent racism of the postwar Deep South, schools for black children were almost nonexistent. Sarah reached adulthood illiterate.

In 1874, yellow fever swept through the Delta area; among its victims were Owen and Minerva Breedlove. Unable to support themselves in Delta, Sarah and her older sister, Louvenia, traveled to Vicksburg, Mississippi, where they found work as laundresses.

In 1882, 14-year-old Sarah married Moses McWilliams, a Vicksburg laborer. Three years later, she gave birth to a daughter, whom she and her husband happily named Lelia. But soon after the child's second birthday, McWilliams died in an accident, leaving young Sarah an impoverished single mother.

Told that St. Louis offered more opportunity, Sarah McWilliams bought a boat ticket, put Lelia on her hip, and headed up the Mississippi. She found work as a laundress and soon started Lelia in school, a move that gave her profound satisfaction. Nevertheless, she constantly dreamed of a finer life for her daughter and herself. "But with all my thinking," she said years later, "I couldn't see how I, a poor washerwoman, was going to better my condition."

McWilliams worked and saved and did without all but the bare necessities, and when Lelia graduated from high school, she was able to send her to a small black college in Knoxville, Tennessee. To help pay the tuition, McWilliams started selling hair products from door to door. Like many other black women, she had conformed to fashion by trying to straighten her hair; as a result it was now broken and patchy and revealed her scalp in several places.

Realizing that the product she was peddling did nothing for her hair, McWilliams decided to develop her own. The formula, she said later, came to her in a dream. "In that dream," she recalled, "a big black man appeared to me and told me what to mix up for my hair. Some of it was grown in Africa, but I sent for it, mixed it, put it on my scalp, and in a few weeks, my hair was coming in faster than it had ever fallen out. . . . I made up my mind to begin to sell it."

The 38-year-old McWilliams now decided to change her surroundings and go into business. On July 21, 1905, she arrived in Denver, Colorado, with her hair formula and her life savings: $1.50. She rented an attic room, joined a church, found a job as a cook, and began making small batches of the new potions she had devised: Wonderful Hair Grower, Glossine, and Vegetable Shampoo. Door-to-door sales proved successful; other black women bought Walker's goods as fast as she could make them.

In early 1906, McWilliams married C. J. Walker, a newspaperman with experience in advertising and direct-mail selling. Whites of the era automatically called blacks by their first names: to avoid that irritant, the entrepreneur now called herself Madam C. J. Walker, which also lent an exotic touch to her products. With her husband's help, Walker turned her small business into an industry. The pair developed major differences, however, first about the business, then about personal matters. They divorced in 1912, but Sarah Walker retained her married name.

Meanwhile, A'Lelia Walker Robinson (who had graduated from college, married, divorced, and added an *A* to her first name) had become her mother's right hand. A'Lelia oversaw the moves of the Walker Company, first from Denver to Pittsburgh, then from Pittsburgh to Indianapolis. In 1915, at her daughter's urging, Walker moved to New York City, although she kept her manufacturing base in Indianapolis.

By this point, Sarah Breedlove Walker had become a wealthy woman, well known both for her business success and her extraordinary contributions to black schools, housing projects, old people's homes, orphanages, and civil rights groups. She had hired a nucleus of highly educated aides—attorneys, teachers, accountants, and other professionals—and had learned not only to read and write but to appreciate literature, classical music, art, architecture, and the theater.

After Walker's move to an elegant town house in New York's Harlem, she bought a tract of land in the New York suburb of Irvington-on-Hudson, hired a prominent black architect, and built a mansion. Called the Villa Lewaro (for LElia WAlker RObinson), the huge and stately residence awed even Walker's wealthy white neighbors. At first, some complained. "The villagers, noting her color, were frankly puzzled," reported the *New York Times*. "When it became known that she was the owner [of the mansion], they could only gasp in astonishment. 'Impossible!' they exclaimed. 'No woman of her race could own such a place.'" But she could, and she did. Soon after she settled into Villa Lewaro, her affluent neighbors came to regard her with respect.

Walker's acceptance by her white neighbors pleased her; even more pleasing was her acceptance by black leaders. In 1912, she had addressed the National Negro Business League's annual convention, but only after the frosty disapproval of its president: the great Booker T. Washington showed notoriously little regard for female entrepreneurs. But Walker's star rose so quickly that Washington soon changed his tune; introducing her as keynote speaker at the league's 1913 convention, he called her "one of the most progressive and successful" blacks in American business.

Walker had not only made herself a millionaire; she had also created prosperous lives for the thousands of black women she employed as agents. As the company expanded from its attic-workshop stage in Denver, it steadily enlarged both its product line and its sales force. Leading that force was Walker herself, who traveled almost constantly, making speeches, opening new Walker beauty salons and "colleges" for training operators, and signing up saleswomen.

By 1919, some 25,000 people, almost all of them black and female, sold Walker products. Their enthusiasm seems to have been deep and genuine—as well it might have been, considering the enormous difference a Walker job could make in a woman's life.

At the time, a black woman worker averaged $10 per week in the North and $2 per week in the South. A typical Walker agent or "hair culturist" (beautician) made $23 per week.

"I have all I can do at home and don't have to go out and work for white people in kitchens and factories," wrote one enthusiastic operator to Walker. Another wrote: "You have opened up a trade for hundreds of colored women to make an honest and profitable living where they make as much in one week as a month's salary would bring from any other position that a colored woman can secure."

Concerned about her escalating blood pressure, Walker's doctors constantly begged her to slow down, but she would not or could not. During World War I, for example, she had visited dozens of military bases, talking to black soldiers about their role in the war and the future; in 1917, she had helped organize and participated in the Negro Silent Protest Parade, a massive demonstration against racial violence.

Almost to the end of her life, Walker traveled thousands of miles a year, made dozens of speeches, and oversaw almost every facet of her sprawling empire. But in 1919, her erratic heart finally forced her to rest. Aware that her time was growing short, she made a list of bequests, establishing a $200,000 trust fund to go to "worthy charities" and leaving sums ranging from $2,000 to $5,000 to such institutions as the Colored Orphans Home in St. Louis, the Home for Aged and Infirm Colored People in Pittsburgh, the Haines Institute in Georgia, the National Association for the

Advancement of Colored People, and Tuskegee Institute. That done, she looked up at her nurse and murmured, "I want to live to help my race." Soon afterward, Sarah Breedlove Walker died at the age of 51.

America's first black self-made female millionaire, Walker never forgot her roots. A child of poverty, she eagerly shared her immense wealth with the needy. Deprived of an early education, she made a point of supporting schools. Born to former slaves, she vigorously exercised her rights as an American citizen, using her economic and personal power to strengthen her community and urging others to follow her lead.

Wherever she spoke, Walker encouraged black women and men to pursue their dreams. "I promoted myself," she often told her audiences. "I had to make my own living and my own opportunity! But I made it! Don't sit down and wait for the opportunities to come. Get up and make them!"

IDA B. WELLS-BARNETT

Ida B. Wells-Barnett, jour-
nalist and antilynching activist, was born Ida Bell
Wells on July 16, 1862, in Holly Springs, Mississippi.
A slave at birth, she—along with her family and the
rest of the Confederacy's blacks—became legally free
when President Abraham Lincoln signed the Emancipation Proclamation on January 1, 1863. Ida was the
first of the eight children born to Jim Wells, son of a

white master and a slave mother, and Elizabeth Warrenton Wells.

In the immediate postwar years, the Wells family prospered: Jim's independent carpentry shop did well, and his wife and older children attended Shaw University, a Holly Springs school opened by the Freedmen's Aid Society. Then, in 1876, tragedy struck: a yellow fever epidemic blasted through Tennessee and Mississippi, taking hundreds of victims, among them Jim and Elizabeth Wells and their youngest child.

A shocked 14-year-old Ida now found herself in charge of the family. To support her siblings, she took a job teaching at a country school for blacks, later moving with her two youngest sisters to Memphis, Tennessee. There she found another country-school position and took advanced courses at the city's black college, LeMoyne Institute.

Boarding the train to work one day in May 1884, the 21-year-old Wells seated herself in her usual car, the first-class ladies' coach. A new conductor took her ticket, then demanded that she move to the smoking car, the only one appropriate, he said, for blacks. Wells refused; she had paid for a first-class coach, and that was where she would ride. When two burly guards tried to force her into the smoking car, she left the train, then hired a lawyer and sued the railroad. To the consternation of some local whites, she won; a Minnesota-born judge ordered the Chesapeake and Ohio Railroad to pay her $500. The *Memphis Appeal* reported the news in a headline: DARKY DAMSEL GETS DAMAGES.

Wells's elation in her vindication proved short-lived; the railroad appealed, and the Tennessee Supreme Court reversed the earlier decision. For "colored people," said the court, the smoking car *was* the first-class coach. It ordered Wells to pay $200 in court costs. From that point on, Ida Wells would dedicate herself to the cause of equality and justice for her race.

For the next seven years, Wells continued to teach in the winter and study in the summer. For entertainment, she went to musical evenings and literary-club meetings. At these gatherings, members read aloud from such publications as the literary *Evening Star*, which Wells had begun to edit, the local weekly, *Living Way*, and the *Free Speech and Headlight*, a militantly pro–civil rights newspaper. Impressed with her work in the *Star*, the editor of the *Living Way* asked Wells to write for his paper.

Wells's fiery *Living Way* articles—signed "Iola"— soon attracted the attention of the black intellectual community. The pieces were hard to ignore, containing such lines as: "A Winchester rifle should have a place of honor in every black home, and it should be used for that protection which the law refuses to give." Other black publications, such as the *New York Age*, the *Indianapolis Freeman*, and the *Little Rock Sun*, began to reprint and comment on "Iola's" stories about black life in Tennessee.

In 1889 the owner of *Free Speech and Headlight* offered Wells the editorship of his small but influential paper. She accepted, soon almost doubling the journal's circulation and filling its pages with tough rhetoric about race relations. Under Wells's leadership, the paper earned a reputation for speaking out against injustice, no matter what its source.

In 1891, Wells, who continued to teach full-time, published a highly critical article about the Memphis Board of Education and its short-changing of the city's black schools. The article aimed at reform; instead, it got its author fired from teaching. Wells's next brush with the city's white establishment came a year later. It began when a crowd of whites raided a jail where three black men—all of them friends of Wells's—were being held on trumped-up charges of inciting to riot. The mob dragged the blacks to the outskirts of town and shot them dead.

Responding to the lynching with a burst of fury on her front page, Wells advised the city's blacks to move away from Memphis, which she described as "a town which will neither protect our lives and property, nor give us a fair trial in the courts, but take us out and murder us in cold blood when accused by a white person." Two thousand blacks took her advice, almost crippling Memphis's streetcar company and infuriating whites. Two months later, Wells wrote another editorial, this one provoked by another lynching.

Observing that most lynchings took place to punish black men for raping white women, she implied that many such alleged rapes were no such thing. Instead, she suggested, they were voluntary relationships between people who found each other sexually attractive. This was more than the white male South could tolerate. Mobs burned and looted the offices and presses of the *Free Speech*, and other newspapers ran open threats against Wells, warning her to leave Memphis if she wished to live.

Wells moved to New York City and became a columnist for the *New York Age*, a crusading newspaper owned by black press titan T. Thomas Fortune. Wells started her association with the newspaper by writing a long, frank, and deeply thoughtful article about lynching and its history. The piece, later published in a pamphlet as *Southern Horrors*, drew a tremendous response from the nation's black community. Fortune printed and sold tens of thousands of reprints; even Frederick Douglass took note. Making a special visit to New York, the great abolitionist thanked Wells for setting the record straight on lynching.

Next, Wells began a lecture tour, explaining southern lynching to audiences in the Northeast. Attending one of her speeches in 1893 was Catherine Impey, an Englishwoman who had been fighting discrimination in Britain for years. Impey, impressed with Wells and her message, invited the Memphis exile to repeat her lecture tour in England, Scotland, and Wales.

Britons listened to Wells with sympathetic rage; she listened to them with curiosity. Particularly impressive to the American woman were the civic associations of her British counterparts. In organized groups, she realized, lay strength. On her return to America in May 1893, she began advising American women to do as British women did—advice that would give a strong push to the black women's club movement, eventually a powerful force for change.

Thanks in large measure to Wells, several influential organizations came into being during the next few years: the National Conference of Colored Women, the National Federation of Afro-American Women, the National League of Colored Women. Behind these umbrella groups were countless smaller clubs at church, school, and community levels, many of them also inspired by Wells's speeches.

In 1893, Wells moved to Chicago, which would be her home base for the rest of her life. She took a job with the *Chicago Conservator*, a black newspaper founded by lawyer Ferdinand L. Barnett, and started Chicago's first civic club for black women. Like similar organizations Wells had sparked, this one concentrated on publicizing and trying to halt lynching. In 1894, she returned to England for another round of lectures about lynching; the following year, she married Barnett, a man whose goals and dreams matched her own. For professional reasons, she took the then-unusual step of using both her husband's and her own family name.

At first, Ida B. Wells-Barnett considered leaving public life, but its lure and her sense of duty soon brought her back to the crusade for justice. She would bear four children and maintain a happy marriage, but she would also keep on writing articles, making speeches, attending conferences, reporting on racial violence, and helping to found activist clubs. In 1898, she led a delegation to President William McKinley to protest lynching; in the same year, she became secretary of the National Afro-American Council. In 1908, she founded the Negro Fellowship League; in 1913, she was appointed as a Chicago adult probation officer. Also in 1913, she founded the first black woman suffrage organization, the Alpha Suffrage Club of Chicago. In 1915, she was elected vice-president of Chicago's Equal Rights League. Wells-Barnett remained active until a sudden attack of uremic poisoning sent her to the hospital in 1931. She died two days later.

Writing in the *Crisis* newspaper, author, editor, and educator W. E. B. Du Bois said, "Ida Wells-Barnett was the pioneer of the anti-lynching crusade. She began the awakening of the conscience of the nation."

CIVIL RIGHTS LEADERS

JESSE JACKSON

Civil rights leader and politician Jesse Jackson was born Jesse Louis Burns on October 8, 1941, in Greenville, South Carolina. Throughout his youth, he was painfully aware that white supremacy ruled Greenville. Racial segregation touched every aspect of life.

Jesse's mother, Helen Burns, was 16 years old and unwed when he was born; his father, Noah Robinson, was married to another woman. So Helen raised the baby herself, with the help of her own mother.

Two years later, Jesse's mother married Charles Jackson, a 24-year-old postal worker. Jesse soon learned who his blood father was, but he was to experience many years of rejection before Noah Robinson welcomed him into his home. In the meantime, Charles Jackson was an attentive stepfather, and he legally adopted Jesse and gave him his last name in 1957.

From the time Jesse Jackson was a small child, he was bright, industrious, and a devoted churchgoer. He did especially well in school. At all-black Sterling High School, he was an honor student, a top athlete, and a participant in a variety of extracurricular activities.

After graduating in 1959, Jackson received a football scholarship to the University of Illinois. Disturbed at the lack of racial equality he found in the integrated North, he transferred after his freshman year to North Carolina Agricultural and Technical University, a black state college in Greensboro. He was well aware that eight months prior to his arrival, four of the school's freshmen had sat down at a whites-only lunch counter and had requested service. Their protest had sparked the sit-in movement, which had spread quickly over much of the South.

Jackson was welcomed at his new college, where he became quarterback of the football team, an honor student, and student body president. He soon fell in love with fellow student Jacqueline Davis, and they were married shortly after she discovered she was pregnant. She gave birth to their first child in July 1963; four more children would follow.

By 1963, Jackson had become president of the North Carolina A&T student body. He had also turned into a prominent student activist against racial segregation in downtown Greensboro, leading protest marches sponsored by the Congress of Racial Equality (CORE). He was arrested during one of these demonstrations and spent several weeks in jail. The protests were successful, however: the city desegregated its downtown.

After graduating from college in 1963 with a degree in sociology, Jackson turned down a scholarship to Duke University Law School. Instead, he entered Chicago Theological Seminary on a fellowship. He had decided to follow generations of preachers in the Robinson family and make a career in the ministry.

The call of the civil rights movement proved too strong, though, and in the spring of 1965, six months before his graduation, Jackson's life took a bold turn. He decided to drop out of the seminary and join the nation's most influential civil rights leader, the Reverend Martin Luther King, Jr., and many members of the organization King founded, the Southern Christian Leadership Conference (SCLC), in their drive to register black voters. Although the federal civil rights act signed by President Lyndon B. Johnson in 1964 had ended segregation in restaurants, theaters, and hotels throughout the South, blacks were still prevented from voting in many southern states.

On Sunday, March 7, 1965, King and 600 of his supporters attempted to march from Selma, Alabama, to the state capitol in Montgomery to dramatize their mission. Local and state policemen beat them back using tear gas, clubs, and cattle prods. Jackson saw the proceedings on television, followed by an appeal from King to clergymen across the nation to come join the march. Jackson left Chicago and went straight to Selma.

A natural leader, Jackson stepped immediately into the front ranks of the demonstrators and assumed a take-charge role. After a successful march to Montgomery, which ultimately led to the passage of the Voting Rights Act of 1965, he asked to be appointed to the SCLC staff. King, a bit wary of the headstrong 23-year-old, placed him on the payroll in Chicago under SCLC official James Bevel.

Back in Chicago, Jackson took charge of the local Operation Breadbasket, part of the SCLC's effort to force major companies patronized by blacks to return their patronage in the form of jobs and investments. He promptly recruited more than 200 ministers to carry on this campaign throughout Chicago, with resounding success. King was so impressed that he put Jackson in charge of the entire Operation Breadbasket program.

King then turned his attention to the plight of northern blacks, many of whom lived in dilapidated, inner-city slums. He launched a new campaign of nonviolent demonstrations in Chicago in the summer of 1966, leading marches to City Hall and through all-white neighborhoods to lobby against segregated housing. Jackson emerged as a key player in these protests.

He also proved to be an energetic leader. Jackson's fiery speeches at Operation Breadbasket rallies won him a steady stream of supporters across the country and brought him national fame. Finally, in 1971, he announced that he was resigning from the SCLC to form his own organization, Operation PUSH (People United to Save [later changed to Serve] Humanity).

Borrowing Operation Breadbasket's goal of economic growth for blacks, PUSH organized protest marches, trade fairs, and forums on everything from tax reform to voter registration during the 1970s. It also participated in politics, supporting candidates for local, state, and national offices "committed to human, economic, and social programs." And in 1975, Jackson turned the focus of PUSH from economics to education, launching PUSH-Excel, a campaign designed to encourage young blacks to stay in school, abandon drugs, and develop a sense of self-esteem.

Jackson's organizational skills and mesmerizing speaking style eventually propelled him to the national political stage. In October 1983, having witnessed several months of encouraging support for his candidacy—"Run, Jesse, run," they pleaded—he officially announced that he would seek the Democratic party's nomination for president. He had no trouble attracting media attention. At Christmastime, he achieved a stunning coup when he traveled to the Middle East and negotiated the release of a black U.S. naval aviator who had been shot down and held prisoner by Syria.

Jackson's political fortunes plummeted less than two months later, however, when he appeared at a Nation of Islam rally and said nothing in response to Black

Muslim leader Louis Farrakhan's open threats to the nation's Jews. Jackson subsequently denounced Farrakhan's message, but the incident damaged his campaign, and he captured only 21 percent of the popular vote and just 11 percent of the delegates in the Democratic primaries.

Although Jackson did not get his party's nomination in 1984, he was allowed to address its convention. And what a speech it was! Broadcast on prime-time television, it electrified blacks and many whites across the nation as he called for an end to racism and discrimination of every sort—including anti-Semitism—and urged Americans to take the moral high ground. "Our time has come!" he urged.

For the 1988 presidential election, Jackson organized his forces into the National Rainbow Coalition and traveled constantly across the country, building grass-roots support. By the end of March, he was the front-running candidate. He won primaries and swept caucuses.

In the end, Jackson outran and outlasted every Democratic rival but one: Governor Michael S. Dukakis of Massachusetts. At their party's convention, Jackson delivered another spellbinding speech, just like he had done four years earlier, telling America, "Keep hope alive."

In 1989, Jackson and his family moved from Chicago to Washington, D.C. The following year, he was elected "shadow senator" from the District of Columbia, a new post created by the city government to lobby Congress for statehood. He took time out from that post in August 1990, after Iraqi leader Saddam Hussein invaded Kuwait and imprisoned several thousand Americans and other foreigners. Jackson flew to Baghdad and successfully negotiated the release of nearly 300 hostages.

And so Jesse Jackson continues to play a major role on the world stage. From meeting with world dignitaries, to getting blacks to vote in record numbers for the 1992 presidential election, to stumping for Democratic candidate Bill Clinton, he remains America's most powerful presence in the fight for racial justice.

JAMES WELDON JOHNSON

A leading figure in American literature and politics, James Weldon Johnson was born on June 17, 1871, in Jacksonville, Florida. His mother, the former Helen Dillet, was a native of the Bahamas and of mixed black and French descent; his father, James, Sr., was born a free black in Virginia. While James, Jr., was growing up in the booming resort town of Jacksonville, his mother worked as a schoolteacher and his father as the headwaiter at an elegant hotel.

Racial segregation was strictly enforced in Jacksonville. But unlike many southern towns, the city boasted a thriving black community that proved very active in civic affairs. The Johnson children—James Weldon; his younger brother, John Rosamond; and an adopted older girl, Agnes—were taught by their parents to value education. And the local school for blacks that the two boys attended was considered one of the best in the country.

Young Johnson was an avid reader, played the piano and guitar, and frequently joined in neighborhood games of baseball and marbles. Because Jacksonville did not have a high school for blacks, he was sent by his parents to the preparatory division of Atlanta University, in Georgia, to get the equivalent of a high school education after graduating from primary school in 1887. Johnson thrived at his new school and entered the university three years later.

In college, Johnson excelled in his studies, sang in the glee club, wrote poetry, and emerged as an outstanding orator. While teaching in a rural Georgia school during summer vacations in 1891 and 1892, he observed the difference between his cultural and educational background and that of the black sharecroppers' children. Yet he felt a bond with them and began to consider making the fight for racial equality his life's mission.

Johnson graduated from Atlanta University in 1894 at the top of his class and was offered a scholarship to Harvard Medical School. He chose instead to accept the principalship of his primary school back in Jacksonville. A career in education, he believed, would be of greater service to his people.

Johnson succeeded in improving the school during his five years as principal. But he would always be a man of many interests, and so he continued to write poetry, founded a daily newspaper for Jacksonville's black community, and became one of the first blacks to pass the Florida bar exam. He opened a law office with the help of a friend in the summer of 1898 but soon discovered that he lacked a passion for legal work.

To divert himself from his duties as principal and his law practice, Johnson began writing the lyrics for *Tolosa*, a comic opera his brother was composing. Rosamond, who had studied at the New England Conservatory of Music and had become an accomplished pianist and music arranger, worked as a music teacher, choir director, and organist in Jacksonville. In mid-1899, shortly after the opera was completed, the two brothers traveled to New York City to have the songs from *Tolosa* published as sheet music.

While in New York, the Johnsons befriended musician Bob Cole and teamed up with him to write a love song, "Louisiana Lize." A well-known singer bought the rights to the tune, and it became a hit. There would be many others, for the two brothers soon formed a successful songwriting partnership with Cole. By the early 1900s, royalty payments for their work were beginning to roll in, and Cole and the Johnson Brothers was recognized as one of the leading songwriting teams in New York.

All of the Johnsons' tunes were popular, but a song that they cowrote back in Jacksonville proved the most lasting of them all. "Lift Every Voice and Sing," which evokes racial pride and the hope for a better future, was finished in early 1900, while James was still serving as a public school principal. In the years that followed, black organizations across the nation adopted the song and turned it unofficially into the black national anthem. It later became the official song of the National Association for the Advancement of Colored People (NAACP).

By 1905, Johnson was pursuing other interests besides music. He was serving as president of New York's Colored Republican Club and was taking courses in literature at Columbia University. One of his professors encouraged him to write about the lives of black Americans, and Johnson began work on a novel. Eventually published in 1912 as *The Autobiography of an Ex-Colored Man*, Johnson's first book strongly influenced the writers who took part in the Harlem Renaissance during the 1920s.

In the spring of 1906, Johnson decided to end his collaboration with Cole and the Johnson Brothers, and pursue a career that would be of greater service to his race. Through contacts in the Colored Republican Club, he received a diplomatic appointment as U.S. consul in Puerto Cabello, Venezuela, and served there for three years. In 1909, he was promoted to a more important diplomatic post in Corinto, Nicaragua. He performed his duties skillfully, hoping that he would eventually be transferred to a post in Europe.

When the Democratic party came to power in 1912, Johnson realized that his chances for promotion were slim. The following year, he resigned from the diplomatic corps and returned to Jacksonville with his wife, Grace. They had married three years earlier, after a lengthy courtship.

For a year, the 42-year-old Johnson tried to decide what line of work to pursue next. In late 1914, he and his wife moved to Harlem, which was in the midst of becoming the center of New York City's black community, and he became an editorial columnist for the *New York Age*, a leading black weekly newspaper. Over the next 10 years, he penned a number of editorials that sought to reverse the lowly status of black Americans.

Johnson's interest in black affairs soon led to his involvement with the recently founded NAACP. He began attending NAACP meetings in 1916 and was promptly elected vice-president of the local branch. That August, he even traveled to Amenia, New York, for an NAACP-sponsored black rights conference attended by more than 50 of the nation's most prominent black leaders. In the fight for black rights, Johnson's star was clearly rising.

It did not take long for him to impress the NAACP's leaders. In December 1916, Johnson was named the association's field secretary. His duties included traveling throughout the country on behalf of the organization, setting up new branches and recruiting new members. After three years of tireless effort, he had helped the NAACP to grow from 70 to 310 branches and its membership to increase from 9,000 to 100,000 members.

During America's participation in World War I, Johnson also served as the NAACP's acting executive secretary, the association's top position. In this role, he investigated acts of racial violence, led protests against lynching, and coordinated the NAACP's legal assistance for black defendants and funding for the homeless. He returned to his duties as field secretary in the spring of 1918 and recruited additional blacks to serve on the NAACP executive board, including Walter White, who became his chief assistant and was put in charge of investigating lynching cases.

In November 1920, Johnson was officially installed as the new executive secretary. During his 10 years in office, he skillfully coordinated the efforts of an underfinanced organization and an overworked staff. He relentlessly lobbied Congress for passage of antilynching legislation and led the NAACP in bringing suit against school boards to increase funding for black education. He also sponsored successful lawsuits to end housing discrimination, helped guarantee black voting rights in Texas, and supported labor organizer A. Philip Randolph's efforts to create a union of railway sleeping car porters.

Johnson's schedule became more and more taxing, and in 1929 he fell ill from exhaustion. He resigned as executive secretary in December 1930 to become professor of literature at Fisk University. He had maintained his literary interests while he worked at the NAACP: his books published in the 1920s were *The Book of American Negro Poetry* (1922), *The Book of American Negro Spirituals* (1925), and a collection of his own poetry, *God's Trombones* (1927). *Black Manhattan* (1930), an account of the Harlem Renaissance; his autobiography, *Along This Way* (1933); and *American Negroes: What Now?* (1934) were his final publications.

In his last years, Johnson and his wife divided their time between the Fisk campus, an apartment in Harlem, and a summer home in Massachusetts. He was driving in a heavy rainstorm in Maine on June 26, 1938, when a train struck his car at a railroad crossing. The collision instantly killed the 67-year-old James Weldon Johnson, who had devoted his life to racial equality so completely and in so many different ways.

MARTIN LUTHER KING, JR.

Civil rights leader Martin Luther King, Jr., was born on January 15, 1929, in Atlanta, Georgia. His father, Martin Luther King, Sr., was pastor of the Ebenezer Baptist Church, a leading black congregation in the city. His mother, Alberta Williams King, was the daughter of a former pastor of Ebenezer Baptist Church. Martin, Jr., his brother, Alfred, and sister, Willie Christine, grew up, as their parents and grandparents had, in the segregated South, where blacks learned about racial discrimination at an early age.

The warmth and support of his family and his father's church strengthened King while he was growing up. Friends and relatives recall that he was a normal boy who enjoyed sports, liked to read, and occasionally played pranks, which were promptly punished by his stern father.

After King graduated from high school in 1944, he entered Atlanta's Morehouse College, an all-male, all-black school. His parents had assumed that he would study for the ministry, but King was puzzled by "the emotionalism of Negro religion, the shouting and the stomping" that he saw in his father's church. "I didn't understand it," he said, "and it embarrassed me."

King changed his mind after hearing Morehouse College president Benjamin Mays preach. A Baptist minister, Mays was quiet and dignified, and from his pulpit in the college chapel he called for the black church to put aside some of its religious fundamentalism and lead the protest for social change. In February 1948, the 19-year-old King was ordained a minister and made assistant pastor at Ebenezer. He graduated from Morehouse several months later.

King's next stop was Crozer Seminary, near Philadelphia, to earn a degree in theology. Crozer presented a new world to him: nearly all its students were white. But by the end of his first year, he had become one of the most popular students at the seminary. His excellent grades also showed him to be among the brightest.

Meanwhile, King was developing a personal philosophy that would burn inside him for the rest of his life. A lecture on Indian leader Mahatma Gandhi provided the spark. Unique among political leaders, Gandhi stressed the power of love and nonviolent resistance as a means for changing people's opinions. Deeply impressed by this concept of peaceful defiance, King saw it as a way that black Americans might be able to break the shackles of segregation.

King received his bachelor's degree from Crozer in 1951, graduating at the top of his class. He was then awarded a scholarship to the School of Theology at Boston University. By the middle of his first year in Boston, he had met the woman who would become his wife: Coretta Scott, an Alabama native and an Antioch College graduate who was studying voice at the New England Conservatory of Music. They were married in June 1953 and had four children.

In the spring of 1954, after completing his classes for a doctorate, King was hired as the pastor of the Dexter Avenue Baptist Church in Montgomery, Alabama. He could not have chosen a more segregated city in the nation. Most of its black residents lived in ramshackle houses that did not have electricity or running water. Whites governed the city with an iron fist.

To King, the blacks of Montgomery seemed resigned to their fate. But change was coming: in May 1954, only a few months before his arrival, the U.S. Supreme Court had struck a severe blow against segregation. In its decision in the landmark case of *Brown v. Board of Education*, the Supreme Court declared that segregating school children by race was illegal.

Throughout the South, angry whites vowed to ignore the Supreme Court ruling. King responded by encouraging his parishioners to join the country's leading civil rights organization, the National Association for the Advancement of Colored People (NAACP). He also called on them to exercise their right to vote.

The battle for racial equality in Montgomery began in earnest on December 1, 1955, when Rosa Parks, a black seamstress, refused to obey a city ordinance that she give up her bus seat to a white passenger. She was arrested and jailed; in protest, the NAACP orchestrated a boycott of the city buses. The city's black pastors, including King, endorsed the protest, and the Montgomery bus boycott was born, with King hand-picked as the leader.

King's message of nonviolent resistance soon reached an audience that stretched far beyond Montgomery. By late 1956, the boycott had led to the desegregation of the city's buses, and King had emerged as a leading spokesman for civil rights. He took advantage of his growing fame in 1957 by organizing a public demonstration in Washington, D.C., to encourage congressional approval of a civil rights bill, the first of the 20th century. Held at the Lincoln Memorial on May 17, the Prayer Pilgrimage for Freedom attracted a crowd of 25,000 people and stamped King as the nation's most influential black leader.

To help spread the message of nonviolent resistance across America, King conferred with leading black clergymen and formed a new and powerful civil rights organization, the Southern Christian Leader-ship Conference (SCLC). As head of the Atlanta-based SCLC, he conducted a persistent campaign of nonviolent social protest, including sit-ins, in-terstate bus rides, and voter registration drives. Arrests and death threats did not deter him; he con-tinued to inspire his supporters to fight for racial equality.

King took on all comers. In Birmingham, Alabama, a fortress of white supremacy, he began demanding that public facilities be desegregated. By the time his clash with city officials had ended in mid-1963, the local police's brutal handling of King and his dem-onstrators had shocked the entire nation and had resulted in a settlement in Birmingham.

Nowhere did King reach a larger audience than during his speech at the March on Washington for Jobs and Freedom, held in the nation's capital on August 28, 1963. Nearly 250,000 civil rights marchers gathered at the Lincoln Memorial to hear him pro-claim at the end of the day-long demonstration, "I still have a dream. It is a dream deeply rooted in the American dream." His dream of a just society seemed all the more possible after he and his legions of supporters helped bring about the passage of the land-mark Civil Rights Act of 1964, which made segre-gation a federal crime.

In honor of his peaceful efforts to end segregation, King earned the 1964 Nobel Peace Prize. At age 35, he was the youngest recipient in history.

The award was soon followed by additional political action. In 1965, he spearheaded a voting rights campaign in Selma, Alabama, that state troopers did their best to stamp out; yet their vicious thrashing of the protesters served only to speed the passage of voting rights legislation. In 1966, he launched the Chicago Freedom Movement, an attempt to win civil rights for urban blacks, and another voter registration march, the James Meredith March Against Fear. In 1967, he again took a stand against violence by publicly proclaiming his opposition to the Vietnam War.

Sadly for King, his message of nonviolence seemed to be doing little good by the middle of 1967. The Vietnam War was escalating, and America's black ghettos, filled with frustration over the slow pace of change, were exploding in violence.

In response, King began a new effort, the Poor People's Campaign, to call attention to the desperate need for economic justice. He called for another march on Washington, D.C., this time to bring thousands of the impoverished to the nation's capital. There, in direct sight of the Capitol, they would build a poor people's city of shacks and tents and shame Congress into aiding the poor.

In the middle of his planning for the Poor People's Campaign, King traveled to Memphis, Tennessee, in support of the city's striking garbage collectors. He addressed the congregation at Mason Temple on the night of April 3, 1968, returned to his room at the Lorraine Motel, and spent all of the next afternoon organizing the march supporting the garbage collectors. At precisely six o'clock, as King stood on the motel's balcony to head off to dinner, he was felled by assassin James Earl Ray's bullet.

Martin Luther King, Jr., was just 39 years old at the time of his death. But his vision of a prejudice-free society—the greatest of all American dreams—will endure forever.

MALCOLM X

Racial spokesman Malcolm X was born Malcolm Little on May 19, 1925, in Omaha, Nebraska. The fourth of Earl and Louise Little's eight children, he entered a world full of violence and fear.

Only a few weeks before Malcolm's birth, his father narrowly escaped being lynched by the nation's most notorious white supremacist group, the Ku Klux Klan.

Earl Little was an outspoken Baptist preacher from Georgia who had grown up surrounded by racial violence and had become a fierce opponent of discrimination. The Klan had targeted him because he had emerged as a spokesman for the Universal Negro Improvement Association (UNIA), founded by black nationalist leader Marcus Garvey to heighten black pride and promote black rights.

When Malcolm was still an infant, the Littles moved to the Midwest, finally settling in East Lansing, Michigan. There Earl Little eked out a living as the Great Depression spread across the nation. He also continued his black activist work for the UNIA, until a bitter day in 1931, when he was found beaten and run over by a trolley car. His murderers, most likely a white lynch mob, were never found.

In the aftermath of her husband's death, Louise Little struggled to support her children and finally went on welfare. Continually confronted with his family's poverty, Malcolm began to drift away from home. Occasionally he was caught performing petty criminal acts. When his mother suffered a breakdown and was committed to a mental hospital in 1937, he became a ward of the state and was placed in a foster home. A short time later, 13-year-old Malcolm Little was put in a juvenile detention center.

In school, Little encountered few problems. He ranked third in his junior high school class and was popular enough to be elected student body vice-president by his predominantly white classmates. But the die was already cast. Deep down, he did not feel accepted in the white world.

Little welcomed the change of scenery that accompanied his half-sister Ella's invitation to spend the summer of 1939 at her well-to-do home in Roxbury, a largely black section of Boston. There he learned what life was like for privileged blacks. He returned to the city the following spring and moved in with Ella.

Having little confidence that his schooling would lead to any sort of bright future, Little decided to go to work instead of continuing his education. His first job was as a shoe shiner at the Roseland State Ballroom, one of Boston's most popular dance halls. He supplemented his income by selling marijuana to some of the customers; and as the days passed, he became increasingly involved in the world of drugs, drinking, and gambling. The more spending money he had in his pockets, it seemed, the more his appetite for vices grew.

At the end of 1941, Little moved to the Harlem district of New York City and was soon drawn into the black community's underworld of hustlers and thieves. He became known on the streets as a drug peddler, Detroit Red.

Little thrived for a while as a hustler. Then the police began to watch him closely, forcing him to find another way to obtain money. He turned to armed robbery and numbers running.

Scrapes with rival hustlers sent Little back to Boston, where his criminal past finally caught up with him. The police hauled him from the streets, and in February 1946 he was sentenced to 10 years in prison. At first, he remained a wildly angry, antisocial young man who took great pride in being an outcast. But as his prison term wore on, he began to listen to three of his siblings as they encouraged him to embrace the black separatist religious movement known as the Nation of Islam, with its message of black superiority and resistance to white domination.

The Nation sought to instill racial pride and promote self-sufficiency while offering its legions of disciples, particularly the black urban poor, a sense of mission in life. Elijah Muhammad, the head of the Nation, and his followers, known as Black Muslims, claimed that all whites were devils who were about to fall from their positions of power. In their place would rise the black community.

As Little learned more about Muhammad, he saw parallels between the Black Muslim leader's work and his own father's social activism. In 1949, Little wrote a long letter to Muhammad and was welcomed into the sect. In keeping with the Nation's custom, Malcolm Little replaced his surname with the letter *X*.

Malcolm X was paroled from prison in 1952 and immediately set out on a mission to use the teachings of the Nation of Islam "to stir and wake and resurrect the black man." His blistering attacks on America's long-standing racial attitudes and his success in recruiting new members—in pool halls, barrooms, and on street corners—soon established him as the ministry's chief operative. A spellbinding public speaker, he urged his fellow blacks to battle racial oppression with militant action.

In June 1954, as a reward for his hard work, Malcolm X was appointed the head of Temple Number Seven in Harlem. Its membership grew swiftly, and during the rest of the decade he organized new temples in cities along the East and West Coasts, drawing converts from the more prosperous and educated middle class. Members were required to make monetary contributions to the Nation, which began buying real estate and starting small businesses. Profits from these ventures enabled the Nation to expand greatly.

At the same time that the number of Black Muslims was growing, the Reverend Martin Luther King, Jr., and other civil rights leaders were challenging racial segregation in the South by holding nonviolent protests. Malcolm X had nothing but contempt for their passive approach to the problems facing black society. He began spreading his message of revolt to crowds in the northern ghettos, telling his listeners that they could not afford to wait any longer for racial justice to be won.

By the early 1960s, Malcolm X and the Nation of Islam had become well known to both whites and blacks throughout the United States. Critics charged that he was a hatemonger who preached violence and destruction. He replied that only radical tactics would cure America's racial problems. "Yes, I'm an extremist," he said. "The black race here in North America is in extremely bad condition."

In 1962, the ailing Elijah Muhammad named Malcolm X as the acting head of the Nation. This appointment aroused the jealousy of other Black Muslims, who attempted to turn the older man against his protégé by spreading rumors that he was trying to usurp Muhammad's power.

Before long, a serious rift developed between Malcolm X and Muhammad. Following President John F. Kennedy's assassination in November 1963, Malcolm

X declared that "the chickens [have] come home to roost," meaning that whites were being repaid for creating a climate of violence in America. This time, Malcolm X had gone too far. The comment created an uproar throughout the United States and provided Muhammad with an opportunity to deal with the supposed threat to his own leadership. He promptly suspended Malcolm X from his duties for the next 90 days.

Toward the end of his suspension, Malcolm X learned that a high-ranking Black Muslim had instructed that the fiery, 38-year-old minister be killed. Malcolm X believed that the only person in the organization with the authority to order such an act was Elijah Muhammad himself, and he responded by announcing in March 1964 that he was leaving the Nation to form Muslim Mosque, Incorporated. This new group was organized to push for black self-determination, but it also represented a shift in Malcolm X's thinking in that it was willing to work in cooperation with less radical civil rights organizations and to accept money and ideas from whites.

After leaving the Nation, Malcolm X developed an interest in Orthodox Islam, and less than a month after organizing Muslim Mosque, he quietly left the country to embark on a spiritual pilgrimage to Mecca, the Islamic holy city. There he was embraced by Muslims of every race and saw that a doctrine of black supremacy was not part of traditional Islam. Before returning to America, Malcolm X traveled through Lebanon and Africa. In a speech made before the Ghanaian parliament, he linked the struggle of black Americans for justice with the struggle of black Africans for political and economic independence, a philosophy he called "global black thinking."

It was a changed Malcolm X who returned to the
United States in May 1964—though still a militant
leader, he was now secure in his decision to work with
civil rights organizations to build a better way of life
for blacks. In addition, he had a new perspective on
global economics and wished to link the black power
movement with the empowerment of the poor and
working class. To help achieve this goal on a
worldwide scale, he founded a nonreligious branch of
Muslim Mosque, the Organization of Afro-American
Unity (OAAU).

To raise funds for the OAAU, Malcolm X went on
an extensive speaking tour. He traveled again to
Africa, where he addressed a conference sponsored by
the Organization of African Unity and met his
longtime hero, leader of the African independence
movement and president of Kenya, Jomo Kenyatta.
But Malcolm X's renewed effort to break the shackles
of white supremacy made him the target of death
threats. He assumed his rivals in the Nation were
behind the warnings.

Both the Nation and federal agents kept Malcolm X
under close surveillance, and he began to suspect that
a conspiracy was being organized against him. This
concern deepened when he traveled to Paris in early
February 1965 to speak at a rally protesting U.S.
involvement in the Vietnam War. He was quickly
deported as a security threat, but rumors reached him
that French officials had discovered a plot to kill him
in Paris and had deported him in order to avoid an
international incident on their soil.

On the night of February 13, Malcolm X's home in
East Elmhurst, New York, was firebombed; he and his

family barely managed to escape from the flaming house. Then, barely a week later, on February 21, during a rally at the Audubon Ballroom in Harlem, three gunmen—allegedly Black Muslims—shot him dead. His New York City headquarters was burned down two days after the shooting. In the wake of Malcolm X's death would remain his call for sweeping changes in American society.

ADAM CLAYTON POWELL, JR.

Political leader Adam Clayton Powell, Jr., was born on November 29, 1908, in New Haven, Connecticut. Shortly after his birth, he and his older sister, Blanche, moved with their parents, Mattie and the Reverend Adam Clayton Powell, Sr., to Harlem, the New York City district that was just emerging as the nation's largest black community.

A Baptist minister, the senior Powell became pastor of the century-old Abyssinian Baptist Church in midtown. He immediately set to work revitalizing it by increasing the church's membership and improving its financial resources. With the help of local reformers, the dynamic Powell also made the church a center for the entire black community. It fed the poor, offered recreation to the young, and presented musical and dramatic performances.

As the influential pastor's son, Adam, Jr., enjoyed a privileged upbringing. He lived in a spacious brownstone and, being the baby of the family, was constantly pampered, especially by his mother. Gradually, he emerged from her shadow.

Fair skinned with straight black hair, Powell could, in the phrase of the day, "pass for white." But his father, being an advocate of black pride, made sure that Adam, Jr., understood his roots. And when his son was 14 years old, the senior Powell moved his church uptown, to a new building in the heart of Harlem.

The Abyssinian Baptist Church thrived in its new location. The congregation grew to more than 10,000 members, the largest of any Protestant church in America. Adam, Jr., the reverend hoped, would one day preside over the church.

The younger Powell was a good student in elementary school. But he saw his grades drop almost as soon as he entered Townsend Harris High School. Fancying himself a ladies' man, he led an active social life. Prodded by his father, he enrolled at the City College of New York in 1925, only to flunk out of school that spring. A busy social calendar was not the only reason for this lapse: his sister died after an operation that March, leaving him devastated.

In the fall, Powell tried college once again. He attended Colgate University, studied reasonably hard, and graduated in 1930. He promptly became assistant minister and business manager of the Abyssinian and also entered Columbia University's Teachers College, from which he received a master's degree in religious studies in 1932. The next year, he married singer Isabel Washington.

By then, Powell had thrown himself completely into his work. Seeing the Great Depression leave an alarming number of Harlemites without jobs, he launched a campaign to help the local black community. He proved to be an extremely capable leader, organizing boycotts and pickets to combat the racial discrimination and despair that plagued Harlem. "My father said he built the church and I would interpret it. This I made up my mind to do," he said. "I intended to fashion that church into a mighty weapon, keen-edged and sharp-pointed."

In 1937, the 29-year-old Powell succeeded his father as the Abyssinian's minister. He used his position as the nation's best-known and most influential black clergyman as a springboard to political office. In 1941, he ran as an independent candidate for a seat on the New York City Council. "I am not seeking a political job," he claimed. "I am fighting for the chance to give my people the best representation in the affairs of their city, to help make Harlem the number one community of New York."

That November, New York's voters made him the first black city councilman ever.

In 1943, Powell decided to go after a larger political prize. The U.S. Congress had recently created a new congressional district in Harlem, and Powell announced his intention to run for the seat as a Democrat. The following year, he was elected to Congress by an overwhelming majority and thus became the first U.S. congressman to represent the district of Harlem.

Soon after taking his seat in the House of Representatives, Powell divorced his wife Isabel and married Hazel Scott, a well-known jazz pianist and singer. They had one child, Adam Clayton Powell III, who was born in 1946. (Powell was married for a third time in 1960, to Puerto Rican native Yvette Marjorie Flores Diago; their son, Adam Clayton Powell IV, was born in 1962.)

As a congressman, Powell quickly established a reputation as a militant, uncompromising champion of black rights. He became especially noted for attacking southern congressmen who supported segregation. In 1945, he even went so far as to publish *Marching Blacks*, a book that urged southern blacks to move north, where they would find greater economic opportunities and be allowed to vote, a right often denied them in the South.

Powell was nothing if not politically independent and disdainful of congressional protocol, and his crusade to foster black rights wore thin on many of his colleagues. One of the things that annoyed them the most was his constant use of what came to be known as the Powell amendment. He employed this legislative tactic for the first time in 1946, when he attached to a bill an amendment that denied federal money to any state that excluded black schoolchildren from its food fund program. The bill—with its attached Powell amendment—was passed.

After that, Powell decided to try to repeat his success. As a member of the House Education and Labor Committee, he attached an amendment to nearly every education bill that denied federal funds to any state that practiced segregation. He carried this practice well into the 1960s, as the South continued to resist every attempt to integrate its schools. Southern congressmen refused to support any bill that included the Powell amendment, and without their votes, federal aid to education suffered. Powell, however, maintained that making use of the Powell amendment was one of the best ways a black politician could agitate for black rights.

As a leader in the fight against segregation and an irritant to the powerbrokers in Congress, Powell was beloved by his constituents. He fought for new social welfare programs and, as chairman of the House Education and Labor Committee in the 1960s, he helped guide important civil rights bills through Congress. He was a pioneer in fostering black solidarity.

But the early 1960s, a number of dark clouds had already begun to appear on Powell's horizon. The Justice Department and the Internal Revenue Service had begun digging into his affairs a decade earlier, and in 1958 he had been indicted for tax evasion. His case was dismissed when it was brought to trial two years later, but the storm was still brewing.

It finally broke in 1967, at the tail end of a House committee's investigation of Powell's congressional payroll. It was revealed that he was paying salaries to his wife Yvette, his companion Corinne Huff, and several other nongovernment people. And he had been illegally spending the taxpayers' money in a host of other ways.

Armed with the investigative committee's findings on Powell's misconduct, the House of Representatives voted on his fate. The verdict was overwhelmingly against him. Twenty-three years after he was first voted into Congress, Powell was stripped of his congressional seat by his fellow representatives. He immediately appealed the decision in the courts.

Meanwhile, a special election was held in April 1967 to fill Powell's now-vacant seat in Congress. The Harlem voters reelected him, and then handed him a 13th term in the 1968 elections.

Back in Congress, Powell was fined $25,000 by his colleagues, who also took away his seniority. His spirits picked up somewhat half a year later, when the U.S. Supreme Court ruled in favor of his appeal, declaring that "the House was without power to exclude him from membership." But the summer of 1969 was hardly a time for celebration. His doctors had just informed him that he was seriously ill with cancer.

Throughout the following year, Powell hardly spent any time at all answering the congressional roll call. And when the Democratic primary for Congress was held in June 1970, Harlem turned against him for the first time. His political career was over.

Powell's life came to an end on April 4, 1972, following an emergency operation in Miami. His body was returned to Harlem for a funeral service at the Abyssinian Baptist Church, where his remarkable career as a crusader for black rights began.

ASA PHILIP RANDOLPH

Labor leader Asa Philip Randolph was born on April 15, 1889, in Crescent City, Florida. His family moved north to Jacksonville when he was two years old, and it was there that he spent the rest of his childhood.

Asa and his older brother, James, were taught by their parents, Elizabeth and James Randolph, Sr., to be proud and independent, to stand up to racial discrimination, and to help the needy. Their father was a minister in the African Methodist Episcopal (AME) church and led a small congregation. He also preached to blacks in rural communities near the city.

Jacksonville at the time was one of the most integrated towns in the South. But as Randolph grew older, instances of racial violence began to increase, until tensions heightened following a fire in 1901 that destroyed two-thirds of the city and led to scenes of looting. The crimes were attributed to blacks, and laws were passed to enforce segregation and to deprive blacks of the positions of authority they held. The Reverend James Randolph promptly forbade his sons from using any segregated public facilities, including the streetcars and the library.

A solid student, Randolph enrolled in Jacksonville's Cookman Institute when he was 14 years old. There he shone in the choir and on the baseball team. He graduated in 1907 as the head of his class and delivered a valedictory address on racial pride.

Lacking the money to go to college, Randolph held a variety of jobs. All the while, he resolved to fight in some way for the improvement of conditions for black Americans. He had already decided not to follow in his father's footsteps and become a minister, but he did have a strong social conscience.

In 1911, shortly after celebrating his 22nd birthday, Randolph left Jacksonville and moved to New York City, settling in the Harlem district. During the next three years, he worked at a series of low-paying jobs: telephone switchboard operator, dishwasher, floor scrubber, porter. He divided his spare time between the public library, a discussion group at a local

Methodist church, and night classes at the City College of New York, where he studied public speaking and social sciences.

Randolph's studies led him to the writings of Karl Marx, the German political philosopher who advocated a society in which everything is owned and controlled by the state. Randolph believed that Marx's socialist system provided the best means for achieving greater racial equality in America. Because most blacks belonged to the working class, they had much to gain in a society in which there was no such thing as private property.

Randolph made his first inroads into labor organization while at City College. He formed a discussion group, the Independent Political Council, that supported the American labor movement and its demands for higher wages and better working conditions. Through this group, he wound up meeting Lucille Campbell Green. The two were married in 1914 and spent nearly 50 years together.

Shortly after his marriage, Randolph befriended Chandler Owen, a Columbia University sociology student who also believed strongly in socialism. Together, they stopped attending classes, joined the Socialist party, and took to the streets of Harlem, becoming streetcorner orators preaching social reform. They soon attracted the attention of William White, who invited them in 1917 to edit a magazine, the *Hotel Messenger*, intended for black waiters working in the city's hotels.

The venture came to an end seven months later, but by then the two men had ideas for a new magazine that would serve as a voice for black workers. The first issue was published in November 1917, and Randolph and Owen called it *The Messenger*, subtitling it the "only radical Negro magazine in America." Published monthly, it quickly gained a prominent place among New York's political journals, being considered among the most intellectual and the most controversial. The editorials called for cooperation among workers of all races and for a relentless assault on racism. Above all, it promoted racial pride.

"We were young, we were against everything, and we weren't going to back down from anything," Randolph said of his early days with *The Messenger*. And he was true to his word. He argued that black Americans should not fight in World War I so long as they were being subjected to racially discriminatory laws. He said that blacks should use arms, if necessary, to defend themselves. He was also outspokenly critical of black nationalist leader Marcus Garvey as well as more mainstream black leaders, such as Booker T. Washington and W. E. B. Du Bois, claiming that their policies encouraged blacks to patiently accept oppression. By 1919, the U.S. State Department had declared Randolph "the most dangerous Negro in America."

The labor movement remained one of Randolph's greatest passions. He wrote many editorials criticizing the American Federation of Labor (AFL), the labor unions' governing body, because blacks were excluded from its unions. But by the mid-1920s he finally had to admit to himself that neither the AFL nor the Socialist party was interested in helping black workers. Discouraged, he quit the Socialist party and decided to take matters into his own hands.

In 1925, Randolph was asked to organize the porters of the Pullman Company, which owned and operated the sleeping cars used on long-distance passenger routes, into the Brotherhood of Sleeping Car Porters. All of the company's porters were black, underpaid, and overworked. During the months that followed, Randolph and several associates traveled around the country establishing branches of the union. By the end of 1926, it claimed a membership of nearly 6,000—more than half the number of porters who worked for the Pullman Company.

It took 12 long years for the Randolph-led Brotherhood of Sleeping Car Porters to win the battle for better working conditions. But on August 25, 1937, when a labor pact was finally reached with the company, giving the porters the wage and work-hour concessions they had demanded, the union became the first group of blacks to sign a labor agreement with a major corporation.

Randolph's triumph elevated him to national prominence and labeled him the leader of America's black community. He tried to use his newly won influence to integrate all of the AFL's unions and to end the nation's racially segregated armed forces, but nothing seemed to work. In 1941, he began to organize a massive protest march on Washington, D.C., to "shake up America." He said that the "leaders in Washington will never give the Negro justice until they see masses—10, 20, 50 thousand Negroes on the White House Lawn!"

The threat of the march on Washington brought about the end of racially discriminatory employment policies in the defense industry and the federal government. In 1948, Randolph's lobbying brought about the desegregation of the armed forces and the creation of a Fair Employment Board to eliminate racial discrimination in government agencies.

By the 1950s, the labor movement finally began to accept the principles that Randolph had been championing for decades, and more and more unions became integrated. In 1955, when the AFL merged with the other leading labor federation, the Congress of Industrial Organizations (CIO), Randolph was elected to the newly formed AFL-CIO's executive council. Two years later, he was voted in as the federation's vice-president.

A tireless champion of the working man, Randolph carried on his fight into the 1960s, helping to form the Negro American Labor Council, which sought to increase the role of blacks in labor unions, and serving as its president. And he remained a guiding light of the nation's civil rights movement. In 1963, he again issued the call for a march on Washington. This time the march took place on August 28, and the massive demonstration, called the March on Washington for Jobs and Freedom, proved to be the crowning event of the civil rights effort, highlighted by the Reverend Martin Luther King, Jr.'s "I Have a Dream" speech. Less than a year later, President Lyndon B. Johnson awarded Randolph the Medal of Freedom for his service to his country.

Randolph continued as president of the Brotherhood of Sleeping Car Porters until 1968. He died 11 years later, on May 16, barely a month after his 90th birthday. His passing recalled the words of journalist Murray Kempton, who said, "It is hard to make anyone who has never met him believe that A. Philip Randolph must be the greatest man who has lived in the United States in this century. But it is harder yet to make anyone who has ever known him believe anything else."

WALTER WHITE

Civil rights leader Walter
Francis White was born on July 1, 1893, in Atlanta,
Georgia. His father, George White, was a mailman;
his mother, Madeline, was a former schoolteacher.
Walter and his six brothers and sisters grew up in a
two-story house that stood on the border between the
city's black and white communities.

The Whites' light skin color also put them on a border of sorts. Although they considered themselves black, they could have easily passed for white, which they refused to do.

The White children were taught to regard friends, family, and faith more highly than material possessions. Education was deeply prized, and Walter's early interest in learning was encouraged by both parents. He constantly borrowed books from the library at the church he attended. And every day after school, he rode with his father on his mail route and engaged in long-running debates. Whenever Walter's knowledge seemed hazy on a subject, George White sent him to the church library to learn more about it.

One night in September 1906, racial hatred erupted in Atlanta, with white mobs attacking blacks. The Whites were initially spared from the violence because they were not recognized as being black. But a mob marched toward their street on the second night of the riot. Only a volley of gunfire from neighbors saved the family from harm.

The incident left a deep impression on Walter White. "I knew who I was," he said. "I was a Negro, a human being with an invisible pigmentation which marked me a person to be hunted, hanged, abused, discriminated against."

To rise above his station in life, White chose to excel. He graduated from high school in 1912 and enrolled at Atlanta University. There he played football, won awards for his debating skills, and was elected president of his class. Upon graduating in 1916, he went to work for an insurance company.

Meanwhile, a city government plan to limit black children to a sixth-grade education attracted White's attention. He and a number of Atlanta's educated blacks protested the proposal, arguing that the city had a legal obligation to provide equal schooling to blacks and whites. The plan was scrapped, prompting White and his allies to press for improvements in the educational system. To marshal support, they formed a chapter of a new and growing civil rights organization, the National Association for the Advancement of Colored People (NAACP). White was elected the branch's secretary.

In 1918, White moved to New York City and became assistant secretary of the entire NAACP. One of the association's chief aims was to put a stop to the racial violence that was occurring throughout the United States, especially in the South. Between 1910 and 1920, almost 900 blacks died at the hands of lynch mobs.

One of White's first assignments was to investigate a lynching in Estill Springs, Tennessee. Letting local residents assume he was white, he tricked them into revealing the details of the murder, then returned to New York to publish the entire story. It received widespread attention and helped recruit many new members to the NAACP and its antilynching campaign.

White involved himself in a broad range of NAACP activities, including the ongoing battle to desegregate schools, hospitals, and neighborhoods. Lynchings and race riots, however, became his specialty. He traveled to Chicago in the summer of 1919 to investigate a series of riots. Then he headed to Phillips County,

Arkansas, where roving white mobs had massacred perhaps as many as 200 black sharecroppers. Posing as a northern newspaper reporter, White uncovered the truth about the killings.

In 1922, White married NAACP staff member Leah Gladys Powell, with whom he had two children: a daughter, Jane, and a son, Walter, Jr. The Whites became part of the social and intellectual life then thriving in Harlem, the black New York City district where they made their home. White himself contributed greatly to the black community's cultural life. By the end of the decade, he had published three books that brought him great acclaim: two novels, *The Fire in the Flint* (1924) and *Flight* (1926), and *Rope and Faggot*, a study of lynching in America.

White's literary successes did not slow him down. He continued his rigorous schedule of NAACP activities, traveling thousands of miles each year while serving as a major fundraiser for the association and continuing his investigations of racial injustice. All told, he personally investigated 41 lynchings and 8 race riots.

One of White's major battles began in 1930, when President Herbert Hoover named a circuit court judge from North Carolina, John J. Parker, to fill a vacancy on the U.S. Supreme Court. White investigated the judge's record and discovered that, in his unsuccessful bid to become governor in 1920, Parker had called for an end to black voting rights. White sent Parker a telegram, asking if he still held such a belief. When Parker failed to respond, White and the NAACP board of directors decided to oppose Parker's appointment.

First, the NAACP asked Hoover to withdraw his nomination. When the president refused, the association took the fight to the U.S. Senate, which must confirm all Supreme Court nominees, and then to cities around the nation. White testified against Parker before the Senate committee considering the appointment, then dispatched NAACP officials to the organization's regional branches to inform black voters of the threat Parker posed to their rights. The black community was encouraged to contact their senators and urge them to oppose Parker.

A flood of protest, in the form of letters, telegrams, petitions, telephone calls, and demonstrators, descended on Washington, D.C. Newspapers throughout the country debated the Parker appointment. On May 7, 1930, the voice of black America was heard. The Senate voted 41–39 to deny Parker a seat on the Supreme Court.

In 1931, White was rewarded for his hard work. James Weldon Johnson, who had served as the NAACP's executive secretary since 1920, stepped down from his post because of poor health. White was named to replace his mentor and close friend as the association's top official.

White had his work cut out for him as head of the NAACP. The Great Depression, the worst economic collapse in the country's history, was producing more social unrest and racial violence. After Franklin D. Roosevelt became president in 1932, White repeatedly urged the nation's leader to speak out in favor of antilynching legislation. Finally, in early 1934, Roosevelt delivered a radio address in which he denounced lynching as murder, and public support increased for a federal antilynching bill. Although Congress failed to pass legislation that outlawed lynching, White's relentless campaign steadily caused the grim practice to diminish.

White worked to ease racial tensions on all fronts. In 1943, when riots erupted in Detroit, his appeal to the president succeeded in bringing federal troops to the city to restore order. That same year, he helped bring calm to Harlem following an outbreak of violence.

In early 1944, White took a leave of absence from the NAACP to travel abroad as a correspondent during World War II and to observe the treatment of black servicemen serving in segregated combat units. For more than a year, he visited military installations in Europe, the Middle East, North Africa, and the Pacific, and sent back reports of racial discrimination.

Back home after the war ended in 1945, White served as a consultant to the American delegation at the founding meeting of the United Nations. Meanwhile, he discovered that outbreaks of violence directed against blacks were on the rise. In 1946, he worked with President Harry S. Truman to establish the Committee on Civil Rights, a group to investigate civil liberties violations. The committee's subsequent report called for sweeping reforms, including the passage of 27 civil rights acts.

In 1948, Truman sent Congress a massive program of civil rights legislation. Southern senators hastily defeated each measure. But the president would not be deterred. He issued two historic executive orders:

one of them desegregated the armed forces, the other called for all federal agencies to practice fair employment.

Truman's actions were crowning triumphs for White. The NAACP chief had spent decades championing greater legal protection of black rights. At last, he had succeeded in pushing a racist, segregated United States into an era of integrated education, housing, employment, military service, and public facilities.

White's achievement did not come without a price. In 1947, he suffered a heart attack and was forced to cut back on his busy schedule. His duties at the NAACP were reduced, and he devoted his last years to writing his autobiography, *A Man Called White* (1948), as well as an evaluation of the civil rights movement.

Walter White died of a heart attack on March 28, 1955, at the age of 61.

PIONEERS OF DISCOVERY

BENJAMIN BANNEKER

Astronomer and mathematician Benjamin Banneker was born on November 9, 1731, in what was then the British colony of Maryland. His father was a former slave, born in Africa, who had bought his freedom. Benjamin's mother was the daughter of a white Englishwoman, Molly Welsh, and a freed African slave.

In 1682 Molly Welsh had been falsely accused of stealing milk on the farm in England where she worked as a dairy maid. She was put on trial and convicted, and as her punishment she was deported to the English colonies in North America. In 1683 Welsh settled on a farm in Maryland as an indentured servant, a person who was legally bound to work for an employer for a certain number of years.

Welsh's term of servitude was seven years. When she received her freedom in 1690, she rented a small plot of land and grew tobacco. After several years she had made enough money from the sale of her crop to buy a small patch of land near the Patapsco River. A few years later Welsh bought two slaves to help her farm the land. One of the slaves, named Bannaka, told Welsh that he had been a prince in Africa. This may have been true, because during this time, rival African states at war often captured the opposing tribe's royal family and sold them to European slave traders.

Bannaka was said to be "a man of bright intelligence, fine temper, with a very agreeable presence, dignified manners, and contemplative habits." He held pride in his African heritage, maintaining his faith while other slaves converted to Christianity. He also kept his African name, although it was changed slightly.

By 1696 Welsh had freed both of her slaves. About this time she married Bannaka, and the couple took the surname of Banneky. They operated a prosperous tobacco farm and eventually had four children, all of whom worked on the farm. The oldest, Mary, married a freed slave named Robert from a neighboring farm in 1730. Their first child, Benjamin, was born a year later. The couple took Mary's surname, which was later changed to Banneker.

Throughout his childhood Benjamin and his three younger sisters worked on the family farm. They helped with the household chores and sowed the tobacco seeds. Although tobacco farming took up most of Benjamin's time, he did not like it very much. Whenever he was able to take a break from farm work, he read. His grandmother Molly Welsh taught him how to read and write and to perform simple arithmetic. She also arranged for him to attend classes for several years at a local Quaker school, and his interest in mathematics and science grew. He enjoyed calculating mathematical problems and figuring out statistics.

At the age of 21, Banneker decided to build a clock, even though he did not know how one worked. Mechanical timepieces were rare in colonial America, but Banneker managed to borrow a pocket watch to use as a model. He took the watch apart and made drawings of its interior to teach himself how it worked. He then reproduced the watch parts by carving them from wood, making them considerably bigger, and assembled them into a large clock. He even added a bell, so that the clock chimed on the hour. Neighbors often came to see it, and Banneker himself became celebrated locally for his mathematical ability.

In 1759, following the death of his father, Banneker became responsible for running the family tobacco farm. During the next 20 years he spent most of his time doing farm work; for relaxation he bought a flute and violin and learned to play both instruments. He liked to sit on the porch and play music in the evening. Being a free black, Banneker led a lonely life. He did not have many friends, and he never married. However, neighbors did visit to have him help make mathematical computations on deeds and other things.

In the 1780s Banneker became acquainted with the Ellicotts, a white Quaker family who lived nearby. One of the family's sons, George Ellicott, was a surveyor, and when he learned of Banneker's interest in mathematics and mechanics, he lent Banneker a telescope, drafting instruments, and several books on surveying and astronomy. Using all these materials, Banneker proceeded to teach himself both surveying and astronomy.

Soon Banneker was able to predict when eclipses of the sun and moon would occur. (An eclipse of the sun, or solar eclipse means that moonlight is blocked by the passage of earth between the moon and the sun.) Banneker also calculated a table showing the locations of celestial bodies—the sun, moon, stars, and planets—at different times of the year. Such a table is called an ephemeris; the plural is *ephemerides*.

In 1791 a cousin of George Ellicott's, Andrew Ellicott, became the chief surveyor of the nearby federal territory. A new national capital was being created on this land that later became Washington, D.C. Andrew Ellicott, hearing of Banneker's skills, invited him to help with the survey.

Several months later, after finishing this work, Banneker returned to his farm and calculated an ephemeris for the following year. In August of 1791 Banneker sent a copy of his ephemeris to Thomas Jefferson, who was then Secretary of State. Along with the calculations he enclosed a letter that complained about the "abuse and censure" of African Americans by whites, and he criticized Jefferson for not opposing slavery. In his letter, Banneker compared the enslavement of blacks to the way in which England had treated the American colonies before the colonies declared their independence.

Jefferson wrote back to Banneker, acknowledging the receipt of his letter and calculations. The future president, who was also an amateur scientist, then sent Banneker's calculations to an acquaintance, the head of the French Academy of Sciences in Paris. Jefferson's and Banneker's letters were later published in pamphlet form and received wide publicity.

In December 1791 Banneker published his ephemeris as part of an almanac entitled *Benjamin Banneker's Pennsylvania, Delaware, Maryland and Virginia Almanack and Ephemeris, for the Year of Our Lord, 1792; Being Bissextile, or Leap-Year, and the Sixteenth Year of American Independence, Which Commenced July 4, 1776.* In addition to the ephemeris, the almanac included several essays on scientific topics.

The publication of Banneker's almanac was sponsored by several abolitionist societies—groups of men and women who worked for the abolition of slavery. At that time many people who supported slavery believed that Africans were not as intelligent as people of European ancestry. Abolitionists used Banneker's work to show that blacks had abilities equal to those of whites.

The first edition of the almanac sold out quickly, and a second edition was printed. The book's widespread popularity freed Banneker from heavy farm work. Instead of raising cash crops, he kept only a small home garden and raised bees. This gave him more time to continue his calculations and to chat with the many visitors who flocked to his cabin, for Banneker had become a celebrity.

Banneker published a new *Almanack and Ephemeris* each year for several years. The *Almanack* for 1793 included copies of Banneker's letter to Jefferson and Jefferson's response. The last known issue of Banneker's *Almanack and Ephemeris* appeared in 1797, probably because support for the antislavery movement was then declining. However, Banneker continued to prepare an ephemeris for each year until 1804. He also published a book about bees and calculated the life cycle of the seventeen-year locust.

One of Banneker's closest friends in his later years was Susanna Mason, a cousin of the Ellicotts. Mason was the founder of an association for the relief of the poor in Baltimore. She met Banneker in 1796, and the two wrote letters to one another. Mason wrote a poem in one of these letters:

> *But thou, a man exalted high,*
> *Conspicuous in the world's keen eye*

On record now thy name's enrolled
And future ages will be told,
There lived a man called Banneker,
An African Astronomer.

Banneker died at his cabin on October 9, 1806, one month before his 75th birthday. He had left many of his personal effects, including his journals and scientific instruments, to George Ellicott, and these were quickly carted away. Banneker's funeral service was held on his farm two days after his death. As the body was being buried, his cabin nearby burst into flames and burned to the ground. Everything remaining in the structure was destroyed—including the famous clock that he had built many years before.

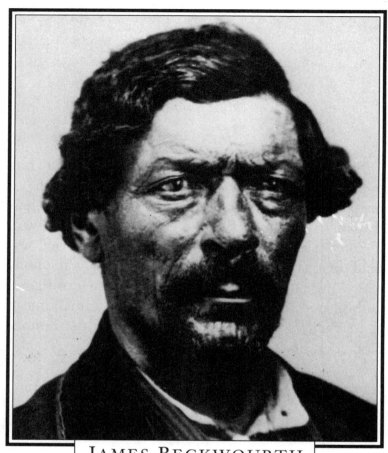

JAMES BECKWOURTH

Frontiersman James Pierson Beckwourth was born in Frederick County, Virginia, around the year 1800. His father was Jennings Beckwith, a member of a prominent landholding family in Virginia. James's mother was probably a light-skinned slave on the Beckwith plantation. After Beckwith's legal wife died in 1808, Beckwith, his son James, and James's mother moved west to a farm near St. Charles, Missouri, to start a new life.

Although James was legally a slave, his father treated him kindly. When James was 10, Jennings Beckwith sent him to school in St. Louis, where he learned to read and write. When he was not attending school, James loved to be outdoors with his father, traipsing through the acres of wilderness surrounding their home.

About 1819 James was apprenticed to a pair of blacksmiths in the city. However, James was more interested in his social life than the daily drudgery of blacksmithing. He frequently got into arguments with his employers over his behavior. One day, in the midst of an angry dispute, a passing constable tried to intervene. James Beckwourth knocked out the policeman and fled the scene.

After several days in hiding, Beckwourth returned to his father, who arranged for his release from the apprenticeship. At this time Jennings Beckwith decided that it was time to free his son, and he went to court to sign papers that formally released Beckwourth from slavery. For several years James Beckwourth worked on the family farm. In the early 1820s he traveled up the Mississippi River to Fever River, Illinois (later renamed Galena), to work in the nearby lead mines.

During these years Beckwourth's love of the wilderness had increased, and he began to dream of a life of solitude and freedom as a trapper and trader on the western frontier. That opportunity came in

1823, when he joined a fur-trapping expedition sponsored by two entrepreneurs named William Ashley and Andrew Henry. Ashley and Henry's venture later became the Rocky Mountain Fur Company.

Beckwourth's activities during the next few years are not known in detail, although he presumably lived as a "mountain man," as frontiersmen were known, hunting and trapping. In June 1825 he attended a gathering of more than 100 American trappers at Henry's Fork, a settlement on the Green River in the Rocky Mountains. For the next 15 years these "conventions," or rendezvous, of mountain men became annual events at different prearranged locations throughout the Rockies. During several days of revelry at Henry's Fork in 1825, Beckwourth established what became a lifelong reputation as a talented raconteur, or storyteller.

Like all successful trappers, James Beckwourth was well-versed in the habits and customs of Native American tribes in the West, and many Indians respected him for his prowess. In fact, friendly Indians could be especially helpful to trappers because they often knew the best sources of game. Not long after attending the 1828 rendezvous of mountain men, Beckwourth and his close friend, the celebrated frontiersman Jim Bridger, were trapping beaver one day near the Powder River when they encountered a party of Crow Indians. Beckwourth knew of his favorable reputation among the Crows, who were generally friendly to white men, and he allowed himself to be "captured" by them. The curious and delighted Crows took Beckwourth back to their camp.

During the next eight years Beckwourth lived with the Crows in the region of what is now Montana and Wyoming while he continued his life as a fur trapper and trader with a new employer, the American Fur Company. The Indians believed that Beckwourth himself was part Crow, an impression that he did not correct. Beckwourth enjoyed the relative freedom of Native American society and took many Indian wives over the years. He engaged in the common Crow practice of stealing horses from white men and earned the nickname Enemy of Horses. Beckwourth earned another nickname, Bloody Arm, for his frequent participation in Crow war parties.

The American Fur Company terminated Beckwourth's employment with them in 1836, and shortly afterward he left the Crows and drifted back to St. Louis. He remained there for several months with little to occupy his time except heavy drinking and street fights. In 1837 Senator Thomas Hart Benton of Missouri called for the formation of a brigade of experienced volunteers to fight the Seminole Indians in Florida. Beckwourth promptly joined up and served in the brigade as a mule skinner and messenger.

Eager to get back to the mountaineering life he preferred, Beckwourth returned to St. Louis in the summer of 1838. After several days in the city he headed west with two male companions to resume his work as a fur trader. This time he was after buffalo skins, and during the next few years he established a flourishing business in Colorado and New Mexico by trading whiskey to the Cheyenne Indians for the skins.

In the early 1840s he established a general store in Taos, New Mexico, and married a woman named Luisa Sandoval. In the fall of 1842 Beckwourth and his wife set up a trading post in south-central Colorado that soon became the settlement of Pueblo. Not long afterward, Beckwourth left to head a trading expedition to southern California, abandoning his wife and their infant daughter in Pueblo.

Beckwourth arrived in California just in time to participate in the Bear Flag Rebellion, an uprising of mountain men who were trying to free California from Mexican rule. During the uprising he stole 2,000 horses from several Mexican-owned ranches near Los Angeles and drove them back to Pueblo, where he sold them. With the proceeds, Beckwourth bought a hotel and saloon in Santa Fe, New Mexico, which he ran successfully for several years. When war broke out between Mexico and the United States in 1846, Beckwourth volunteered as an army messenger, carrying communications between Santa Fe and Fort Leavenworth, Kansas, on horseback.

In the late summer of 1848 Beckwourth moved back to California and became a mail courier for the government, riding a regular route nearly 200 miles long between Monterey and Dana's Ranch, the site of present-day Santa Maria. By 1849 Beckwourth had resigned this job and become a familiar figure in the gold-mining camps of northern California, earning his living by playing cards and occasionally prospecting.

Soon Beckwourth had resumed his familiar occupation as a horse "trader." His horse-stealing and selling activities took him into the valley of the Sierra Nevada, the mountain range lying along the eastern border of California. Sometime during the winter of 1850 he discovered a pass through the mountains that was later named the Beckwourth Trail.

Eventually thousands of pioneers would follow the Beckwourth Trail to California, which had become a state following its cession to the United States by Mexico in 1848.

Beckwourth established a combination ranch, trading post, and hotel along the trail that became famous as the Beckwourth Ranch. Nicknamed the emigrants' landing place, the ranch provided food and lodging to many new settlers. Even those who had no money to pay were welcomed by their gracious host, who entertained his guests with many stories of his adventures as a mountain man.

During the winter of 1854 Beckwourth dictated his life story to a guest at the ranch named T. D. Bonner, a would-be poet and journalist from Massachusetts. Bonner turned Beckwourth's tales into a book, *The Life and Adventures of James P. Beckwourth, Mountaineer, Scout, Pioneer, and Chief of the Crow Nation,* which was published in 1856 by Harper Brothers in New York City following Bonner's return to the East Coast. Although Beckwourth made no money from the sale of the book—Bonner pocketed all the royalties and then disappeared—he did become something of a celebrity, and many visitors came to the ranch to catch a glimpse of him.

In 1858 the footloose Beckwourth abandoned the ranch and traveled for a while as far east as St. Louis. He then settled in Denver, where he opened a general store that became a frequent stopping place for Cheyenne Indians. Beckwourth became an outspoken defender of the rights of the Cheyenne, who were being displaced from their lands by new white settlers from the East. Beckwourth's friendly relations with the Indians ended in the fall of 1864, however, when he was forced by U.S. Army troops to lead them to an encampment of Cheyenne and Arapaho at Sand Creek, Colorado. The troops massacred most of the Indians, and the survivors blamed Beckwourth for betraying them, although he claimed that he would have been hanged had he not cooperated with the troops.

The details of Beckwourth's last years are not known. He apparently worked for a while as a scout and dispatch rider at Fort Laramie, Wyoming. Sometime in 1866 he began a new trading venture with his old friend Jim Bridger. He died in October 1866 while visiting a tribe of Crow Indians along the Bighorn River.

GUION BLUFORD

Aerospace engineer and astronaut Guion Stewart Bluford, Jr., was born in Philadelphia, Pennsylvania, on November 22, 1942, the oldest of three brothers. His mother taught special education classes in the Philadelphia public schools, and his father was a mechanical engineer. As a child Guion—pronounced Guy-on—was nicknamed Guy.

Guy Bluford collected numerous mechanical toys which he enjoyed taking apart and putting back together. He was especially interested in flying, and he built model airplanes and collected pictures of planes. He also liked to study the flight of other objects, including table tennis balls and the folded newspapers he delivered every day. Bluford decided at an early age that he wanted to build planes when he grew up.

Bluford was raised in an integrated Philadelphia neighborhood and attended integrated schools, and his parents taught him and his brothers that they were capable of accomplishing anything they wished, provided they worked hard enough. During the early 1950s scientists in both the United States and the Soviet Union were working on artificial earth satellites, spacecraft that would be launched into orbit around the earth to gather information on space. The goal of scientists in both countries was to eventually send human beings into space to explore the universe. Bluford, who was then in junior high school, was excited by stories of space exploration and began to focus seriously on a career as an aerospace engineer, a person who works on the design, construction, and operation of spacecraft.

In the fall of 1957, shortly before Guy Bluford's 15th birthday, the Soviet Union launched the satellite *Sputnik I*, ushering in the space age. The United States immediately stepped up its space program and in 1958 created NASA, the National Aeronautics and Space Administration. The government also encouraged renewed interest in mathematics and the sciences in the nation's schools in order to catch up with the Soviets. Bluford eagerly followed newspaper and television accounts of missile launches by NASA in Cape Canaveral, Florida, but in the high school he attended no one seemed especially interested in the space race.

At Overbrook High School, Bluford was an average student, and his guidance counselors did not encourage his interest in aerospace engineering or even in attending college. Instead, they advised him to enroll in a technical school after graduation and learn a mechanical trade. Both Bluford and his parents ignored the advice of the counselors, who seemed unaware of the fact that several generations of family members had attended college and in many instances earned advanced degrees. In the fall of 1960 Bluford enrolled in the aerospace engineering program at Pennsylvania State University.

For the first time, Bluford later recalled, he began to realize that he was different because he was black. There were relatively few African American students at Penn State, and some of them were active participants in the civil rights movement that had begun in the late 1950s. While Bluford supported the movement, he concentrated on his education, which included numerous courses in math and science. When both the Soviet Union and the United States launched men into space in 1961, the spring of his freshman year, Bluford had an even greater incentive to remain focused on his goal of building spacecraft.

During his four years at Penn State, Bluford was a member of the air force ROTC (Reserve Officers' Training Corps). He decided in his senior year that he would become an air force pilot to fulfill his required military service obligation. Bluford graduated from Penn State in 1964 and received the ROTC's Distinguished Graduate Award. He had married a fellow student during his last year at college, and shortly after graduation their first son, Guion III, was born.

With his wife and son, Bluford moved to Arizona for pilot training at Williams Air Force Base. He received his pilot wings in 1965, the same year that his second son, James Trevor, was born. Bluford had little time to spend with his family, however. The United States was engaged in the Vietnam War, and during the next few years Bluford flew 144 combat missions in Southeast Asia, piloting an F-4C Phantom jet. He logged 3,000 hours of flying time and received 10 air force medals for competence and bravery.

After Bluford returned to the United States, the air force sent him to teach cross-country and acrobatic flying at Sheppard Air Force Base in Texas, where he accumulated 1,300 hours of instructing. Bluford still hoped to become an aerospace engineer, and he applied to the Air Force Institute of Technology for further training. Despite stiff competition, he was accepted in 1972 and graduated two years later, receiving a master's degree with distinction.

Bluford continued graduate studies in aerospace engineering at the Institute during the next four years while he worked at the Air Force Flight Dynamics Laboratory at Wright-Patterson Air Force Base in Ohio. In 1978 he received a Ph.D. in aerospace engineering with a minor in laser physics, the study of light and energy. As part of his requirements for the doctorate, Bluford developed a computer program that could calculate the pressure, density, and velocity of the air surrounding the wings of a plane as it moved through space.

About the time he received his doctorate, Bluford applied for the U.S. astronaut program, under the direction of NASA. He believed that NASA was the best place to learn about the latest developments in aerospace technology, and as an astronaut he could combine his interests in flying and engineering. Several weeks after submitting his application Bluford was notified of his selection as an astronaut candidate and invited to work at the NASA-sponsored Johnson Space Center in Houston, Texas. In 1978 nearly 9,000 other Americans applied for the astronaut program; Bluford was one of only 35 men and women chosen that year.

Bluford moved his family to Houston and began a year of training. Upon his completion in 1979 he was officially made an astronaut and during the next few years learned how to fly a space shuttle. NASA had first begun developing space shuttles in 1972. Part rocket, part spacecraft, and part airplane, shuttles were designed to carry human beings out into space for exploration and scientific investigation. Other uses were developed for shuttles, including the launching of communications satellites and the creation of space stations. Shuttles are propelled by rockets and have wings like airplanes so that they can glide on air currents. Like airplanes—but unlike most rockets—they can also navigate in outer space.

The first space shuttle, *Columbia*, was launched in April 1981. During the following year it made three more flights. In the spring of 1983 the second space shuttle, *Challenger*, was launched. Bluford was selected to fly on *Challenger*'s third flight, scheduled for that summer. Although Bluford was not the first black man to be selected for the astronaut program, he would make history as the first black American in space.

In the early morning darkness of August 30, 1983, Lieutenant Colonel Guion Bluford, Jr., was one of five astronauts aboard the *Challenger* as it rose from the launchpad at Cape Canaveral and moved into orbit around the earth. As a mission specialist, Bluford experimented with the Canadian-built remote manipulator arm during *Challenger*'s six-day flight. He also had chief responsibility for one of the major goals of the mission: the deployment of a communications satellite sponsored by the Indian government.

Bluford made the first nighttime launch and landing in the history of the shuttle program. His second flight was aboard the Mission 61-A/Spacelab D1 in

October and November 1985. Bluford was one of eight people on this scientific mission. Upon landing, he had logged 314 hours in space.

Since his historic flight on the *Challenger*, Bluford has continued to work as an aerospace engineer at the Johnson Space Center. In 1987 he earned a master's degree in business administration from the University of Houston. Bluford has received numerous awards for his achievements, including several honorary degrees from American universities, and has published several scientific papers. Bluford lives in Clear Lake, Texas, with his wife and two sons.

Botanist George Washington Carver was born into slavery around 1864 on a farm near Diamond Grove, Missouri, owned by a white man named Moses Carver. When George was only a few weeks old, slave raiders from Arkansas attacked the farm and carried off George and his mother. Moses Carver was able to rush George's brother, Jim, to safety, but could not save the others. Moses

Carver negotiated with the raiders and swapped a racehorse for the infant's return. His mother was never found.

George took the surname of Moses Carver and grew up with the Carver family. Since the Carvers had no children, the couple raised George and his brother as their own. He was no longer a slave—slavery had been legally banned in 1865 by the Thirteenth Amendment to the U.S. Constitution—but he worked on the farm throughout his childhood. Because George was often sick, his duties were limited to doing work around the house, such as cooking and tending the family garden. When he was not helping with the housework, he explored all aspects of nature. "I literally lived in the woods," he said. "I wanted to know every strange stone, flower, insect, bird, or beast."

In his early teens he left Diamond Grove to get a formal education, since there were no schools for blacks near his home.

For several years Carver worked at odd jobs while he attended grade schools for African Americans in Kansas and in other Missouri communities. He eventually completed high school in Minneapolis, Kansas, where he had taken the middle name Washington to distinguish himself from another George Carver in the class. In 1885, he applied by mail to Highland College, a small school in Highland, Kansas. He was accepted, but when he went to register for classes and school officials saw that he was black, he was turned away. Carver was disappointed and decided to put off continuing his education for a few years.

For a while Carver homesteaded on the Kansas plains. His health was frail, however, and the work proved too hard for a lone man. In the late 1880s he moved to Iowa and eventually gained admission to Simpson College in Indianola, a small school operated by the Methodist church. Although Carver was the only African American enrolled at the school, he was treated kindly by his teachers and fellow students. "The students are wonderfully good. . . . I have the name unjustly of having one of the broadest minds in school," he said. Carver supported himself by doing laundry as well as intricate needlework—tatting, knitting, and embroidery. At Simpson he developed his aptitude for painting and for a while considered becoming an artist.

Carver's teachers, however, encouraged him to consider a more practical career, out of concern that a black man might not be able to earn a living as an artist. Carver showed a strong interest in plants and often painted flowers, so botany and agriculture seemed a logical choice. Carver himself believed that he had a responsibility to improve the lives of other black men and women, and helping them to grow better crops seemed one way of accomplishing this goal.

In 1891, following the recommendations of several teachers, Carver transferred to the Iowa State College of Agriculture (now Iowa State University), in Ames. Carver had trouble adjusting to his new college—unlike those at Simpson, the students did not all make him feel welcome. However, he soon became involved in all aspects of college life—he made new friends and joined many campus activities. Carver participated in the campus debate club, the German club, and the art club, organized an agricultural society, became the first trainer and masseur for the football team, served as missionary chairman of the Young Men's Christian Association, and joined the National Guard Student Battalion, in which he was made captain, the highest student rank. Academically, his abilities were quickly recognized by the faculty; he worked as an assistant to several professors and was eventually put in charge of the college greenhouse, where he conducted experiments in plant fertilization.

Carver received bachelor's and master's degrees in science from Iowa State. He could have remained at the college as a faculty member, but he believed even more strongly that he had to help his fellow blacks. The opportunity he was looking for came in 1896, when he was invited by the famous African American educator Booker T. Washington to become director of agricultural work at the Tuskegee Institute. Washington had founded Tuskegee in 1881 as a center for the education of African Americans, who had very few opportunities for learning.

From the moment he arrived at Tuskegee, Carver used every opportunity to make himself useful. He even played the piano in concerts to raise funds for the school. In addition to his regular teaching duties, he began a series of conferences at Tuskegee to teach African American farmers better agricultural methods. He also taught them nutrition and the importance of eating healthful foods.

Carver set up farm demonstration programs, including the training of extension agents—men who visited farmers and advised them on how to increase crop yields, prevent erosion, and control pests. To carry his program to outlying areas, Carver created what he called a movable school of agriculture. Teachers and equipment traveled in wagons to remote rural areas to give lessons in agricultural methods, nutrition, and home economics. Carver's concept of a movable school was later adopted in underdeveloped areas around the world.

Carver was shy and hardworking, and he had little concern for pleasure, personal comfort, or financial success. He was very religious, and though he often suffered from the consequences of segregation, he refused to give up his goal of promoting human welfare. He became increasingly convinced that the problems experienced by southern farmers—both black and white—were the result of several factors. Most important was the fact that they did not diversify their crops. Instead, they grew the same plant, cotton, year after year, which depleted the soil of essential minerals and attracted a specific pest, the boll weevil. Farmers also neglected soil conservation and did not know how to protect their plants against the ravages of pests.

To counter these problems, Carver launched a campaign to persuade farmers to grow other crops, including peanuts, sweet potatoes, and cowpeas. In order to do so, he knew that he had to create a demand for them. Farmers had concentrated on growing cotton because it had many commercial uses. Peanuts, sweet potatoes, and cowpeas were then grown by farmers only in their own home gardens, as food to feed their own families.

In his crude laboratory, which he had assembled from cast-off materials he found in trash piles, Carver began to develop new products from these crops. During his lifetime he introduced 325 different peanut derivatives, ranging from beverages to ink to synthetic rubber, using all parts of the plant, including the shells. In addition, he discovered more than 100 uses for sweet potatoes and made many other new products from cowpeas, soybeans, pecans, and other plants.

In his laboratory Carver made pioneering studies of crop disease and found ways to make plants resistant to attack. He also experimented with various inexpensive ways to replenish worn-out farmland. He concluded that the best method was the cheapest—recycling discarded plant material by turning it into compost and working it back into the land. Carver taught farmers that the debris they had hauled away and burned for generations was in fact a valuable resource.

Carver's numerous contributions to agriculture ultimately benefited the entire South. He was widely hailed as both a scientist and a humanitarian and given many honors, including membership in the Royal Society of London. Carver received many offers from business leaders to work for them at enormous salaries, but he always refused. Any financial rewards for his various discoveries were turned over to the Tuskegee Institute. Instead of publishing accounts of these discoveries in scientific journals, he wrote about their practical applications in numerous agricultural bulletins for farmers and housewives.

Carver remained at Tuskegee for 47 years, working and writing until shortly before his death on January 5, 1943. Eight years later his birthplace near Diamond Grove, Missouri, was proclaimed a national monument by the U.S. government.

CHARLES DREW

Physician Charles R. Drew was born in Washington, D.C., on June 3, 1904, the eldest of five children. His father was a carpet layer for a furniture company. Charles's mother, a graduate of Howard University and a former schoolteacher, stayed home to raise her children at the insistence of her husband. The Drews were a close-knit family and had strong ties to the racially integrated neighborhood of Washington in which they lived.

Charles Drew attended the local elementary school and went on to Dunbar High School, then one of the best secondary schools for African Americans in the United States. At Dunbar, Drew was an excellent student and an outstanding athlete, and upon graduating in 1922 he was awarded a partial scholarship to Amherst College in Massachusetts. Drew enrolled at Amherst that fall, augmenting his scholarship by working as a waiter. He became one of the college's leading athletes, excelling in both track and football, and paid close attention to his studies with the goal of becoming a doctor.

After graduating from Amherst in 1926, Drew needed to earn money to attend medical school. He took a job as a science instructor and athletic director at Morgan College (now Morgan State University) in Baltimore, Maryland, and worked during the summer as a swimming pool manager. By 1928 he had saved enough money to enroll at McGill University in Montreal, Canada. Drew's savings were supplemented by a loan from several of his Amherst classmates, and he also worked again as a waiter to earn extra money.

In addition to his medical studies at McGill, Drew found time for athletics. He joined the university track team and became its captain. Drew became one of Canada's top hurdlers and led McGill to several national championships. He eventually became Canada's all-time leading scorer in intercollegiate track competition.

Drew was an outstanding medical student and graduated near the top of his class in 1933, receiving both M.D. and C.M. (master of surgery) degrees. He then served a year each as intern and resident at Montreal General Hospital, where he specialized in surgery, blood typing, and problems of transfusion and blood storage.

In 1935 Drew returned to Washington and became an instructor in pathology at Howard Medical College. The following year he became resident and instructor in surgery at Freedmen's Hospital, the teaching hospital at Howard, where he continued his research in blood storage. In 1938 Drew received a grant from the Rockefeller Foundation that allowed him to serve a two-year residency in surgery at Columbia Presbyterian Hospital, which is affiliated with Columbia University in New York City.

At Columbia, Drew became the first black American to work toward the advanced degree of doctor of science in medicine. He was assigned to work under Dr. John Scudder, who was doing research in blood chemistry and transfusion.

In 1939, as part of his work at Columbia Presbyterian, Drew established a blood bank, a facility for storing donated blood that could then be transfused to hospital patients. Only two years earlier the first blood-storage facility in the United States had been established at Cook County Hospital in Chicago. When the Columbia blood bank opened in August, Drew became its director.

The previous spring, during a trip to a medical convention at the Tuskegee Institute in Alabama, Drew had stayed overnight with friends in Atlanta. There he met Lenore Robbins, a home economics teacher at Spelman College, the first school of higher education for black women in the United States. In September 1939 the couple were married and then settled in New York City, where Drew continued his graduate work at Columbia. Lenore Drew soon became her husband's research assistant.

Drew's special interest was the preservation and storage of blood. While whole blood could be preserved for up to several weeks if it was stored at a low temperature, its quality deteriorated considerably as red blood cells broke down. Drew carried out research on the use of plasma—the liquid that remained after the solids in the blood had been removed—as a substitute for whole blood in transfusions.

A little more than 50 percent of blood is composed of plasma, which contains nutrients, proteins, antibodies, and hormones. Red blood cells are the only components of blood that break down after a week of storage—and there are no red blood cells in plasma. In early 1940 Drew and Scudder began investigating the possibility of using blood plasma in place of whole blood. Their research was speeded up by pleas from the French government, which was then fighting the Germans in the early days of the Second World War. France asked the United States for help in establishing a blood bank program for its wounded soldiers.

Drew knew that plasma could be kept for as long as a month without being refrigerated. He had also determined that plasma could be dried, then reconstituted as needed by adding sterile distilled water. However, drying plasma was a complex and expensive procedure, and Drew was investigating the possibility of freezing plasma for later use. In the meantime, plans were made to begin shipments of liquid plasma to the French, but before the plan could be put into effect, France fell to the Germans in June and the project was abandoned.

That same month, Drew received his doctor of science degree from Columbia. His dissertation, "Banked Blood: A Study in Blood Preservation," was termed a masterpiece by Scudder and other professors at the medical school. Shortly after graduation, Drew returned to Washington, D.C., where he became a surgeon at Freedmen's Hospital and an assistant professor of surgery at Howard University. However, that fall he came back to New York City to direct Blood for Britain, a blood-collection program to help English war casualties. Using the procedures he had developed for the abandoned French program, Drew arranged for shipments of plasma to be sent to Great Britain for use in transfusions.

The Blood for Britain program ran successfully for five months. After it ended early in 1941 Drew joined the American Red Cross as the coordinator of a blood-banking program for the entire United States. He resigned several months later, after the U.S. War Department called for the segregation of "white" and "black" blood. He said that the War Department's decision was "indefensible" and that "there is no scientific basis for the separation of the bloods of different races." Drew returned to Howard, where he became professor of surgery and chief surgeon at Freedmen's Hospital.

The decade of the 1940s was a period of impressive accomplishments for Drew, who made major contributions to the field of medical education. More than half of the nation's black surgeons who were certified by the American Board of Surgery during the 1940s had studied under Drew at Howard. In 1947 Drew also launched a campaign to open membership in the American Medical Association, the nation's leading professional organization for physicians, to black doctors. Throughout its history the AMA had banned blacks from membership. The AMA refused to change its policies during Drew's lifetime, despite his appeals, and though he published many articles in the AMA's prestigious journal, he was never admitted as a member of the association.

Drew received several awards for his work as a physician and educator, including the Spingarn Medal, presented annually by the NAACP (National Association for the Advancement of Colored People) to an outstanding black American. In addition to his duties at Howard Medical College and the Freedmen's Hospital, Drew served on the boards of the American Cancer Society, the National Polio Foundation, and the National Society for Crippled Children, and also did volunteer work for the YMCA.

He also found time to be a concerned parent to his four young children.

Drew died suddenly on April 1, 1950, in a car accident near Haw River, North Carolina, while traveling to a meeting at the Tuskegee Institute. In the years following his death, Drew's pioneering work in human plasma research, which paved the way for later discoveries of other important uses for blood products, has been widely acknowledged. Many schools and hospitals have been named after him, and in 1976 the Charles R. Drew Commemorative Medal was established to honor exceptional achievements in the advancement of the medical education of black Americans and other minorities. Five years later the U.S. Postal Service issued a commemorative stamp in honor of Drew's contributions to science.

MATTHEW HENSON

Explorer Matthew Henson was born on August 8, 1866, on his parents' farm in Charles County, Maryland. Both of his parents had spent their entire lives as free blacks in the South. In the aftermath of the Civil War, blacks were increasingly terrorized by white supremacist groups, including the Ku Klux Klan. To escape the violence erupting around them, the family sold their farm a year after

Matthew's birth and moved to a poor section of Washington, D.C.

When Matthew was seven his mother died, and his father sent him to live with an uncle who lived nearby. Matthew attended public school for six years, and as he grew older he worked during the summer at a restaurant washing dishes. By the time he turned 13, his father had died and his uncle could no longer care for him. Matthew Henson became a full-time dishwasher and waiter at the restaurant, whose owner let him sleep in the kitchen.

After several months, Henson grew tired of his job. He heard stories of adventure from sailors who frequented the restaurant, and he decided to try for a job as a seaman. In the fall of 1879 he set out on foot for Baltimore, some 40 miles to the north of Washington, and went straight to the harbor. He was soon hired as a cabin boy on a merchant ship called the *Katie Hines*.

For the next five years Henson sailed to ports around the world, performing a variety of duties that ranged from peeling potatoes to mopping the decks. The captain took a special interest in Henson and gave him lessons in history and geography as well as training in carpentry, mechanics, first aid, and other practical subjects.

Following the captain's death, Henson left the *Katie Hines* in 1884. He worked briefly on another ship, then spent the next three years traveling around the eastern United States. By 1887 he had returned to Washington, where he became a clerk in a hat store.

One day in the spring of 1887 a naval officer named Robert Peary came into the store to buy a sun helmet. Peary was about to lead a surveying expedition to Nicaragua, where he hoped to discover a suitable route through the Central American jungle for a proposed canal to link the Atlantic and Pacific oceans. Peary needed a servant to accompany him on the expedition, and on the spur of the moment he hired the clerk who had waited on him—Matthew Henson.

During the yearlong expedition, Henson proved himself to be an invaluable aide to Peary. As part of his duties, he supervised the building of Peary's headquarters in Nicaragua and looked after the lieutenant's personal needs. Peary was so impressed by Henson that he promoted him to a position on the surveying team, where Henson earned high praise from the other crew members.

During the Nicaraguan expedition Henson continued to acquire useful skills, and he became an expert at shooting a rifle and paddling a canoe. On the voyage home, Peary told Henson that he was planning an expedition to Greenland to map unexplored areas of the Arctic. At that time no European or American explorers had gotten within 600 miles of the North Pole, and Peary secretly hoped that he would be the first to reach it. When Peary invited Henson to accompany him on his new expedition, Henson readily agreed. They sailed from the port of Brooklyn, New York, in June 6, 1891, and reached their final destination, McCormick Bay, in Greenland, more than three weeks later.

Henson immediately went to work, constructing a house at the campsite and building sledges—large sleds—to carry the expedition farther north. Henson learned many skills from the Eskimos who visited the campsite, including how to handle a sledge and dog team, and he taught these skills to Peary.

Following the return to New York of the Peary expedition in September 1892, Henson spent several months recovering from an eye injury he had received in Greenland. He then accompanied Peary on a lecture tour to raise money for another trip to the Arctic. Their second trip began in the summer of 1893 and continued for more than two years. Again Henson was an invaluable companion, assisting Peary in his explorations, frequently saving him from near disaster, and helping him to retrieve two large meteorites.

Shortly after their return in September 1895, Henson was hired by the American Museum of Natural History in New York City to help set up an exhibition of animal specimens that the men had brought back from the Arctic. Henson made two more brief trips to Greenland with Peary in 1896 and 1897 to secure a giant meteorite that had to be left behind in 1895. On the second mission they brought back the 35-ton object to the American Museum, where it is still on display.

In January 1897 Peary, who was now a famous figure, publicly announced his intention of reaching the North Pole. The following year Henson accompanied Peary on a four-year expedition to the Arctic.

Despite many attempts, however, they were unable to reach their goal because of hazardous weather conditions. After their return in the fall of 1902, Peary told Henson that it would be several years before he could raise enough money to mount another expedition to the Arctic. Henson took a break from polar exploration and became a porter on the Pennsylvania Railroad, traveling throughout the country for three years.

In the summer of 1905 Henson was summoned back to New York by Peary, who was now ready to embark on another expedition, this time in a boat made especially strong to move through the frozen northern seas. The boat was named the *Roosevelt*, after President Theodore Roosevelt, one of Peary's strongest supporters. Much of the preparatory work for this expedition was done by Henson. This time they got within 175 miles of the North Pole, but the men had to turn back because of poor weather conditions, the loss of many of their sled dogs, and a dwindling supply of food.

In 1907, during preparations for the return journey, Henson married Lucy Ross, a young woman he had met two years earlier in New York. Less than a year later, in July 1908, he was back on board the *Roosevelt*, sailing with Peary for what was to be a final journey northward.

Finally, after months of backbreaking preparation, Peary, Henson, and four Eskimos set out by sledge on the last leg of the journey on April 1, 1909. Henson himself was responsible for breaking the trail through the snow and ice. Six days later they had achieved their goal: all six men had reached the North Pole.

When Peary and Henson returned to the United States that summer, they expected to be feted for their discovery. Instead, they discovered that Dr. Frederick Cook, a physician who had accompanied Peary and Henson on their 1891 trip to the Arctic, claimed that he had reached the North Pole the previous year. Cook's story had already been accepted by the general public, and there was little celebration for Peary, an arrogant man who could easily offend others. As for Henson, he was dismissed as "an ignorant negro" who had probably caused Peary to mistake his location. While asserting that he had indeed reached the North Pole, Peary made no attempt to defend the accomplishments of Henson, and a rift grew between the two men.

By 1910 Cook's claim was shown to be false and Peary was generally acknowledged as the conqueror of the North Pole. Numerous honors were showered on him, and he was promoted to the rank of admiral in the U.S. Navy. Henson, however, was quickly forgotten and took a job parking cars in a garage. In 1912 he published an account of his adventures, *A Negro Explorer at the North Pole*, but it was not popular.

In 1913, through the efforts of a black politician in New York City, Henson was given a job as a messenger in the U.S. Customs Bureau. He was later promoted to clerk and worked at this job until his retirement in 1940, on a pension of $1,020 a year—

a pittance compared with the enormous pension granted to Peary before his death in 1920.

Not everyone had forgotten Henson, however. As the decades passed, black organizations mounted campaigns to win recognition for him. In 1937 Henson was finally admitted to the Explorers Club, and eight years later—36 years after the discovery of the North Pole—he received a medal from the U.S. Navy. In 1954 he and his wife were invited to the White House by President Dwight D. Eisenhower. Henson died less than a year later, on March 9, 1955, in New York City.

ERNEST EVERETT JUST

Zoologist Ernest Everett Just was born in Charleston, South Carolina, on August 14, 1883, the third child of Charles and Mary Just. Ernest's father was a construction worker at the Charleston docks, and his mother worked as a seamstress. Before Ernest was a year old, his older brother and sister died. Within several years his mother had given birth to another son, Hunter, and a daughter, Inez.

When Ernest Just was four years old, further tragedy struck the family. Both his father and grandfather died, and his mother was now the sole support of herself and her three small children. For a while she taught school in Charleston and worked as a miner on nearby James Island. With other African Americans, Mary Just later founded a new town on the island, which was named Maryville in her honor.

Mary Just ran the local school in Maryville, and Ernest attended classes there. During his years on the island he also had to do household chores and help care for his younger brother and sister, but during what little free time he had, Ernest liked to explore the island and investigate the plants and animals that lived there. When he was 13, his mother raised enough money to send him to an all-black boarding school in Orangeburg, South Carolina, to prepare him for a teaching career. When Ernest finished his studies there three years later, he returned home because his mother thought he was not yet old enough to become a teacher.

Believing that her son should get further education, Mary Just tried to find another school for him. In a church newspaper she read about Kimball Union Academy, an institution in Meriden, New Hampshire, sponsored by a religious organization called the Christian Endeavor World Unity Group. According to the article, Kimball Union offered scholarships to exceptional students. She wrote to them about Ernest, but before they received a reply, Ernest decided to visit the school.

There was no money for the trip, so Ernest found a job on a small ship sailing from Charleston to New York. He was paid five dollars when the ship docked in New York. To earn enough money for a train ticket to New Hampshire, he worked for a month as a cook in a New York restaurant. When he finally arrived at Kimball Union, he discovered that he had won a scholarship to the school.

Ernest Just completed Kimball Union's four-year program in three years and graduated in 1903 as the top student—and the only black—in his class. He was now on his own, for his mother had died the year before and relatives were caring for his brother and sister. He received a scholarship to Dartmouth College, where he first studied classical languages and literature. In his second year, Just became increasingly interested in science, especially biology. He was encouraged in his studies by his biology teacher, William Patten, who later became a close friend.

In his junior year, Just was named a Rufus Choate Scholar, the highest award offered by the college. He graduated with high honors in 1907 and was elected to Phi Beta Kappa, the national honor society. Just had decided that he wanted to pursue a career as a research biologist, specializing in the study of small marine animals like sandworms and starfish. However, there were few opportunities in this field for young black men. He took a job teaching biology at Howard University, an all-black institution in Washington, D.C., and tried to do research at the university laboratory. However, the laboratory equipment was inadequate for his experiments, and after he was made head of the department in 1908 he found that he had little time for independent research.

In 1909 Just's former professor and friend William Patten introduced him to Frank R. Lillie, who was the chairman of the biology department at the University of Chicago. Lillie was also the head of the Marine Biological Laboratory at Woods Hole, Massachusetts. Known as Woods Hole, the facility was a famous research center where scientists gathered every summer to do research.

Lillie invited Just to spend the summer of 1909 at Woods Hole as his research assistant. Impressed with Just's work, Lillie invited him back the following summer, and soon afterward Just's work was respected to such an extent that he returned to Woods Hole each summer as an equal participant with other distinguished scientists. In 1912 he published his first research report, an account of the early moments of a sandworm's life. Just became an authority on the embryology of marine animals and published many studies about them.

That same year, in June, he married Ethel Highwarden after a long courtship. Ethel was a teacher of German in the College of Arts and Sciences at Howard. After planning a trip to Europe, the highlight being Germany, where they were both anxious to visit, Ethel gave up her honeymoon so her husband could get on with his career. The couple had three children: Margaret, Highwarden, and Maribel, born in 1913, 1917, and 1922. Even after the marriage broke up, Just attempted to maintain a relationship with his children. His oldest and favorite child, Margaret, accompanied him on his first trip to Europe.

Lillie encouraged Just to work for an advanced degree in biology, and in 1915 he took a leave of absence from Howard and enrolled as a graduate student at the University of Chicago. In one year he completed all requirements for a doctoral degree and received a Ph.D. with high honors in 1916. Even before beginning his graduate studies, Just had become widely known as an outstanding scientist through his research at Woods Hole. In 1915 the NAACP (National Association for the Advancement of Colored People) awarded Just the first Spingarn Medal, given annually to an outstanding black American.

Despite his prominence, Just was unable to get an appointment at a major American university that would allow him time to do research as well as teach. He was married and had a family to support, so he continued teaching classes at Howard University while supporting his research with small grants from major philanthropic foundations.

By the 1920s Just was an internationally known biologist. Because he had a thorough knowledge of French and German, he was able to keep abreast of the work of European scientists in his field and to participate fully in foreign conferences.

The fact that he was treated with more respect abroad than he was in the United States gradually embittered Just. He stopped going to Woods Hole and began spending more time abroad doing research, first at a laboratory in Naples, Italy, and during the early 1930s at the Kaiser Wilhelm Institute in Berlin. He continued to teach part-time at Howard but became increasingly reluctant to encourage black students to receive advanced training. He believed that they would only be frustrated in their attempts to pursue scientific careers because of strong racial prejudice in the United States.

By the mid-1930s Just was doing most of his research at the Sorbonne in Paris. During this time he wrote his best-known work, *The Biology of the Cell Surface*, which was published in 1939. During his lifetime Just published about 60 scientific papers as well as a monograph, *Basic Methods for Experiments on Eggs of Marine Animals*, which also appeared in 1939.

Just had settled permanently in France in the late 1930s and now considered it his home country. However, World War II began in the fall of 1939 and Germany invaded France the following spring. Just offered himself for military service, but the French government turned him down; when France surrendered to Germany, he was imprisoned for a short time. Since the United States was not yet at war with Germany, U.S. government officials were able to free him from prison. However, he had been in poor health for some time, and his prison stay only aggravated his condition.

Just had divorced his wife, Ethel, and remarried Maid Hedwig Schnetzler, with whom he had a daughter, Elisabeth. In the fall of 1940 Just returned to Washington, D.C. Suffering from cancer, his health grew worse and he was unable to pursue further research. He died in Washington on October 27, 1941. Just's pioneering research in embryology and cytology (the study of cells) was the basis for later important studies in genetics and the mechanism of heredity.

Inventor Lewis Latimer
was born on September 4, 1848, in Chelsea,
Massachusetts, a small town near Boston. He was
the fourth child of George and Rebecca Latimer,
who were former slaves. Lewis's paternal grandfather, Mitchell Latimer, had been a wealthy
plantation owner and slaveholder in Norfolk,
Virginia, in the early 19th century and had

sired Lewis's father, George, with one of his slaves.

In 1842 George Latimer and his wife, Rebecca, fled slavery for the safety of Massachusetts, which had banned the selling and owning of slaves some years earlier. They were immediately hunted down as fugitive slaves by their owners, and New England's leading abolitionists—including orator Frederick Douglass and William Lloyd Garrison, editor of *The Liberator*, an antislavery newspaper—fought to keep them from being sent back to Virginia, where they faced imprisonment and possible execution. Funds were quickly raised to purchase George Latimer from his owner—Rebecca had eluded capture—and the couple were reunited in time for the birth of their first child, George junior.

Although George Latimer, Sr., had become a celebrity, earning a living in the North was difficult for him. After the passage of the Fugitive Slave Law of 1850, his life became even more filled with hardship. Although his freedom had been paid for, at any time he might be seized and returned to slavery because, according to the act, any white man could claim ownership of any black simply by swearing that the black had once been his lawful property and had run away; blacks had no legal rights, and their written and verbal claims meant nothing against the sworn testimony of a white man.

George Latimer avoided seizure by moving frequently with his wife and four small children. During the 1850s he ran a barbershop in a black neighborhood of Boston, assisted by young Lewis. Constant worry about his safety preyed on George Latimer, especially after he learned of the famous March 1857 decision by the U.S. Supreme Court to return fugitive slave Dred Scott to his former owner in Missouri. In 1858 George Latimer suddenly disappeared; family and friends assumed that fear of recapture had led him to desert his family. Lewis Latimer did not hear from his father again until many years later.

Lewis and his two older brothers and sister helped his mother support the family. During the Civil War, Lewis lied about his age so that he could fight with the Union against slavery. He served as a seaman aboard a U.S. Navy gunboat that participated in a blockade of southern ports during the final year of the war. Following his discharge in July 1865, Latimer returned to Boston and lived with his mother.

Although jobs for both blacks and whites were scarce, Latimer found employment as an office boy with Crosby and Gould, a firm of patent lawyers. They employed artists who made sketches of inventions—a drawing of an invention had to be submitted to the U.S. government when the inventor applied for a patent. Latimer had a natural aptitude for drawing, and he was eager to learn this trade. While he performed his office duties, he carefully observed the work of the staff artists. From his small salary he saved enough money to buy the instruction books and drawing tools, and at home each night he taught himself basic draftsmanship. After several months, Latimer approached the head draftsman, showed him his work, and was soon allowed to do simple sketches. Latimer eventually rose to become head draftsman at Crosby and Gould.

As he sketched other men's inventions, Latimer began working on some ideas of his own. In February 1874, along with his associate W. C. Brown, Latimer proudly received his first patent—for an improved water closet, or toilet, used on passenger trains. Two years later Latimer participated in a history-making event when he helped Alexander Graham Bell prepare his patent application for a brand new invention, the telephone. Latimer not only executed the drawings of the device but is also believed to have helped Bell with the written description that accompanied the drawings.

Latimer remained at Crosby and Gould for several more years, then worked briefly for another patent lawyer and as a pattern drawer at an iron foundry. In 1879 Latimer and his wife, Mary, whom he had married six years earlier, moved to Bridgeport, Connecticut, where his sister, Margaret, and her husband lived. He worked for a while as a paperhanger, then found work as a draftsman in a machine shop. One day Hiram Maxim, an inventor who owned the U.S. Electric Lighting Company, stopped by the shop. He was impressed by Latimer and promptly hired him to work at his own company as a draftsman. As he made his drawings, Latimer also taught himself everything he could learn about electrical lighting.

A year earlier, Thomas A. Edison had received a patent for an electric light bulb, and there was a growing demand from both businesses and private home owners for electrical lighting. Edison's bulb was not long-lasting, however; the filament, or wire, inside the glass produced light by being heated until it glowed, but filaments burned out after only a few days at most, and then the entire bulb had to be replaced.

Maxim, Edison, and other inventors were trying to create longer-lasting filaments, and Latimer decided that he, too, would make an attempt. After much trial and error, he invented a long-lasting carbon filament that was cheap to produce—and revolutionized the field of electric lighting. He received a patent for the device, but the credit for its invention—and all the profits—went to Hiram Maxim and the U.S. Electric Lighting Company.

Latimer, perhaps realizing that it would be futile to seek proper recognition, continued to work on improvements in electric lighting devices at Maxim's firm. Just a few months after patenting his process for making carbon filaments, Latimer and an associate, John Tregoning, received another patent, this time for an electric arc lamp, a device that did not use a filament.

Latimer soon became recognized as an expert in the electric light industry, and he acted as a consultant in the construction of the first electric plants in Philadelphia, Montreal, and New York City. He also supervised the installation of lights and wiring in public and private facilities in those three cities. His accomplishments in Montreal were especially impressive, since he had to direct a crew of workmen who spoke only

French. Latimer taught himself the language in order to write specific technical directions for the workmen; later he taught himself German, too.

In the spring of 1882 Maxim sent Latimer to England to open a new light bulb factory, but when Latimer returned to the United States several months later, he discovered that his job had been eliminated. About this time, Hiram Maxim wrote his autobiography, taking credit for perfecting the light bulb but not mentioning Lewis Latimer.

For a few months Latimer worked for an electric lighting company in Brooklyn. Then he was hired by Maxim's archrival, Thomas Edison, who worked out of offices in New York City and laboratories in New Jersey. Latimer was put in charge of the company library, and he had the additional duties of collecting information for use in lawsuits to protect Edison's numerous patents. (During his lifetime, Edison received nearly 1,100 patents for various devices, including the phonograph, the microphone, and picture photography.)

During the years that he worked for Edison, Latimer patented other devices of his own invention, including a combination cooling-disinfecting apparatus (the forerunner of a window air conditioner) and a locking coat and hatrack. With encouragement from Edison, Latimer wrote a book, *Incandescent Electric Lighting, A Practical Description of the Edison System*, which was published in 1890. In his spare time he painted and wrote poetry. He also became a strong supporter of equal rights for black Americans and corresponded with black leaders Frederick Douglass and Booker T. Washington.

From 1896 to 1911 Latimer served as chief draftsman of the Board of Patent Control, an organization formed jointly by Edison's organization, now called the General Electric Company, and its chief rival, the Westinghouse Company, to avoid costly legal battles between the two companies over patent rights. After the board was abolished in 1911, Latimer became a patent consultant for an engineering firm headed by Edwin Hammer. He retired in 1922 because of failing eyesight but received a generous pension from the General Electric Company. Four years earlier Latimer's contributions to General Electric had been officially recognized when he was named a member of the Edison Pioneers, 28 individuals who had been the founders of Edison's company.

Latimer died on December 11, 1928. Nearly 50 years later, during the 1970s, his contributions to science and industry were rediscovered and widely acknowledged. In 1982 a street in Flushing, New York, the community where he lived for many years, was named after him. Six years later, Latimer's house was saved from demolition and moved to a new site, where it will be reopened in 1995 as a museum.

FEMALE WRITERS

MAYA ANGELOU

A multitalented artist and one of the most remarkable personalities on the American scene, Maya Angelou was born Marguerite Johnson on April 4, 1928, in St. Louis, Missouri. Her parents, Bailey and Vivian Baxter Johnson, divorced when Marguerite was only three years old. At that time, she and her four-year-old brother, Bailey, Jr., were sent to live with their paternal grandmother in

Stamps, Arkansas. Annie "Momma" Henderson, the children's grandmother, made a meager living from her small-town general store, but she provided her grandchildren with a warm and loving home. She taught them self-reliance, courage, and faith and gave them the sense that nothing was beyond their ability to achieve if they wanted it enough.

When Marguerite was seven, her life took a strange and terrible detour. During a visit with her mother in St. Louis, she was raped by her mother's boyfriend. The man was convicted of the crime and, according to Angelou, was murdered for his misdeeds before he could begin serving his sentence. Believing that she was somehow responsible for the man's death, Marguerite retreated into silence and did not speak for five years.

Back in her grandmother's house, the young girl found the understanding and support that she needed during her painful withdrawal. "Sister, Mama don't care what these people say about you," her grandmother told her. "Mama know, Sister, when you and the good Lord get ready, you're gonna be a preacher." Marguerite also found an older friend, Mrs. Bertha Flowers, who refused to write her off. Rather than comparing her to other children, Mrs. Flowers treated Marguerite as an individual with her own needs and talents. After five years, the young girl was finally able to emerge from her self-imposed silence. By the time she was finished with the eighth grade, she ranked at the head of her class.

At this point, Marguerite was reunited with her mother in San Francisco, where Vivian was operating a boardinghouse. The atmosphere was quite different from the one she had known in Arkansas. Her mother associated with a sophisticated and fast-living crowd, and Marguerite was soon caught up in her world. She became pregnant and at the age of 16 gave birth to a son, Guy. She later called this event "the best thing that ever happened to me."

Motherhood at such a young age might have led Marguerite to become more dependent on her own mother, but instead it inspired her to make a life for herself and her baby. The road was far from easy. She worked as a cook and a waitress, and even delved into the world of prostitution as a small-time madam. At the age of 22, she married a white man named Tosh Angelos. The marriage ended two and a half years later, but Marguerite came out of it with more life experience and a new identity—Maya Angelou.

Angelou had taken dance lessons while in high school, and now she determined to exploit her talent. She began by performing in a succession of Los Angeles bars and eventually worked her way up to the better night spots. Her career took a major step forward in 1954, when she was chosen to take part in an overseas tour of George and Ira Gershwin's classic musical *Porgy and Bess.*

When she returned from the tour, Angelou was no longer content to be merely a performer. She had developed a keen social awareness, and she was inspired by the work of Dr. Martin Luther King, Jr., who was leading the movement for black civil rights in the South. At King's request, Angelou spent two years in the North seeking support for the civil rights movement. "We are all diminished when one group is diminished," she later reflected. "Can you imagine if this country were not so afflicted with racism? Can you imagine what it would be like if the vitality, humor, and resilience of the black American were infused throughout this country?"

Angelou certainly saw to it that her own best qualities came to the fore. Her work as an activist brought her into contact with some of the leading African American writers of the day, including James Baldwin and Paule Marshall, and she developed the desire to become a writer as well.

It was not Angelou's way to shut herself in a room with a typewriter. Instead, she set off boldly for Africa with her son and a South African freedom fighter named Vusumzi Make. The three settled in Cairo, Egypt, where Angelou took a job as an editor with a newspaper entitled the *Arab Observer*. However, Make resented Angelou's desire for a career of her own, and the couple eventually split up. Angelou and her son then went to live in the West African nation of Ghana, where Angelou found steady employment as both a journalist and a teacher.

By the mid-1960s, Angelou decided that her true home was the United States. When she returned, her career exploded in a breathtaking number of directions. She began to both write plays and act in them, and in 1971, when she wrote the script for the film *Georgia, Georgia*, she became the first black woman to have a screenplay produced.

The achievement that brought Angelou national attention was the 1970 publication of *I Know Why the Caged Bird Sings*, an account of her life up to the birth of her son. Nominated for the prestigious National Book Award, the book was followed by four more volumes of autobiography: *Gather Together in My Name* (1974), *Singin' and Swingin' and Gettin' Merry Like Christmas* (1976), *The Heart of a Woman* (1981), and *All God's Children Need Traveling Shoes* (1986).

"I don't tell everything I know," Angelou said of her autobiography, "but what I do tell is the truth. There's a world of difference between truth and facts. Facts can obscure the truth. You can tell so many facts that you fill the stage but haven't got one iota of the truth."

Angelou also became well known to television viewers because of her role in the 1977 production of *Roots*, Alex Haley's saga of his family's history from its African origins through the days of slavery. Angelou's performance in the ground-breaking miniseries earned her a nomination for an Emmy Award. In 1979, *I Know Why the Caged Bird Sings* was adapted into a television movie, for which Angelou not only wrote the script but also composed the sound track.

As her artistic career flourished, Angelou continued to concern herself with social issues. In recognition of her growing stature, President Gerald Ford appointed her to the commission charged with coordinating the celebration of the U.S. bicentennial in 1976. Two years later, President Jimmy Carter named her as a member of the Commission of International Woman's Year, which culminated in a major conference sponsored by the United Nations in Nairobi, Kenya.

Angelou's intellectual achievements were signally honored in 1981, when Wake Forest University, in Winston-Salem, North Carolina, granted her a lifetime appointment as Reynolds Professor of American Studies. In addition to continuing her autobiography with such volumes as *The Heart of a Woman*, Angelou devoted much of her energy to poetry and published several verse collections, including *Just Give Me a Cool Drink of Water 'fore I Diiie*, *And Still I Rise*, and *I Shall Not Be Moved*.

With the conservative administrations of Ronald Reagan and George Bush holding power in Washington, the 1980s were not an enjoyable decade politically for the outspoken and progressive Angelou. With the election of Bill Clinton to the presidency in 1992, however, Angelou emerged with more stature than ever. At President Clinton's inauguration ceremony on January 20, 1993, Angelou was chosen to read her poem "On the Pulse of Morning" on the steps of the Capitol just before the new president took his oath of office. It was an event that thrilled her many fans and brought her squarely back into the public eye.

Shortly after the inauguration, Angelou was appointed chairwoman of the annual Horatio Alger

Award dinner in the nation's capital. She herself had been a 1992 recipient of the award, which honors individuals who have overcome adversity to become major achievers. Angelou declared that she was "bowled over by the honor" of organizing the prestigious dinner but also acted swiftly to put her own mark on what was traditionally a sedate and formal social function. Under her supervision, the dinner was enlivened by strolling musicians playing a wide variety of music, and the menu was changed to include some of Angelou's favorite southern dishes.

Throughout her extraordinary and adventurous life, Angelou has drawn strength from her unquenchable optimism, a quality she offered to the entire nation in the conclusion of her inauguration poem:

Here on the pulse of this new day
You may have the grace to look up and out
And into your sister's eyes, into
Your brother's face, your country
And say simply
Very simply
With hope
Good morning.

GWENDOLYN BROOKS

The first black American writer to win a Pulitzer Prize, Gwendolyn Brooks was born in Topeka, Kansas, on June 7, 1917. Her parents, David Anderson Brooks and Keziah Corinne Wims Brooks, provided her with a loving and stimulating home life.

Young Gwendolyn began writing when she was seven. By the age of 11, she was collecting her poems in composition books. Her parents, convinced that she had an exceptional talent, encouraged her to believe that anything was possible.

By the time she was 15, Brooks was boldly sending her manuscripts to well-known writers. Among them was James Weldon Johnson, the eminent poet, novelist, diplomat, educator, and civil rights leader. Then a professor of literature at Fisk University in Nashville, Tennessee, Johnson took the trouble to send the manuscripts back with comments and suggestions. "He thought I was talented and hoped that I would keep writing," Brooks later recalled. "My parents were delighted with all of this attention. . . . But I would have gone on writing. I didn't care what any of them said."

Though her mother had gone home to Topeka to give birth to her, Brooks grew up in the city of Chicago. When she attended high school, she was surrounded by large numbers of whites for the first time and found the experience disturbing. Accustomed to attention and support in her early years, Brooks now found that she was shunted to the side. She observed that society was divided along racial lines; rather than creating a desire to be accepted by the dominant group, the experience taught her to value her own personality and racial identity. Concentrating on her studies, she became a keen student of literature and delved into the work of all the leading modern poets.

After graduating from high school, Brooks enrolled in Woodrow Wilson Junior College. In 1938, when she was 21, she met Henry Lowington Blakely II and married him shortly afterward. The couple separated briefly at the end of the 1960s, but in 1989 they celebrated their 50th wedding anniversary.

Nothing in Brooks's life was more important to her than her poetry. "In writing poetry you're interested in condensation so you don't try to put all of a particular impression or inspiration on a single page. You distill. Poetry is life distilled."

In 1941, her writing received a major stimulus when she attended a poetry workshop in Chicago's South Side Community Art Center and shared her work and ideas with other writers. Two years later, her work earned her a prize from the Midwestern Writers' Conference. When in 1945 the prestigious firm of Harper & Brothers published her first collection of poems, *A Street in Bronzeville*, her career was definitely launched. Critics were deeply impressed by this young poet who had mastered all the complicated techniques of modern poetry but firmly focused her gaze on the trials and tribulations of her people. Distinguished African American writers of the earlier generation, such as Claude McKay and Countee Cullen, and those of her own generation, such as Ralph Ellison and Richard Wright, enthusiastically welcomed Brooks into their ranks.

With the success of her first book, many doors opened to Brooks. In 1946 and 1947, her work was aided by Guggenheim Fellowships, and she also received financial support from the nation's most prestigious cultural associations, the American

Academy of Arts and Letters and the National Institute of Arts and Letters.

Brooks's second book of poems, *Annie Allen*, was published in 1949 and more than justified the support she had been given. The following year, the book was awarded the Pulitzer Prize. Never before had a black American captured this coveted award.

The Pulitzer spurred an outpouring of work from Brooks. In 1953, she published an autobiographical novel, *Maud Martha*, which was not a record of her life but a distillation of her experience. "I didn't want to write about somebody who turned out to be a star," she explained, "'cause most people don't turn out to be stars. And yet their lives are just as sweet and just as rich as any others and often they are richer and sweeter." Critics later recognized that *Maud Martha* was ahead of its time in its exploration of feminist themes, an approach that was not widely understood until the growth of the women's movement in the late 1960s.

In 1956, Brooks published her first book of children's poems, *Bronzeville Boys and Girls*. She followed in 1960 with another adult verse collection, *The Bean Eaters*. *The Bean Eaters* took a critical view of race relations in America: Among other topics, Brooks's poems dealt with the 1957 school desegregation battle in Little Rock, Arkansas, and the brutal lynching of Emmett Till, a black teenager, in Mississippi in 1955.

In 1968, Brooks made a literary breakthrough with *In the Mecca*, a book that had started out as a novel and ended as a long narrative poem interspersed with ballads. *In the Mecca* recounts a mother's search for her lost child in the Mecca Building in Chicago; the search becomes a rogues' gallery of the people who inhabit the run-down building and exposes the failure of their lives and of the society in which they live. Nevertheless, the poem also carries a positive message.

Build with lithe love. With love like lion-eyes.
With love like morningrise.
With love like black, our black.

Despite the fact that her work was gaining widespread acceptance—*In the Mecca* was favorably reviewed and nominated for a National Book Award, and Brooks was named poet laureate of the state of Illinois—Brooks grew increasingly disenchanted with the white literary establishment. In 1969, she announced that she was leaving Harper & Row and would henceforth deal only with black publishers. Her reason for this, she said, was to "clarify my language. I want these poems to be free. I want them to be direct without sacrificing the kinds of music, the picturemaking I've always been interested in." Changing to black publishers was a way of reaching out to a larger audience of black readers. Her next book of poems, *Riot*, as well as a number of later volumes, were published by Broadside, a Detroit firm run by the prominent black poet Dudley Randall. Later, in 1987, Brooks founded her own press, the David Company.

Riot also marked a change in Brooks's style, as the literary tone of her earlier work gave way to more direct language accessible to the average reader. This was a result of Brooks's decision to focus on the black community—she had abandoned her earlier belief in integration and was now convinced that African Americans needed to build their own institutions. She began to sponsor poetry contests for young people and to conduct poetry workshops, one of which involved a powerful Chicago youth gang known as the Blackstone Rangers. The experience was rejuvenating for Brooks, who later recalled: "The young people that I met in the late sixties . . . educated me. They gave me books to read. We talked and talked. They just absorbed me, adopted me." Brooks also began to spend a good deal of time working with prison inmates, reading them her poems and encouraging them to write.

Following *Riot*, Brooks continued to write prolifically, producing such volumes as *Aloneness, Broadside Treasury, Jump Bad, Beckonings*, and a straightforward autobiography, *Report from Part One*. By the 1980s, her stature as one of America's leading poets was firmly established. In 1989, Brooks's many admirers held a public celebration of her 70th birthday at Navy Pier in Chicago, and the National Endowment for the Arts awarded her a $48,000 Lifetime Achievement Award. In 1990, Chicago State University created a Gwendolyn Brooks Distinguished Chair of Creative Writing and appropriately chose Brooks herself to fill the post.

Brooks made it clear that this new wave of acceptance would not change her attitude or diminish her independence. "There are so many blacks who are denying all blackness. They think they can twinkle their fingers at blackness and it'll just go away and they'll be loved by whites and accepted." She often reiterated her admiration for the assassinated civil rights leader Malcolm X, who, she said, "believed black people should love black people and value them above all others." Even in her seventies, she was still the same fearless poet who had written back in 1949: "First fight. Then fiddle."

NIKKI GIOVANNI

A challenging poet with a powerful social message, Yolande Cornelia "Nikki" Giovanni was born in Knoxville, Tennessee, on June 7, 1943. When Nikki and her older sister, Gary, were still very young, the family moved to Cincinnati, Ohio. Nikki's father, Jones "Gus" Giovanni, worked as a probation officer, and her mother, Yolande Watson Giovanni, was a social worker. When she was

14, Nikki moved back to Knoxville to attend high school, living with her maternal grandparents, John and Louvenia Watson. Originally from Georgia, Louvenia Watson had spoken out so strongly against southern racism that her family had finally smuggled her out of town for her own safety. Her strong-willed, independent nature exerted a powerful and lasting influence on Nikki: even as a youngster, she often stuck up for her older sister.

Giovanni was an excellent student at Knoxville's Austin High School, and at the age of 17 she entered Fisk University in Nashville. However, when she decided to go back to Knoxville for Thanksgiving without asking permission, she came into conflict with the dean of women, who promptly suspended her. Refusing to give in, Giovanni went back to Cincinnati and lived with her parents for the next several years. During that time, she worked in a drugstore, assumed full-time care of her nephew Christopher, and took some courses at the University of Cincinnati. She finally returned to Fisk in 1964, when the university appointed a new dean, Blanche M. Cowan, who became both a friend and a mentor to Giovanni. This time she adapted eagerly to college life and graduated magna cum laude in 1967.

While at Fisk, Giovanni took part in the Fisk Writers Workshop, which was directed by John Oliver Killens, a noted black author with strong opinions about racial and political issues. Giovanni, having grown up in a middle-class professional family, had entered college in 1960 as a conservative Republican.

Responding to the ideas of Killens and to the political upheavals of the late 1960s, she emerged from Fisk as a socially conscious writer and a progressive activist. She was a charter member of the Student Nonviolent Coordinating Committee (SNCC) and organized the Black Arts Festival in Cincinnati. Her first book of poems, *Black Feeling, Black Talk*, published in 1967, took an angry and militant view of race relations in the United States. Some readers were shocked and disturbed by her call for African Americans to combat racism by violent means. However, this was an attitude shared by other young black writers who had grown up during the nonviolent phase of the civil rights movement and saw little real change in American society.

Under a certain amount of pressure from her parents, Giovanni decided to continue her education. With a grant from the Ford Foundation, she enrolled in the University of Pennsylvania School of Social Work. But she soon realized that her true interest was in literature and enrolled in the School of Fine Arts at Columbia University in New York. Though she left Columbia before completing her master of fine arts degree, she was appointed assistant professor of English at Queens College, teaching in the socially progressive SEEK program. During this time, her poetry began to shift away from purely political themes. Her second volume of poems, *Black Judgment*, mixed political concerns with personal issues: the poem entitled "Nikki-Rosa," a tough-minded celebration of childhood memories, emerged as one of her most popular works and has been included in many anthologies:

> *I really hope no white person ever has cause*
> *to write about me*
> *because they never understand*
> *Black love is Black wealth and they'll*
> *probably talk about my hard childhood*
> *and never understand that*
> *all the while I was quite happy.*

During the 1970s, Giovanni's poetry became more spiritual and inward looking. The volumes of poetry she published during the decade—*Re-Creation* (1970), *My House* (1972), *The Women and the Men* (1972), and *Cotton Candy on a Rainy Day* (1978)—do not ignore politics but concern themselves principally with personal relationships. One of the factors in this evolution was the birth of Giovanni's son, Thomas Watson, in 1969. In keeping with her frank and independent personality, Giovanni made it clear in public statements that she had made a conscious choice to have a child without being married.

If motherhood altered Giovanni's approach to writing, it also broadened her range of activities. Long concerned with the self-image developed by black children, Giovanni decided to establish her own publishing company, NikTom, in 1970. She herself wrote three volumes of children's poetry: *Spin a Soft Black Song* (1971), *Ego-Tripping and Other Poems for Young Readers* (1973), and *Vacation Time: Poems for*

Children (1980). One of her principal themes in these poems is the celebration of African roots. In the poem "Ego-Tripping," for example, she evokes the power of African mythology:

I was born in the congo
I walked to the fertile crescent and built
the sphinx
I designed a pyramid so tough that a star
that only glows every one hundred years falls
into the center giving divine perfect light
I am bad.

Though she is best known as a poet, Giovanni's career has many other facets. In 1971, she published her first collection of essays, *Gemini: An Extended Autobiographical Statement on My First Twenty-five Years of Being a Black Poet.* In *Gemini*, she explored the roots of her art, ranging from childhood to the birth of her son. The book impressed readers with its freshness and honesty and was nominated for a National Book Award.

Having both studied and taught literature, Giovanni was always keenly aware of the debt she owed to African American writers of earlier generations. In *A Dialogue: James Baldwin and Nikki Giovanni* (1973) and *A Poetic Equation: Conversations Between Nikki Giovanni and Margaret Walker* (1974), she paid tribute to two of the writers who had most influenced her. At the same time, these books were a valuable study of the changes in thinking and literary technique from one generation of African American writers to another.

Quite early in her career, Giovanni discovered that she had a flair for reading her own work and always relished direct interaction with her audiences. Between 1975 and 1978, for example, she made no fewer than 200 personal appearances. Like many other poets, she also understood the close relationship between poetry and music. In 1972, she made her first record album, *Truth Is on Its Way*, in which she read her poems to a background of gospel music. The success of the album led to several more, including *Like a Ripple on a Pond*, *The Way I Feel*, and *The Reason I Like Chocolate*.

During the 1980s and early 1990s, Giovanni's writing shifted back to larger concerns. Unlike her more racially militant approach during the 1960s, her outlook this time focused more on humanity as a whole and the problems common to all peoples. Her independence often caused controversy: in 1984, she refused to endorse a boycott of the white supremacist regime in South Africa, declaring that "a nation 80 percent black cannot be treated as if it were a soft drink or the grocery store on the corner." Her position on this issue drew much criticism from American blacks and even resulted in death threats.

Giovanni's contributions to literature have been increasingly recognized by the academic community. In addition to receiving honorary doctorates from Fisk and Indiana universities, she served as a visiting professor at Ohio State University and at the College of Mount St. Joseph, and in 1989 she took up a permanent faculty position at Virginia Polytechnic Institute.

Throughout her career, Giovanni's versatility led some critics to complain that her writing was not as polished as it ought to be. She responded by admitting that she was not the kind of writer who could confine herself to a room with the idea of producing a perfect work of art: "I like the story and I care more about *what* is being said than about *how* it is said." Giovanni is above all a communicator, and in this role she will continue to be a vibrant influence in American culture:

> *and if ever i touched a life i hope that life knows*
> *that I know that touching was and still is and*
> *always will be the true*
> *revolution.*

LORRAINE HANSBERRY

One of the outstanding play-
wrights in the history of the American theater,
Lorraine Vivian Hansberry was born in Chicago,
Illinois, on May 19, 1930. The youngest of four
children, she was raised in a prosperous and cultivated
environment. Her father, Carl Augustus Hansberry,
was a successful real estate broker who was active in
the Republican party and in civil rights organizations;

her mother, Nannie Perry Hansberry, was a school-teacher and a leader in Chicago's political and cultural life. Adding additional luster to the family, one of Lorraine's uncles, Leo Hansberry, was a professor of African history at Howard University in Washington, D.C.

The Hansberrys enjoyed a prominent position in Chicago's black community and often entertained visiting dignitaries. While growing up, Lorraine met such African American celebrities as the actor Paul Robeson, the composer Duke Ellington, heavyweight boxing champion Joe Louis, and Olympic track star Jesse Owens. She also grew up with an awareness of racism, because her parents actively opposed Chicago's unofficial system of segregated housing, which had created a crowded black ghetto on the city's South Side.

Despite the Hansberrys' affluence, Lorraine attended Chicago's public schools, graduating from Englewood High School in 1947. Her parents were both graduates of all-black colleges in the South and wanted her to enroll at Howard. But Hansberry showed her independence by choosing the University of Wisconsin at Madison, where the vast majority of students were white—indeed, she was the first black student to live in her freshman dormitory. Left-wing political views held sway at the Madison campus, and Hansberry involved herself in such causes as the Young Progressive League and the 1948 presidential campaign of third-party candidate Henry Wallace. She also discovered the power of the drama to convey a social message in poetic form when she saw a production of the Irish author Sean O'Casey's *Juno and the Paycock*. Later on, she was to recapture O'Casey's deep feeling for his native culture in her own portrayal of African American life in Chicago.

After two years at Madison, Hansberry began to find college life too far removed from the political realities that concerned her. She dropped out and moved to New York City, where she went to work for Paul Robeson's radical newspaper, *Freedom*. Writing about politics while also reviewing books and plays, she was promoted to associate editor in 1952. Meanwhile, the experience of living in Harlem, New York's leading black community, stimulated her creative impulses, and she began to produce plays and short stories. Before long, writing would become her main interest.

Before launching her literary career, Hansberry married Robert Nemiroff, a white college student who was an aspiring poet and songwriter. The young couple decided to devote themselves to writing, working at odd jobs to make ends meet. In 1953, Hansberry quit her newspaper job and began to work seriously on three plays that were in the early stages of development. During that time, she made a living by working as a typist, a garment worker, and a camp director.

When Nemiroff and a friend wrote a hit song, Hansberry was able to stop working and write full time. Her efforts now focused on a play she first entitled *The Crystal Stair*, which concerned the struggles of a black family on Chicago's South Side. When she finished the play in 1957, Hansberry read it to a number of friends, and they were deeply impressed by its power and originality. Phil Rose, a music publisher who had worked with Nemiroff, tried to interest Broadway producers in the play, but he could not find anyone willing to take a chance on a serious drama that presented black people as complex, rounded human beings. Rose decided to produce the play himself in association with a group of backers. After a series of successful trial runs in New Haven, Philadelphia, and Chicago, Hansberry's play, now entitled *A Raisin in the Sun*, opened at Broadway's Ethel Barrymore Theater on March 11, 1959.

The cast of the original production was headlined by Sidney Poitier and consisted of other gifted actors, such as Ruby Dee and Ivan Dixon, who were then as little known as the author. That was soon corrected. The play was an instant hit, both with critics and audiences, who responded to the searing truth of Hansberry's portrayal of ordinary people whose dream of a decent life is threatened at every turn by racial and economic oppression. *A Raisin in the Sun* ran for a total of 538 performances on Broadway, an impressive tenure for a serious drama, and won the 1959 New York Drama Critics Circle Award as Best Play of the Year. Columbia Pictures quickly bought the movie rights, and the film version, with a screenplay written by Hansberry and including almost the entire original cast, made its successful debut in 1961.

Raisin, as it came to be called with the familiarity granted to classics, made Hansberry a national celebrity. She used her position of prominence to emphasize the obligation of writers to involve themselves with social issues. She also supported the civil rights movement, lending her support to such groups as the Student Nonviolent Coordinating Committee (SNCC). Hansberry's outspokenness antagonized a number of whites who had expected her commercial success to turn her into a moderate. When she criticized the administration of President John F. Kennedy for not acting vigorously enough on civil rights, the Federal Bureau of Investigation (FBI) began to keep a file on Hansberry, classifying her as an ally of dangerous black militant organizations.

Hansberry privately acknowledged her homosexuality during the 1950s, and effectively separated from her husband. She decided not to make her sexual orientation public for a variety of reasons, among them the negative reaction she anticipated from her family and from the leadership of the black liberation movement. Consequently, she and Nemiroff maintained all the outward appearances of an ongoing marriage and remained close friends, though they lived apart. In 1963, Hansberry purchased a house in Croton-on-Hudson, just north of New York City, and settled in to begin work on another play.

Hansberry's new play, *The Sign in Sidney Brustein's Window*, opened on Broadway in October 1964. The play, which had a mostly white cast and explored the problems confronting modern intellectuals, was a shock to many theatergoers, who had been anticipating a sequel to *A Raisin in the Sun*. The reviews were mixed, and only the dedication of Nemiroff and other supporters kept the play running for the respectable total of 101 performances.

By this time, Hansberry was facing a far graver challenge. She had begun to feel ill in 1963, and her doctors discovered that she was afflicted with cancer of the pancreas. This unpleasant news did not discourage her from writing or engaging in political activities, mainly in support of the civil rights movement in the South. In addition to completing *The Sign in Sidney Brustein's Window*, she worked on a new play entitled *Les Blancs*, which was about revolution in an African nation; a book on the English feminist Mary Wollstonecraft; and a photo essay on the civil rights movement. But there were limits to her strength. Two operations and a course of chemotherapy failed to arrest the cancer, and Hansberry's health began to decline dramatically. On January 12, 1965, she died in University Hospital in New York at the age of 34.

Neither Hansberry's work nor her influence ended with her death. She had appointed Robert Nemiroff her literary executor, and he worked diligently to realize the projects she had left unfinished. Nemiroff's stage adaptation of Hansberry's unpublished writings, *To Be Young, Gifted, and Black*, was a tremendous off-Broadway success in 1969, and *Les Blancs* was produced on Broadway the following year.

Above all, *A Raisin in the Sun* has endured as a dramatic classic. In 1974, Nemiroff produced a musical version of the play on Broadway, and the production earned the coveted Tony Award. In 1987, a new version of the original play was prepared—including the restoration of material that was previously cut—and was staged by leading theater groups throughout the nation. As long as there is an American theater, Hansberry's indictment of racism and her cry for human liberation will continue to move and enlighten audiences.

ZORA NEALE HURSTON

One of the most distinctive
voices in American literature, Zora Neale Hurston
was born in Eatonville, Florida, on January 7, 1891.
Her parents, John and Lucy Ann, were farmers, but
unlike the majority of black farmers in the United
States at that time, they did not work for white landowners. Their town, Eatonville, had been founded in
1887 to provide black Americans with a community in

🐝 309 🐝

which they could prosper and govern themselves. The Hurstons had come to Eatonville from Alabama, bought their own land, and imbued their eight children with a sense of pride and self-worth.

As she grew up, Zora developed a forceful and independent personality that did not easily bend to discipline at home. Restless and imaginative, the young girl was equally in love with roughhousing, reading, and fantasizing. She also delighted in the local general store; whenever her parents sent her there, she eagerly soaked up all the stories, many of them deriving from African legends, that the customers swapped on the front porch. These stories were later to play an important role in her literary career.

When Zora was 13, her rich and varied life in Eatonville was ended by the death of her beloved mother. Shortly after the funeral, Zora joined two of her siblings in the city of Jacksonville, where she continued her schooling. As if it were not bad enough to be away from her cherished Eatonville, living in a city where black people were second-class citizens, Zora soon learned that her father had no intention of paying her tuition or doing anything else to support her. Returning home, she found him remarried to an attractive young woman who had no intention of being burdened with a brood of stepchildren.

Zora was sent off to live with friends of her mother's, but in fact she was alone in the world at the age of 14. For five years she wandered from place to place and from one menial job to another. Then, in 1910, Zora heard that the star of an operetta company that was touring the South needed a lady's maid. She applied for the job and was hired for what was to her the fabulous sum of $10 a week. More important, she entered a world in which her personality and her aspirations could blossom.

Hurston stayed with the operetta company until 1912, and after that there is a tantalizing gap of five years that remain a mystery to her biographers. It is known, however, that in 1917 she enrolled at the Morgan Academy, a secondary school in Baltimore. After earning her high school diploma with distinction in a single year, she became a part-time student at Howard University in Washington, D.C., where she studied English literature and embraced the ideas of W. E. B. Du Bois, who called upon black intellectuals to lead the way to a just society.

Nourishing her intellect and her flair for language at Howard, Hurston developed the ambition to become a writer. Encouraged by the publication of her first short story in the college literary magazine, she submitted a story entitled "Drenched in Light" to the New York–based magazine *Opportunity: A Journal of Negro Life*. When Charles S. Johnson, the magazine's editor, accepted the story and wrote Hurston a letter of praise, she soon decided that if she was going to succeed as a writer, she would have to move to New York.

Hurston arrived in New York in 1925 and became a full-fledged participant in the Harlem Renaissance, a remarkable flowering of African American creativity in art, literature, music, and dance. With her striking appearance, her exuberant personality, and her wealth of vivid stories about life in Eatonville, she was an instant hit with the leading lights of the Renaissance. The exhilarating atmosphere of New York stimulated Hurston's literary efforts; she won an award from *Opportunity* for her story "Drenched in Light" and contributed another story and a play to a new magazine entitled *Fire!!*

Hurston's growing literary stature also won her a scholarship to prestigious Barnard College. While majoring in English, she took a course in anthropology with the eminent scholar Franz Boas. Impressed by Hurston's intellectual abilities, Boas persuaded her to undertake a systematic study of her own heritage. When she finished her course work in 1927, Hurston traveled to the South and tried to collect folklore. She had little success in this venture, but the trip proved important for two reasons: she married her longtime boyfriend, Herbert Sheen, and struck up a friendship with the young black poet Langston Hughes.

Back in New York, Hughes introduced Hurston to Charlotte Mason, a wealthy white woman who had a keen interest in the Harlem Renaissance. The two women hit it off, and Mason offered to sponsor Hurston on another folklore-gathering trip. Hurston set off again at the end of 1927, and this time she found what she was looking for. For the next three years, Hurston visited cities and towns, farms and lumber camps, collecting stories, folktales, songs, and religious rituals. With the help of Alain Locke, who had been one of her professors at Howard, she then began to collect her material for publication.

In 1932, while working on her folklore study, *Mules and Men*, Hurston returned to Eatonville. Living in her hometown stimulated her love of storytelling, and she soon completed a story entitled "The Gilded Six-Bits." The piece was accepted by *Story*, a prestigious literary magazine, and published in 1933. Shortly afterward, Hurston received a letter from New York publisher Bertram Lippincott, praising her story and asking whether she had ever considered writing a novel. Hurston wrote back that she was indeed working on a novel; in truth, she had an idea for a novel but had not yet written a word. With typical energy she rented a little room in the nearby town of Sandford and set to work. Several months later, penniless and on the verge of eviction, she shipped the manuscript of *Jonah's Gourd Vine* off to Lippincott. To her amazement and delight, the publisher accepted her book and sent a check for $200 as an advance.

Published in 1934, *Jonah's Gourd Vine* told the story of a southern couple who were very closely modeled on Hurston's own parents. The novel was almost unanimously praised by book reviewers across the nation; *Mules and Men* appeared the following year, cementing Hurston's reputation as a serious writer and a student of black culture. She soon won a prestigious Guggenheim Fellowship and took off for the Caribbean in order to study voodoo.

Hurston conducted her research in Jamaica and in Haiti, where she claimed to have met a zombie. In addition to collecting a wealth of material on voodoo, she found time to write her second novel, *Their Eyes Were Watching God*, which was published in 1936. Relating the romantic and spiritual history of a young woman named Janie Crawford, *Their Eyes Were Watching God* endures as one of the masterworks of American literature. But its reception in the politically charged climate of 1936 was curiously mixed: white critics praised the book, but many black intellectuals attacked Hurston for writing romances instead of grappling with social problems.

Although hurt by the criticism, Hurston worked on, publishing a book on voodoo, *Tell My Horse*, in 1938. Like Janie Crawford, she also continued to search for personal fulfillment. Her marriage to Herbert Sheen had ended in 1931, and in 1939 she married a man named Albert Price III. This match proved no more satisfactory than the first, and Hurston and Price soon began to live apart, finally divorcing in 1943.

By 1940, Hurston was a nationally known writer, but she had never been able to earn a steady income from her books. Attempting to take advantage of her celebrity, she published her autobiography, *Dust Tracks on a Road*, in 1942. Her best-known work along with *Their Eyes Were Watching God*, the book got rave reviews and won her a $1,000 award from a prominent magazine. Money in hand, Hurston bought a houseboat in Daytona Beach, Florida, and settled in to continue writing. Though she sold a number of articles and another novel, she was out of money again by the end of the decade. At one point she was obliged to work as a maid, but after selling an article in 1951 she was able to rent a small house and get back to work.

Unfortunately, Hurston's ambitious new novel, *Herod the Great*, was rejected by publishers, and she continued to struggle against poverty. By 1959, suffering from a variety of ailments, she was obliged to move into a welfare home, where she died on January 28, 1960. The 69-year-old writer was buried in a segregated cemetery, in a grave that was unmarked until 1973, when writer Alice Walker discovered it and placed a headstone on it. For Hurston's epitaph, Walker chose a simple but indisputable phrase: A Genius of the South.

TONI MORRISON

One of America's literary
giants, Toni Morrison was born Chloe Anthony
Wofford in Lorain, Ohio, on February 18, 1931, the
second of four children. Her parents, George and
Ramah Wofford, had grown up in Georgia and
Alabama, respectively. Their own parents had been
sharecroppers, and they had vivid memories of the
grinding poverty and racial intolerance endured by

black people in the rural South. As a result, they took great pains to instill in their children the virtues of self-reliance and pride in their African-American heritage.

It should not be supposed, however, that the Woffords' home was a somber, joyless place to grow up. On the contrary, Toni's parents were deeply imbued with the richness of African American culture. They related many folktales and African myths to their children and stressed the importance of learning. As Morrison later recalled: "I remember myself as surrounded by extraordinary adults who were smarter than me. I was better educated, but I always thought that they had true wisdom and I had merely book learning. It was only when I began to write that I was able to marry those two things: wisdom and education."

Morrison's ability to acquire that education was a direct result of her parents' urging. They made sure that she knew how to read before she entered the first grade and encouraged all of her intellectual aspirations. In high school, Morrison devoured the classics of European literature and absorbed ideas and techniques that she would eventually put to use in her own books.

In 1949, Morrison entered Howard University in Washington, D.C., where she began calling herself "Toni," a shortened version of her middle name. Majoring in English, she expressed her flair for drama by joining the Howard Repertory Theater. Upon graduating she went on to Cornell University, where she earned a master's degree in English in 1955. After teaching for two years at Texas Southern University, she returned to Howard as a member of the faculty. For the first time she began to work seriously on her own writing and joined a group of black writers who read and discussed one another's efforts. While at Howard, she married Harold Morrison, a Jamaican-born architect. The couple had two children, Slade and Harold, but their marriage ended in divorce in 1964.

Following the breakup of her marriage, Morrison faced the challenge of supporting her two young sons alone. She soon found a job as a textbook editor with a division of Random House in Syracuse, New York. After putting in a full workday and then getting her children off to bed, she began writing late into the night. "Writing for me was the most extraordinary way of thinking and feeling," she said. "It became the one thing I was doing that I had absolutely no intention of living without." Morrison found a story she had written a few years back about a young black girl in the Midwest, Pecola Breedlove, who yearns to have blue eyes, which she considers the symbol of beauty. She turned the story into a full-length novel that explored the deep-seated effects of racism, *The Bluest Eye*. When the manuscript was completed she sent it to Holt, Rinehart & Winston, a major New York publisher. Holt agreed to publish the book, but Morrison's satisfaction was dampened by her feeling that the publishers did not really believe in her as a writer but merely wanted to capitalize on the growing interest in black literature.

Shortly after her novel was accepted, Morrison moved her family to New York City, where she began to work as a trade book editor for Random House. It was the beginning of a 16-year tenure at the publishing house, during which Morrison rose to the position of senior editor and had the opportunity to nurture and publish the work of other black writers.

Despite the demands of her job and the responsibilities of child rearing, Morrison was determined to pursue her career as a novelist. In 1973, she published her second novel, *Sula*, the tale of a young black woman determined to live by her own rules. In the book, Morrison explored the relationship between two black women—something that had rarely been attempted in American fiction. Neither *Sula* nor *The Bluest Eye* was a commercial success, but the books were well received by reviewers and established Morrison as an emerging talent.

One of Morrison's most satisfying projects at Random House was *The Black Book*, a compilation of materials on black history from the point of view of ordinary people. Acting as the coordinator of the project, Morrison helped a group of scholars and volunteers collect an array of documents and mementos from black families throughout the country. Though the resulting book was not published under her name, Morrison gained a broad and intimate view of African American life that provided powerful stimulus to her fiction.

Morrison's breakthrough into the front rank of American writers occurred in 1977 when she published her third novel, *Song of Solomon*, the story of a young African American who strives for material wealth and discovers in the process that his most valuable possession is the heritage of his people. *Song of Solomon* was hailed by critics and became a major best-seller, eventually selling 3 million copies. The novel earned Morrison the 1978 American Academy and Institute of Arts and Letters Award and also the National Book Critics' Circle Award.

Morrison's acceptance by the predominantly white, male literary elite was all the more significant in light of her racial pride and intellectual independence. As she explained to an interviewer, "My job is to not become anybody's creature, not the critical establishment's, not the media's, not anybody's. I'm not doing anyone justice, not the women's movement, not the black movement, not novels, not anyone, if I toe the line. I want to write better. Think better. I don't know how not to want that. And better for me may not be in step with what is current and prevailing."

Following the success of *Song of Solomon*, the appearance of a new novel by Morrison became a literary event. Her next work, *Tar Baby*, published in 1981, was set in the Caribbean and explored the relationship between a black woman who wants to merge herself with the affluent culture of mainstream America, and her lover, who is intent on preserving his racial and cultural identity. *Tar Baby* spent four months on the

New York Times best-seller list and confirmed Morrison's standing as a literary superstar.

With two best-sellers under her belt, Morrison was able to leave her job at Random House and devote herself to writing and teaching. In 1984, she was appointed to the Albert Schweitzer Chair of the Humanities at the State University of New York at Albany. While teaching courses in literature, Morrison completed her fifth novel, *Beloved*, in 1987. In this book, Morrison addressed the issue of slavery, telling the story of an escaped slave who, when caught, kills her daughter rather than have the child return to the South to grow up a slave. Hailed as both a brilliant work of fiction and a powerful exploration of American history, *Beloved* had an even greater impact than Morrison's previous books and earned her a coveted Pulitzer Prize.

In 1989, Morrison was appointed to a professorship at Princeton University, making her the first black woman to have an endowed chair at an Ivy League college. The academic environment stimulated her to write critical essays, and in 1990 she was invited to deliver the Massey Lectures in American Civilization at Harvard University; the text of these lectures was published in book form under the title *Playing in the Dark: Whiteness and the Literary Imagination*. While teaching and lecturing, Morrison continued to write fiction, and her novel *Jazz*—the exploration of a romantic triangle in 1920s Harlem—was published in 1992.

The crowning achievement of Morrison's literary career occurred on October 7, 1993, when the Nobel Committee of the Swedish Academy, which awards the Nobel Prize, announced that she had won the 1993 Nobel Prize in Literature. Toni Morrison "gives life to an essential aspect of American reality" in novels "characterized by visionary force and poetic import," the academy said. "She delves into the language itself, a language she wants to liberate from the fetters of race. And she addresses us with the luster of poetry." Morrison became the eighth woman—and the first black woman—to receive the Nobel Prize in Literature.

Her overall achievement as a writer is remarkable in equal measure for her creative skill and for the courage and determination that brought her gifts to fruition. If there is any single phrase that could typify Toni Morrison as an artist, it may be this simple but far-reaching declaration: "I never played it safe in a book."

ALICE WALKER

A Pulitzer Prize–winning author and a forceful advocate of women's rights and social justice, Alice Malsenior Walker was born on February 9, 1944, in the small Georgia town of Eatonton. Alice was the eighth child of Willie Lee and Minnie Walker, sharecroppers who struggled to survive by working the land of an elderly white woman. The family's children helped work the fields and do the farm chores, but the Walkers always believed strongly in the value of education. When little Alice was four years old, her parents entrusted her to Mrs. Reynolds, the local first-grade teacher. In Reynolds's school, the young girl discovered the magic of learning and quickly proved that she had a keen intelligence.

Alice suffered a devastating blow in 1952 when she was struck in the right eye by a pellet from her brother's BB gun. Because her parents were unable to get her to a doctor right away, she lost the sight in her right eye and was disfigured by a bulbous growth of scar tissue. Previously outgoing, she now became self-conscious and withdrawn, avoiding social contact as much as possible. She lived with this burden until she was 14; at that time, while visiting one of her brothers in Boston, she consulted a doctor who removed the scar tissue. Although her right eye remained sightless, it was at least restored to its normal appearance.

Filled with renewed self-confidence, Walker returned to Eatonton and became one of the most popular students in her high school. For a time she wondered what to do with her life after graduation. That difficult question was settled one day in 1960 when she saw a civil rights demonstration led by Dr. Martin Luther King, Jr., on a television news broadcast. She understood that it was possible to struggle against the poverty and racism her own family had endured, and she vowed to dedicate her life to the cause.

When she graduated from high school in 1961, Walker entered Atlanta University's Spelman College, the nation's foremost college for black women, on a scholarship. She reveled in the study of literature, but she chafed at the conformist atmosphere of the college. Before long, however, many of Spelman's students were swept up in the battle against racial segregation, and Walker enthusiastically took part in marches and sit-ins. The crowning event of this time in her life was the March on Washington for Jobs and Freedom, which took place in the nation's capital on August 28, 1963. Perched on the limb of a tree above the crowd of 250,000 marchers, Walker heard every word of Dr. King's memorable "I Have a Dream" speech.

When the atmosphere at Spelman continued to restrict her, Walker transferred to Sarah Lawrence College in Bronxville, New York, where the study of literature awakened her interest in writing. When she graduated in 1965, Walker was committed to being an author, but she had not forgotten her devotion to civil rights. Spurning writing grants and a safer existence in New York, she returned to the South to work in voter registration drives, a project that required great physical courage in that hostile environment. While fighting segregation, she fell in love with a young law student named Mel Leventhal, and the two eventually returned to New York together.

Back in the North, Walker applied herself to her writing and published her first piece, an essay on the civil rights movement, in 1967. In the same year she married Mel Leventhal, and when he graduated from law school the couple returned to Mississippi to continue the struggle for racial justice. In 1968 Walker became writer-in-residence at Jackson State University and published her first book of poems, *Once*. The following year she published her first novel, *The Third Life of Grange Copeland*, an exploration of the lives of southern sharecroppers that revolved around a man who murdered his wife. Three days after finishing the novel, Walker gave birth to a daughter, Rebecca.

Despite her growing list of accomplishments, the pressures of work and child care—added to the hostility her interracial marriage aroused in many southerners—began to take a toll on Walker. In 1971, she accepted a short-term teaching position at Wellesley, the prestigious women's college near Boston, not realizing that she was saying good-bye to the South for good.

At Wellesley, Walker created a ground-breaking course on women writers whose work had been unjustly neglected. Her classes electrified the students who attended them and inspired Walker to produce more work of her own. In 1973, she made her first real impact on the literary scene with a book of stories, *In Love & Trouble: Stories of Black Women*, and a collection of poems, *Revolutionary Petunias & Other Poems*. Both works were praised by reviewers; the volume of stories won an award from the American Academy and Institute of Arts and Letters, and the book of poems was nominated for a National Book Award.

When Walker resettled in New York with her family in 1974, she took a job with *Ms.* magazine and continued to write. Though she soon had to cope with the death of her father and the breakup of her eight-year marriage, she worked with unflagging energy, and her second novel, *Meridian*, appeared in 1976. *Meridian*, which tells the story of a young southern woman caught up in the civil rights movement, was praised by critics and led to a Guggenheim Fellowship. Walker traveled to San Francisco in search of inspiration for a new book, and while there she fell in love with a writer and political activist named Robert Allen. When the couple settled into a cabin in northern California and were joined by Walker's daughter, a new chapter in the writer's life and career began.

Walker had been thinking about writing a historical novel for some time, and as soon as she got her bearings she threw herself into the project. The book took shape as a series of letters detailing the struggle of a young woman to overcome the brutal circumstances of her life in the rural South. Completed after a year of intensive work, *The Color Purple* was an immediate sensation. Hailed by critics as a major event in American literature, the novel captured both the 1983 American Book Award and the Pulitzer Prize. It also became a phenomenal commercial success, selling nearly 2 million copies in two years. Following up on her new status as a major author, Walker published a book of essays, *In Search of Our Mother's Gardens*, and another volume of poems, *Horses Make a Landscape Look More Beautiful*.

In 1985, director Steven Spielberg began shooting the film version of *The Color Purple*, starring Whoopi Goldberg. Walker, who had done the first draft of the screenplay, assisted the production crew on location in North Carolina, making sure that all the details of the characters' lives were accurately rendered. The film, nominated for 11 Academy Awards, not only propelled Walker's novel back onto the best-seller lists but also made her an international celebrity.

When Walker attended the film's premiere in her hometown of Eatonton, Georgia, the enthusiastic response of her former neighbors, both black and white, had long-lasting and beneficial effects. Walker's sister Ruth Walker Hood built upon the outpouring of emotion to establish The Color Purple Educational Fund Foundation, Inc., a nonprofit charitable and educational organization based in Eatonton. With Walker contributing her own time and money, the organization has, among other activities, provided scholarships to promising students in financial need.

Walker's sense of social responsibility was clearly not diluted by her newfound fame and wealth, and her creative drive was similarly undiminished. Settling back into her northern California home, Walker plunged into an ambitious new novel that attempted to retell the history of the world through the eyes of an African goddess. Published in 1989 as *The Temple of My Familiar*, the novel delighted many readers, puzzled some, and made it quite clear to everyone that Walker was a writer who would always be forging ahead and breaking new ground. Continuing her work as a poet as well, Walker collected all the poems she had written between 1965 and 1990 and published them in a single volume in 1991.

Firmly rooted in northern California, Walker has involved herself in a great variety of social and literary issues, always championing the cause of the dispossessed and neglected. In one of her essays, she eloquently described the principles that motivate her: "I have been helped, supported, encouraged, and nurtured by people of all races, creeds, colors, and dreams; and I have, to the best of my ability, returned help, support, encouragement, and nurture."

PHILLIS WHEATLEY

Phillis Wheatley, America's first black author, was born in 1754 on the west coast of Africa. When she was a young girl she was captured by slave traders, who shipped her to the British colonies in America to be sold. In 1761, she was unloaded from a slave ship onto Boston's Beach Street wharf, thin and frail, with nothing to cover her but a scrap of dirty carpet. In the slave market she attracted the attention of Susannah Wheatley, the wife of a Boston merchant, who was looking for a servant and was somehow drawn to the unpromising-looking girl. The merchant's wife purchased the young slave for a small sum. The seven-year-old African thus acquired a new name, derived from the family that had purchased her and from the name of the ship that had brought her to America, the *Phillis.*

Though Phillis Wheatley was now the property of another person, she was luckier than most other enslaved Africans. Of the 230,000 or so blacks in the American colonies at that time, all but about 16,000 lived in the South, where they toiled on plantations and often endured harsh treatment. In the North, the Africans were usually employed as household servants and treated with less brutality.

As she assumed her duties in the Wheatley household, young Phillis quickly showed evidence of an unusual intelligence. She grasped spoken English in a remarkably short time and soon began to read and write. Most masters, even in the North, would have been alarmed at any evidence of intellectual ambition on the part of their slaves and would have stifled it at once. But John and Susannah Wheatley were people of unusual humanity—they believed that the young girl's talents were a divine gift and that it was their duty to nourish them. Phillis later wrote of Susannah Wheatley: "I was a poor little outcast and stranger when she took me in; not only into her house, but I presently became a sharer in her most tender affections. I was treated by her more like her child than her servant."

At her parents' request, 18-year-old Mary Wheatley became Phillis's tutor. Instead of working constantly, Phillis spent several hours a day with Mary, reading the Bible and studying poetry. By the time she was nine years old, Phillis could read English fluently and even understand some of the most difficult passages in the Scriptures.

When she was 12, Phillis began to write poems. The Wheatleys were delighted to discover this talent in her; they provided her with all the comforts and materials she needed and took special precautions to protect her delicate health. At the same time, Susannah Wheatley did all she could to promote Phillis's career as an author. She invited the leading thinkers of Boston to converse with the young African and sent her to the homes of prominent citizens. To the Wheatleys' great satisfaction, Phillis proved that she could hold her own in conversation with anyone.

Phillis quickly gained a host of admirers, including Thomas Hutchinson, the governor of the Massachusetts colony, and John Hancock, who was to be a prominent signatory of the Declaration of Independence. Nevertheless, Phillis remained a slave, and as such she could never be accepted as an equal in white society. Because the Wheatleys considered her far superior to other Africans and would not allow her to associate with members of her own race, she occupied a peculiar—and lonely—position between two worlds.

At this time, Phillis developed a powerful religious faith, based upon the teachings of the Great Awakening, a movement that swept the colonies during the 18th century. The new doctrine was especially appealing to her because it promised salvation for all believers and held that everyone was equal in the eyes of God. Phillis embraced these beliefs with all her heart and expressed them in her poems. One of her earliest poems, written at the age of 14, was titled "An Address to the Atheist": "Thou who dost daily feel his hand, and rod/Darest thou deny the Essence of God!/If there's no heav'n, ah! whither wilt thou go . . . ?"

As Phillis Wheatley entered adolescence, the American colonists' desire for independence from Great Britain began to reach the boiling point, with occasional riots occurring over burdensome taxes imposed by the British crown. Though some colonists declared their loyalty to the mother country, Wheatley was firmly on the side of the rebellious Patriots; when British redcoats shot down five protesters in March 1770, Wheatley wrote a poem commemorating the event that became known to history as the Boston Massacre.

Wheatley achieved international notice at the age of 17 when she wrote her first major work, a poem lamenting the death of George Whitefield, a dynamic preacher who was one of the leaders of the Great Awakening. The elegy begins: "Hail, happy saint, on thine immortal throne,/Possest of glory, life and bliss unknown;/We hear no more the music of thy tongue. . . ." Published as a pamphlet and circulated among Whitefield's followers throughout the colonies and in England, the poem brought Wheatley to the attention of a wide public.

With the enthusiastic support of Susannah Wheatley, Phillis collected all the poems she had written and sought to have them published as a book. When backers could not be found in Boston, Susannah secured a publisher in England. In order to promote the project, Phillis and young Nathaniel Wheatley sailed for England in May 1773. In London, Phillis found herself an instant celebrity, but her trip was cut short after a month when news arrived that Susannah Wheatley was seriously ill. Despite Phillis's hasty departure, the publication of her book, *Poems on Various Subjects, Religious and Moral*, was a notable event. It was only the second book published by an American woman and the first by an African American.

The book received enthusiastic reviews in the British press, and not long after its publication the Wheatleys granted Phillis her freedom. She continued to live in their household, though she was now responsible for her own upkeep. In May 1774—in the midst of her deep sorrow over the death of Susannah Wheatley—Phillis finally received 300 copies of her book from London, just before the British government imposed a naval blockade on its American colonies. A year later, when redcoats and Patriots exchanged fire at Lexington and Concord, the American Revolution was under way.

Wheatley's sympathies were still fervently with the Patriots, and in 1776 she wrote a poem supporting the revolutionary cause. But the war brought her only hardship. She found it difficult to sell her books, and when John Wheatley died in 1778, he made no provision for her in his will. Perhaps as a means of survival, she married John Peters, an educated black man who ran a grocery in Boston. Wheatley appears to have lived in comfort with Peters, though she found it difficult to interest the residents of war-torn Boston in a second volume of poems.

In the early 1780s, the Peters family, which now included three children, moved from Boston to the nearby village of Wilmington. The reason for the move, apparently, was Peters's financial difficulties, and the hardships of a relatively poor life in a small village took its toll on Wheatley's health. The family moved back to Boston after the triumph of the revolution, but they did not regain their former prosperity. Records indicate that Wheatley's husband was imprisoned for debt on at least one occasion.

Despite her tribulations, Wheatley continued to write. In January 1784, she published a poetic tribute to the late Samuel Cooper, a prominent Bostonian who had been a sponsor of her first book. In September, the *Boston Magazine* carried her elegy comforting a family on the loss of a child; it was a heartfelt poem, for she had lost two of her own children. Toward the end of the year, she produced "Liberty and Peace," a poem celebrating the end of the Revolutionary War.

When "Liberty and Peace" was published, its author was unable to read it. Ill and exhausted, Phillis Wheatley had died on December 5, 1784, in a run-down boardinghouse. She was only 31 years old. No one attended her funeral, and she was buried in an unmarked grave, next to her third child, who had survived her by only a few hours. Her contemporaries did nothing to honor Phillis Wheatley, but succeeding generations have cherished her as the founder of black literature in America. There is now a monument to her in the city of Boston, honoring the remarkable woman who once wrote, "In every human breast, God has implanted a principle, which we call love of freedom; it is impatient of oppression, and pants for deliverance."

MALE WRITERS

JAMES BALDWIN

Novelist, essayist, and passionate critic of American race relations, James Arthur Baldwin was born on August 2, 1924, in the black community of Harlem in New York City. He was the oldest in a family of nine brothers and sisters, and his childhood was one of poverty and hardship. His stepfather, a part-time preacher who worked in a local bottling plant, nurtured a fierce hatred of white people and was a stern disciplinarian whom the young James could never please. His mother worked as a maid. A small, frail-looking boy with wide eyes and a broad grin whose classmates at Frederick Douglass Junior High School would often bully, James took refuge from the bleakness and cruelty of his environment by immersing himself in reading and writing. He discovered the New York Public Library in midtown Manhattan and went there frequently, and he began to write stories and essays on Harlem life for his school paper.

At the age of 14, Baldwin experienced a religious conversion and began to preach at the Fireside Pentecostal Assembly, one of Harlem's many storefront churches. At the same time, he also began to attend De Witt Clinton High School in the Bronx, where he befriended a group of white students who shared his growing interest in literature and avant-garde ideas. By the time he graduated from high school in 1942, he had abandoned his preaching and determined to become a writer.

In the summer of 1943, with Harlem shaken by riots as a result of the shooting of a black man by white police officers, Baldwin, as he wrote in his famous essay "Notes of a Native Son," decided that he would have to leave the community or be consumed by the poverty, desperation, and rage he saw all around him. He moved into a small apartment in Greenwich Village in lower Manhattan. During the day he worked as a waiter, busboy, and dishwasher in local restaurants, and at night he continued to write.

In 1945, Baldwin met the novelist Richard Wright, whose *Native Son* was the most critically acclaimed and commercially successful novel ever written by a black American. Wright offered the aspiring writer much encouragement, and Baldwin began to write book reviews for such prominent journals of ideas as the *Nation*, the *New Leader*, and the *Partisan Review*. In 1948 his first major essay, "The Harlem Ghetto," was published in *Commentary* magazine. The essay tackled the difficult and painful issue of the origins of black anti-Semitism, and it caused considerable controversy.

Though he was beginning to establish himself as a writer, Baldwin was exhausted and depressed. He had failed to finish a novel that Wright had urged him to complete, he was not making any money, and he felt alienated in the mostly white community of Greenwich Village. At the end of 1948, he decided to leave the country to live in Paris, France, which black American artists had long regarded as a haven from racial prejudice.

In spite of its reputation as a center of world culture, Paris in 1948 was a bleak city still recovering from the effects of World War II. Baldwin, who had arrived in France with just $40, lived in a series of cheap hotel rooms and at one point even pawned his clothes and his typewriter to pay his bills. He found that when he owed someone money, the supposed French indifference to skin color quickly gave way to intolerance. But gradually he established a circle of friends, one of whom took him to

Switzerland, where in several months he completed his acclaimed first novel, *Go Tell It on the Mountain*, an autobiographical story about a Harlem youth trying to escape the despotism of his stepfather and the suffocating influence of religion. In 1955, he followed with *Notes of a Native Son*, a collection of essays that examine the subtle ways in which racial prejudice damages both blacks and whites. A year later, Dial Press published his second novel, *Giovanni's Room*, a bold exploration of a homosexual relationship. In 1957, eager to take part in the growing civil rights movement and having established himself as a successful writer, Baldwin returned to the United States.

Soon after arriving in the United States, Baldwin toured the South to witness firsthand the wave of sit-ins, demonstrations, boycotts, and marches that were beginning to crack the barriers of discrimination. In Atlanta, Georgia, he met the Reverend Martin Luther King, Jr., and heard him give sermons to black congregations. Overwhelmed by the courage and dedication he saw around him, Baldwin began to write about the ordinary black people who risked beatings and bombings to change their lives. These essays were published in the collection *Nobody Knows My Name: More Notes of a Native Son* in 1961. In 1962, he published his third novel, *Another Country*, which concerned the suicide of jazz drummer Rufus Scott and interracial and bisexual relationships among a circle of friends in Greenwich Village and Harlem. Though controversial, both books were best-sellers.

At this time, Baldwin was becoming more and more involved in the civil rights movement, writing essays and traveling around the country giving lectures on its significance. In 1962, he met Elijah Muhammad, the leader of the Nation of Islam (the so-called Black Muslims), who urged that blacks separate themselves from white society. Though Baldwin himself believed in the integrationist strategy of Martin Luther King, Jr., he was able to understand the forces that drove some blacks to become militant separatists. Out of his experiences with the Black Muslims came *The Fire Next Time*, an apocalyptic vision of the destruction that faced American society if it could not solve its racial problems. The book made Baldwin a national figure and he appeared on the cover of *Time* magazine. In 1963, in the wake of police beatings of civil rights workers in Birmingham, Alabama, Baldwin brought together a group of prominent black artists and educators—including Lena Horne, Harry Belafonte, Lorraine Hansberry, and Kenneth Clark—to urge U.S. attorney general Robert Kennedy to put the full force of the federal government behind new civil rights legislation. On August 28, 1963, he attended the huge "March on Washington for Jobs and Freedom" organized by labor leader A. Philip Randolph and Martin Luther King, Jr., to exert pressure on Congress for a new civil rights bill.

These were heady times for Baldwin. In 1964, he was elected to the National Institute of Arts and Letters. In January 1965, at Cambridge University in England, he won a debate against William F. Buckley of the *National Review* on the need for revolutionary change in American race relations. In March 1965, he joined Martin Luther King, Jr., on his second, successful attempt to march from Selma, Alabama, to Montgomery, Alabama, to pressure President Lyndon Johnson for a new voting-rights act, and he protested America's growing involvement in the war in Vietnam.

At the same time, Baldwin was coming under criticism from more radical black leaders, such as Eldridge Cleaver and Imamu Amiri Baraka, because of his integrationist views and the sympathetic portraits of white characters in some of his works. There were terrible tragedies as well—in the 1960s, Baldwin lived through the assassinations of John and Robert Kennedy, Medgar Evers, and Malcolm X, and in the opinion of several of his friends, he never fully recovered from the murder of Martin Luther King, Jr., in 1968. Despite all this, he refused to abandon his commitment to nonviolent protest and racial harmony.

During the 1970s, Baldwin lived well, even extravagantly, on the income from his books, maintaining residences in New York City, France, and Istanbul, Turkey. He wrote three more novels, *Tell Me How Long the Train's Been Gone*, *If Beale Street Could Talk*, and *Just Above My Head*. He published *A Rap on Race* with anthropologist Margaret Mead, *A Dialogue* with the poet Nikki Giovanni, and a book of essays, *The Devil Finds Work*. But despite this productivity, many critics felt that his creative fire was flickering. In 1981, he traveled to Atlanta, Georgia, to cover the trial of child murderer Wayne Williams for *Playboy* magazine. The resulting essay, "The Evidence of Things Not Seen," raised disturbing questions about the racism that still lingered in American society.

In his last years, Baldwin divided his time between teaching at various American universities and relaxing at his farmhouse in the south of France. In 1986, the French government awarded him the medal of the Legion of Honor. He died in France on December 1, 1987, of cancer. With his bright, wide eyes, his broad grin, his warm, animated face, and his articulate and passionate speaking voice, Baldwin always made a strong impression on those who knew him. In his writing, he always confronted the complex issues of racial and sexual relations with searing honesty and much hope.

CHARLES CHESNUTT

America's first published black novelist, Charles Waddell Chesnutt, was born in Cleveland, Ohio, on June 20, 1858. Charles's father, Andrew—the son of a white southern tobacco farmer and his black housekeeper—soon moved his family to Fayetteville, North Carolina, where his own father lived, and opened a grocery store. When Charles was growing up, he spent his free time working in the store, and the countless stories he heard from the customers stayed with him all his life. An avid reader as well as a keen listener, he spent most of his earnings in the local bookstore.

Young Charles was an excellent student, but when he was 14 his father decided that it was time for himto leave school and get a full-time job. Charles went to work for a saloon keeper, but before long his high school principal, Robert Harris, got him a position as a student teacher. Two years later, in 1872, Harris's brother Cicero hired the 16-year-old Chesnutt to be the assistant principal of his school in the city of Charlotte, North Carolina. Chesnutt continued to be a voracious reader, devouring books on literature, history, mathematics, and education. In 1875, feeling lonely while on a teaching assignment in South Carolina, he began to keep a journal in which he developed ideas that would later appear in his writings.

Chesnutt's solitude was to end a year later when he returned to Fayetteville to take a job at the State Colored Normal School, a new college designed to train black teachers. There he met Susan Perry, a Fayetteville native who shared his intellectual interests and greatly admired his energy and accomplishments. The two young teachers began to spend their free time together, and in June 1878, they were married. Their first child, Ethel, was born the following year.

Though he now had much to be pleased about, Chesnutt was deeply troubled by the racial situation in the post–Civil War South. The end of the war and the freeing of the slaves more than a decade earlier had not ushered in an era of social equality; the old injustices remained in slightly less obvious forms. Chesnutt himself, with his fair skin, blue eyes, and brown hair, was in a particularly difficult position. Racist whites still considered him inferior because of his African blood; his fellow blacks, knowing that he could easily "pass" for white whenever he chose, often regarded him as an outsider. Believing that he could escape this dilemma in the North, Chesnutt took leave of his family temporarily in 1878 and traveled to Washington, D.C., in search of work.

Chesnutt could not find a decent job in the nation's capital, and he soon returned to Fayetteville, taking over as principal of the Normal School upon the death of Robert Harris. Shortly thereafter, Susan Chesnutt gave birth to another daughter, Helen. Chesnutt was earning enough to support his growing family in comfort, but his glimpse of life in the big city had left its mark. Chesnutt wanted more than a secure position—he wanted fame, and he wanted to give his children more opportunities than he had enjoyed. The only way to achieve this, he decided, was by establishing himself as a writer. Against the advice of many friends and relatives, Chesnutt again said good-bye to his family and boarded a train for New York City.

Chesnutt had taken great pains to learn the art of shorthand, and his skills as a stenographer earned him a job with a New York financial newspaper. But he soon realized that New York was a very expensive place in which to raise a growing family. (While there, he received news of the birth of a son, Edwin.) Chesnutt then decided on Cleveland, the city of his birth, as the most likely place to settle. He quickly established himself in the midwestern metropolis, working as a stenographer in a judge's office and studying law at night. In 1884, he was finally able to send for his family.

Throughout his time in Cleveland, Chesnutt had worked on his writing whenever possible, refining his skills and hoping for a break. His opportunity arrived in the form of a story contest sponsored by S. S. McClure's newspaper syndicate. Chesnutt submitted a story entitled "Uncle Peter's House," and although he did not win the contest, the story impressed McClure, who bought it for $10 and then resold it to a Cleveland newspaper.

Published in 1885, Chesnutt's story was the first work of fiction in decades to depict blacks as ordinary human beings rather than scoundrels or likeable fools. In the two years following his breakthrough, Chesnutt sold seven more stories to McClure, published a number of poems and sketches in various magazines, and passed the Ohio bar exam with the highest score among all the applicants.

When one of Chesnutt's stories was published in the influential *Atlantic Monthly*, he began to attract a wider following. In addition to his stories, he also published essays on the racial situation in the South. Before long, his fiction began to deal almost exclusively with racial themes.

Despite his success in selling his stories and his flourishing stenographic practice, Chesnutt was still dogged by an unfulfilled ambition—he wanted to see a book with his name on it. It took him nearly a decade to achieve this goal, but at last, in March 1899, the distinguished Boston firm of Houghton Mifflin and Company brought out *The Conjure Woman*, a collection of Chesnutt's stories retelling the tales of African sorcery he had absorbed during his days in the South.

Chesnutt's first book broke the dam. Within the space of a year, he found publishers for two other works, a biography of the antislavery activist Frederick Douglass and a second book of fiction, *The Wife of His Youth and Other Stories of the Color Line*. In this story collection, Chesnutt explored his most important theme, the fate of mixed-bloods in a racist society. Many reviewers—among them William Dean Howells, the nation's most influential man of letters—praised Chesnutt's writings for their quality and their subject matter. But in the straitlaced atmosphere of the age, others condemned his frank treatment of racial issues, especially the intermarriage of whites and blacks. Nevertheless, Chesnutt made an indelible mark on the literary scene—by publishing a book of fiction, he had achieved something no other black American had previously been able to accomplish.

Never afraid to take risks, Chesnutt decided in 1899 to abandon his stenographic business and devote himself completely to writing. His faith in his ability was quickly rewarded, for in the following year Houghton Mifflin decided to publish his first novel, *The House*

Behind the Cedars. Though the book's treatment of racial issues again aroused resistance and held down sales, the publishers were committed to Chesnutt. In 1901, they published his second novel, *The Marrow of Tradition*, which was based on a race riot that had taken place in North Carolina three years earlier. Predictably, the book was violently condemned in the South and praised in the North. When sales fell far short of the 20,000 copies the publishers had hoped for, Chesnutt reopened his stenography business. By any standard, he was a successful man. His daughters were educated at Smith College and his son at Harvard University, and in 1904 he moved his family into a spacious home on one of Cleveland's most appealing residential avenues.

As racial questions began to be discussed with more candor and urgency in the early years of the 20th century, Chesnutt's voice was one of the most eloquent to be raised in support of social and political equality. By the 1920s, when black culture began to emerge in a burst of pride and artistic achievement, Chesnutt was the dean of African American literature, respected by the younger generation as well as his own. In 1928, the 70-year-old author was awarded the Spingarn Medal by the National Association for the Advancement of Colored People (NAACP) in recognition of all his varied achievements.

Energized by the award and the praise it brought him, Chesnutt set to work on a new novel, entitled *The Quarry*. Unfortunately, Chesnutt's writing style was out of step with the times, which demanded more realism than romanticism, and the book was turned down by publishers.

Disappointed but not discouraged, Chesnutt continued to maintain his lively interest in a variety of subjects and to enjoy his hobby of fly-fishing, which he indulged at his family's summer retreat in Michigan. In 1932 his health began to fail, and upon returning from the office one afternoon he was forced to take to his bed. Four days later, on November 15, he died painlessly in the presence of his wife and daughters. Through his energy and courage, Charles Chesnutt advanced the still-unrealized goal of a just society, one in which, in his words, "men will be esteemed and honored for their character and their talents."

PAUL LAURENCE DUNBAR

The first black American to gain international recognition as a poet and novelist, Paul Laurence Dunbar was born on June 27, 1872, in Dayton, Ohio. His father, Joshua Dunbar, had been a slave on a Kentucky farm until he escaped to Canada and freedom by the Underground Railroad. During the Civil War, he returned to the United States and joined the all-black 55th Massachusetts

Infantry Regiment and fought with distinction near Jacksonville, Florida, and Charleston, South Carolina, rising to the rank of sergeant. After the war, remembering the kindness shown him as a fugitive slave by the people of Ohio, he moved to Dayton. Paul's mother, Matilda, was also a slave, a domestic servant on a Kentucky farm who had been sold away from her family when still a child. She tried to run away in 1863, but while on the run she heard about President Abraham Lincoln's Emancipation Proclamation and returned to the farm to await the Union victory. After the war, widowed with two children, she moved to Dayton, Ohio, where she met and married Joshua Dunbar. His parents never let Paul forget that he was one of the first generation of black Americans born in freedom.

Paul's parents divorced when he was still young, but they continued to live near each other and both took an interest in his education. Dunbar excelled in all-black elementary schools and at the age of 12 began to show an interest in writing poetry. "I rhymed continually," he said, "trying to put together words with a jingling sound." In 1885, he entered an all-white Dayton high school, but he continued to do well and had no difficulty making friends and winning the respect of his fellow students. One of his close friends was Orville Wright, who with his brother Wilbur would go on to invent the airplane. At the time, the Wright brothers were thinking of going into the bicycle business, and they had also built their own printing press and were publishing a local newspaper,

the *West Side News*. Dunbar wrote articles for the
paper, and soon the Wrights were also printing the
Dayton Tattler, aimed at the town's black readership
and edited and almost entirely written by Dunbar.

After graduation, Dunbar tried to get a job as
a reporter for one of Dayton's newspapers, but he
quickly discovered that black journalists were not
in demand. Instead, he went to work as an elevator
operator in a local bank building, but his poems,
published in the newspapers that would not hire him,
began to attract attention beyond Dayton, and Orville
Wright urged him to publish a collection of his works
in book form. In 1892, encouraged by a letter of
admiration from the esteemed poet James Whitcomb
Riley, he published at his own expense an anthology
of 56 poems under the title *Oak and Ivy*. Dunbar wrote
in the romantic, lyrical style of his favorite poets,
Percy Bysshe Shelley, John Keats, and Alfred Lord
Tennyson, but he celebrated the nobility of ordinary
people leading ordinary lives, and he successfully captured the sounds and rhythms of black speech. Many
of the poems were nostalgic in tone and looked back
toward a simpler country life, a popular theme in the
post–Civil War period of industrial expansion and
rapid change.

Dunbar's reputation began to grow, and in 1893
the editors of the *Dayton Herald* asked him to go to
Chicago to report on the nation's first World's
Fair, the World's Columbian Exposition. In Chicago,
he worked briefly as a secretary for the fiery antislavery activist Frederick Douglass, recently retired as

foreign minister to Haiti. The experience encouraged Dunbar to seek a wider audience for his work and to write more poems dealing with the struggle for racial equality.

The Wrights printed a flier for him, advertising his skills as a poet and lecturer, and Dunbar began to give poetry readings in many cities. He worked briefly as a law clerk for a prominent Dayton attorney but soon found that the work interfered with his writing and abandoned it. In 1894, the prestigious literary magazine *Century* published three of his poems, and he determined to find some way to make a living as a poet. In 1896, he published a second anthology of poetry, *Majors and Minors*, which was favorably reviewed by the novelist William Dean Howells in *Harper's Weekly*, bringing Dunbar to national attention. According to Howells, Dunbar was "so far as I know, the first man of his color to study his race objectively, to analyze it to himself, and then to represent it in art as he felt it and found it to be; to represent it humorously, yet tenderly, and above all so faithfully that we know the portrait to be undeniably like . . . intellectually Dunbar makes a stronger claim for the Negro than any Negro has yet done."

In the summer of 1896, Dunbar traveled to New York City to meet Howells, who was then regarded as America's foremost man of letters. While there, he signed a contract with Dodd, Mead & Company for his third anthology, *Lyrics of Lowly Life*, which gained him an international reputation as a poet. In 1897, he traveled to London, where he met the black composer Samuel Coleridge-Taylor, and the two men collaborated on a number of choral works that set Dunbar's poetry to music. In 1898, he returned to the United States, married the poet Alice Ruth Moore, and accepted a position as an assistant librarian at the Library of Congress in Washington, D.C. He worked with the black musician Will Marion Cook on *Clorindy*, a musical about the popular dance craze the cakewalk, wrote a volume of short stories about the Deep South entitled *Folks from Dixie*, and published his first novel, *The Uncalled*. But one of the main characters of *The Uncalled* was a white man, and critics attacked Dunbar for not sticking to what he knew best—the lives of black folk. Angry that he was being narrowly defined as a black writer, Dunbar began to speak and write more forcefully about racism and prejudice in American society.

In 1899, Dunbar published his fourth book of poetry, *Lyrics of the Hearthside*, but he found himself increasingly bothered by a hacking cough that would not go away. Widely heralded as the "poet laureate of the Negro race," he gave up his job with the Library of Congress and tried to support himself with lecture tours and poetry readings, but his health did not improve. In April 1899, while in New York City on his way to Albany to meet with Governor Theodore Roosevelt, he collapsed in Grand Central Terminal. He was diagnosed as suffering from pneumonia and underwent a long period of recuperation in the Catskill Mountains of upstate New York and in Denver, Colorado, but his real ailment—

tuberculosis—had been misdiagnosed, and he never fully recovered.

Though Dunbar cut down on his poetry readings and speaking engagements, he continued to write. In 1901 and 1902 he completed two novels, *The Fanatics* and *The Sport of the Gods*, both of which, unlike some of his earlier sentimental writing, took a harsher and more realistic look at race relations in the United States. These books were pioneering works that would greatly influence Claude McKay, James Weldon Johnson, Langston Hughes, and other young black writers of the Harlem Renaissance of the 1920s and encourage them to speak bluntly about problems of race.

By 1903, Dunbar's already precarious health had been further undermined by a drinking problem, which was aggravated by his doctors' prescription of wine and whiskey to treat his respiratory problems. He had separated from his wife and returned to live with his mother in Dayton, Ohio. He had witnessed race riots and subtle forms of segregation in northern cities, and his writings grew angrier and more despairing. He published several more collections of poetry—*Lyrics of Love and Laughter* and *Lyrics of Sunshine and Shadow* in 1903 and *L'il' Gal* in 1904—that revealed the poet's darker mood, but his energies were waning. "Something within me seems to be dead," he said. "There is not spirit or energy left in me."

Upset at the breakup of his marriage, at his publishers (who seemed only to want more verse in black dialect), and at his own failing health, Paul Laurence

Dunbar died of tuberculosis on February 9, 1906. He was survived by his mother, who lived to the age of 95 in the house that is now a public museum dedicated to the poet. His *Complete Poems* was published posthumously in 1913. Though his style of poetry is unfashionable today, Paul Laurence Dunbar was the first black writer to be accepted as an American man of letters and the first to teach that the lives of black people were an integral part of the American experience.

RALPH ELLISON

The author of one of the most important American novels of the 20th century, Ralph Waldo Ellison was born on March 1, 1914, in Oklahoma City, Oklahoma. At the turn of the century, Oklahoma was a new, sparsely settled territory, and Ralph's parents, along with thousands of other black Americans, had migrated there from the Deep South in search of a better way of life. Ralph's father, Lewis

Ellison, had high hopes for his son and named him after the 19th-century poet and philosopher Ralph Waldo Emerson, whose notion of "self-reliance" seemed to the father the key to success. Lewis Ellison died three years after his oldest son was born; after reading several of Emerson's works in school, Ralph, unduly burdened by his father's expectations, refused to use his middle name and vowed never to read Emerson again.

After the death of his father, Ralph's mother, Ida, worked as a maid and building superintendent to support Ralph and his younger brother. She brought home old books, magazines, and records to encourage her children's interests in whatever fascinated them. "They spoke to me of a life which was broader and more interesting," Ellison said of the things his mother brought him, "and although it was not really a part of my own life, I never thought they were not for me simply because I happened to be a Negro. They were things which spoke of a world I could someday make my own." One of Ralph's first loves was music. He worked in a drugstore where local jazz musicians often came by, and at Douglass High School he learned to play the trumpet and the saxophone. From his mother's African Methodist Episcopalian church he learned black spirituals and hymns, and he dreamed of becoming a musician and composing a symphony.

In 1933, Ellison received a state scholarship to study music at the prestigious all-black Tuskegee Institute in Alabama. Ellison was never comfortable at Tuskegee, and he could not adjust to the intense racial segregation off campus. But while there, he developed an interest in literature, discovering the modernists of the world literary scene—Ernest Hemingway, T. S. Eliot, Ezra Pound, and James Joyce. He perceived in the works of these writers new rhythms and a new use of language that reminded him of jazz and could be adapted to express the black experience. In Ellison's third year at Tuskegee there was a problem with his scholarship, and in the spring of 1936 he decided to go to New York City, partly to earn the money to continue school and partly to experience the cultural life of the city's famous black community, Harlem.

In the 1920s, a new generation of black writers, musicians, and artists launched the Harlem Renaissance, exploring the black experience with a new intellectual freedom, supported by a large, sophisticated urban black audience. By the time Ellison arrived in New York City in 1936, the Great Depression had sapped some of Harlem's vitality, but it was still a stimulating environment for a would-be artist, and such prominent black writers as W. E. B. Du Bois and Arna Bontemps were still active. "I thought of it," Ellison said, "as the freest of American cities and considered Harlem as the site and symbol of Afro-American progress." Ellison studied briefly with the black sculptor Augusta Savage and met the novelist Richard Wright and the poet Langston Hughes, who introduced him to the politically engaged novels of the French writer André Malraux.

To this point in his life, Ellison had planned on becoming a composer, but his new friendships, especially with Wright, gradually convinced him to make literature his vocation. "He had as much curiosity about how writing is written as I had about how music is composed," Ellison later wrote about Wright, "and our curiosity concerning artistic creation became the basis of our friendship." When an audition for Duke Ellington's Orchestra failed to work out, Ellison gave up music and any plans to return to Tuskegee, now determined to become a writer. "My ambitions as a composer had been fatally diverted," Wright later said about this period of his life.

In 1938, Ellison went to work for the Federal Writers' Project, a division of the Works Progress Administration (WPA), a depression-era program designed to alleviate unemployment. His assignment was to interview hundreds of black New Yorkers and help prepare a living history of their experiences. In 1939, he began to publish short stories. In 1942, he left the Federal Writers' Project to become managing editor of the new radical magazine *Negro Quarterly*. Many young black artists of the period were attracted to the radical ideas of the Communist party, but when the party, during World War II, refused to protest segregated army units, Ellison lost interest in the organization. In 1943, he joined the racially mixed merchant marine and worked for two years as a ship's cook and baker, continuing to write stories throughout the war. In 1946, he married Fanny

McConnell, a Fisk University graduate with a strong interest in his writing.

After the war, Ellison began to work seriously on the novel that would make him famous, *Invisible Man*. Parts of the book were published in British and American literary magazines as early as 1947, but the finished novel was first published in 1952. *Invisible Man* is an allegory, a symbolic story deeply influenced by surrealist trends in modern European literature. It tells of an unnamed southern black youth trying to survive in a world of white hypocrisy that denies him a sense of individual identity. Forced to compete in a world where whites make the rules and blackness must be denied, the hero comes to think of himself as "invisible," a nonperson not only to others but to himself. "At first you tell yourself it's all a dirty joke, or that it's due to the 'political situation,'" Ellison's narrator explains, "but deep down you come to suspect that you've yourself to blame, and you stand naked and shivering before the millions of eyes who look through you unseeingly."

Ellison hoped that the novel would speak as profoundly to whites as it did to blacks. "I conceived of the novel," he said, "as an account, on the specific level, of a young Negro American's experience. But I hoped at the same time to write so well that anyone who shared everything except his racial identity could identify with it, because there was never any questions in my mind that Negroes were human, and thus being human, their experience became metaphors for the experiences of other people."

Invisible Man was an immediate success, and in 1953 it won the National Book Award, making Ellison the first black writer so honored. In 1955, Ellison received a fellowship from the American Academy of Arts and Letters and spent two years in Rome, Italy, trying to write a second novel on similar themes. When the novel simply would not come together, he published various parts of it as short stories. In 1964, he published *Shadow and Act*, a collection of essays on how deeply all of American culture had been influenced by the black experience. During the 1960s, an increasingly militant civil rights movement, embittered by the assassinations of its leaders and anxious to build a separate black culture, turned away from Ellison, who was steadfast in his refusal to adopt political labels. He saw the black struggle for racial equality as a uniquely American experience, for example, and showed little interest in its African roots. But *Invisible Man* continued to sell and has not been out of print since it first appeared.

In the late 1960s, Ellison began to lecture at major American universities. He and his wife bought an old farm in Plainfield, Massachusetts, hoping to retire to the country. But in 1967 the farm burned down, destroying much of his work in progress. In 1970, he received a literary award from the French government, which was presented to him by the writer who had so excited him as a young man, André Malraux, who was now the French minister of cultural affairs. In 1975, he returned to Oklahoma City for the dedication of the Ralph Ellison Branch Library. He received several honorary degrees and participated in many arts councils and foundations that created opportunities for new black artists. In 1985, Ellison published *Going to the Territory*, another collection of essays about the nature of American literature and artists such as Richard Wright and Duke Ellington. Ellison continues to act as a spokesman for black artists, but always on his own terms. "My problem was that I always tried to go in everyone's way but my own," Ellison had written in *Invisible Man*. "I have also been called one thing and then another while no one really wished to hear what I called myself. So after years of trying to adopt the opinions of others I finally rebelled."

Alex Haley, who electrified the American public with his award-winning family saga, *Roots*, was born on August 11, 1921, in Ithaca, New York. At the time of his birth, his parents, Simon Haley and Bertha Palmer Haley, were both graduate students. Because it was difficult for the young parents to care for an infant while pursuing their education, they brought baby Alex to Henning, Tennessee, so that he could be cared for by his maternal grand-parents, Will and Cynthia Palmer.

The family was eventually reunited, but when Alex was 10, his mother died. Simon Haley, now a college dean, carried on as best he could and pushed his children to excel, but his message was not well received by Alex, who missed his mother and resented his father for remarrying after two years. Though he was bright enough to graduate from high school and enter college at the age of 15, Alex had no idea what he wanted to do with his life. After two years of study, he dropped out and enlisted in the U.S. Coast Guard for a three-year hitch.

In the Coast Guard, Haley was assigned to a cargo-ammunition ship on duty in the Southwest Pacific, where he served first as a messboy and then as a cook. Bored by the long periods of inactivity common in shipboard life, Haley read everything in the ship's library and wrote long letters to all of his friends and relatives. When his shipmates discovered that Haley had a way with words, he began tapping out love letters to women all over the globe on his small portable typewriter. Having started in this vein, Haley began to write sentimental love stories, which he hoped to sell to various romance magazines. The editors sent back a steady stream of rejection slips, but Haley had begun to think of himself as a writer.

The Coast Guard made use of Haley's writing skills by shifting him to a public relations job in New York City. While writing speeches for other officers, he grew interested in the history of the Coast Guard and began to write adventure stories based on the yarns he had heard from former shipmates. When three of these pieces were accepted by *Coronet* magazine, Haley's literary fortunes took a major turn for the better.

In the end, Haley's 3-year hitch in the Coast Guard turned into a full 20-year career. When he retired from the service in 1959, he applied for work with a number of advertising and public relations firms in New York. Though he had first-rate qualifications, it became clear that big-time public relations was a whites-only affair. Haley then decided to go for broke: he found a dingy one-room apartment in Greenwich Village and spent all his waking hours at the typewriter.

The determined author endured some hard times ("One day I was down to 18 cents and a can of sardines," he later recalled), but by the end of the year the popular magazine *Reader's Digest* commissioned him to write a series of celebrity profiles. This led to an assignment from *Playboy*, the successful men's magazine, for a series of interviews with notable African Americans. Haley proved to be highly adept in this forum, and his lengthy conversations with such important figures as Miles Davis, Jim Brown, and Leontyne Price were a great hit with the magazine's editors and readers.

The turning point in Haley's career came in 1962 when *Playboy* suggested that he interview the controversial Black Muslim minister Malcolm X. Haley, who had first met Malcolm in 1959, had a difficult

time gaining the militant leader's trust, but when
the interview was finally published, its uncensored
presentation of Malcolm's fiery antiwhite and anti-
Christian views caused a national sensation. As a result, Haley was approached by Grove Press with the
proposal that he do a full-length book on Malcolm.

Reluctantly at first and then with great frankness,
Malcolm told Haley the story of his life in a series
of long conversations, describing his progress, under
the influence of the Nation of Islam, from street
criminal to civil rights activist. As the book developed,
it charted Malcolm's evolution toward a more universal view of race relations and his growing estrange-
ment from the Nation of Islam. Just two weeks after
the completion of the manuscript, Malcolm was assassinated by Black Muslim gunmen in New York City.
Published in 1966, *The Autobiography of Malcolm X, As
Told to Alex Haley* was immediately recognized as a
unique document of a remarkable American life.

One of the things Haley had learned from Malcolm
X was the necessity for African Americans to take
pride in their identity and their history. Recalling
all the stories he had been told as a boy about his
own family's experiences, Haley resolved to turn
these recollections into a book. He soon interested
Doubleday, one of the nation's leading publishers, in
the project, and received a $5,000 advance. He ex-
pected to have a manuscript in a year's time.

As Haley worked on the book, however, he was
drawn deeper and deeper into the past, puzzled by
certain unintelligible words his grandmother had used

in her stories. After consulting scholars, he learned that these words derived from the Mandingo language of West Africa, and he decided that he could not tell his family's story without delving into its African origins.

After securing a grant from his old employers at *Reader's Digest*, Haley traveled to Africa and painstakingly tracked down a tribal historian, or griot, in a small village on the Gambia River. After the elderly griot had recited various incidents of tribal history for two hours, he mentioned a man named Kunta Kinte, who had disappeared from the village a long time before, shortly after the "King's soldiers" came to the village from abroad.

Haley was electrified. Kunta Kinte was the same man his grandmother had told him about, the ancestor who had been taken from his country by slave traders and brought to America in chains.

Deeply moved and excited by his discovery, Haley also understood the enormous labor involved in reconstructing the saga of Kunta Kinte and his descendants in the New World. He began by taking a freighter from Gambia to the United States, trying to relive the journey of the slave ship, and went on to talk with thousands of people and visit more than 50 libraries and archives throughout the world. Finally, in February 1976—10 years past its original due date—Haley delivered his manuscript to the editors at Doubleday.

The wait was worth it, both for the publishers and for Haley. *Roots: The Saga of an American Family* appeared in the nation's bookstores on September 17 and became an instant sensation. By the end of the year, more than 500,000 copies were in print, and ABC television had signed a deal to produce a 12-hour miniseries based on the book. The agreement included a payment to Haley of $1 million, a staggering fee for an author at that time.

The money did not immediately change the simple life-style of the 55-year-old Haley, but when ABC aired "Roots," he soon became a public figure of major proportions. The miniseries, aired on six successive evenings, was watched by 90 million viewers, the largest audience for a single program in television history. Boosted by the success of the program and the sequel that aired a year later, Haley's book was translated into 31 languages and sold more than 8 million copies worldwide. The author was showered with awards, citations, and honorary degrees, capped by a special Pulitzer Prize awarded him in 1977 for his "important contribution to the history of slavery."

Unfortunately, Haley soon learned that celebrity has its drawbacks. Following Haley's Pulitzer Prize, critics began to attack the historical validity of *Roots*. Haley had quite candidly stated that although the dates and major events in his book were accurate, he had made up incidents and dialogue in order to flesh out the story. Nevertheless, he was sued by two prominent black novelists who claimed that he had improperly used passages from their work. One suit was dismissed; in the other case, Haley decided to make an out-of-court settlement, against the advice of his publishers.

Haley was deeply hurt by the accusations, and his search for personal contentment continued to be a difficult one. His lifelong devotion to writing had caused three marriages to end in divorce; aside from meeting the countless people inspired by *Roots*, his main enjoyment derived from entertaining friends at the splendid estate he had bought in Tennessee.

By the 1990s, Haley found the time to begin another serious project, this one centering on an ancestor who was a slave owner of Irish descent. A television version of the story "Queenie" was broadcast with great fanfare in 1993, but the novel remained unfinished—Alex Haley had died of a heart attack on February 10, 1992. Though his final years were troubled by controversy, he will always be remembered for inspiring black Americans with a new sense of pride in their heritage.

CHESTER HIMES

Criminal, convict, black protest writer, and master of the detective novel, Chester Bomar Himes was born on July 29, 1909, in Jefferson City, Missouri, the youngest of three brothers. His father, Joseph, was a skilled blacksmith and wheelwright who taught at Lincoln Institute. His mother, Estelle, was also a teacher. In 1919, Chester's father accepted a teaching position at Alcorn A. & M.

College and moved his family to Alcorn, Mississippi, a move that appalled his wife because it exposed the family to the institutionalized segregation of the Deep South. Believing that Mississippi's segregated schools were worthless, Chester's mother, who was light-skinned and often passed as white, tutored him at home. One night, as a gesture of protest, she checked into a whites-only hotel; the scandal that resulted when she announced in the morning that she was black cost Chester's father his job and forced the family to leave town.

The Himes family settled first in Pine Bluff, Arkansas, where an accident in a high school chemistry lab blinded Himes's brother, Joe. The family then moved to St. Louis, Missouri, to obtain better medical treatment for Joe. In 1923, the family moved again, this time to Cleveland, Ohio. After graduating from high school, Himes went to work as a busboy in a hotel to save money for college, but he was seriously injured when he fell down the hotel's elevator shaft. After being denied treatment at a whites-only hospital, he suffered through a long and painful recovery. In 1926, he finally enrolled at Ohio State University in Columbus, but he could not adjust to the segregated life on campus and did poorly. At the end of his first year, at the age of 18, he dropped out of school.

With his parents continually fighting and his home life in disarray, Himes spent his time in the streets and fell in with the Cleveland underworld. He became involved in gambling, prostitution, check forging, and the illegal sale of liquor. He began to carry a gun. In late 1928, he broke into a house and stole some jewelry. He was arrested, tried, and sentenced to 25 years of hard labor at the Ohio State Penitentiary. In prison, Himes started to write short stories to pass the time. They were cynical stories of criminals and convicts trapped by their circumstances and driven to commit acts of violence. In 1934, two of his stories, "Crazy in the Stir" and "To What Red Hell," were published by *Esquire* magazine under the byline "Prisoner No. 59623."

In 1936, after seven years in jail, Himes was paroled. He came out of the penitentiary in the middle of the Great Depression, and work was hard to find. In 1937, he married his longtime girlfriend, Jean Johnson, and took a succession of jobs as a waiter and bellhop at several Cleveland hotels and country clubs as he tried to support himself as a writer. More of his stories were published by *Esquire* and *The Crisis*, the journal of the National Association for the Advancement of Colored People (NAACP), but there was little money to be made. In 1943, at the suggestion of the poet Langston Hughes, Himes went to Los Angeles to try to write for Hollywood, but in the film industry blacks were wanted only for menial labor. He got a job in the Los Angeles shipyards and after hours began to work on his first novel. During a three-year period, while continuing to write short stories, essays, and his novel, Himes held 23 different jobs.

In 1944, Doubleday published Himes's *If He Hollers Let Him Go*, a bitter novel about a black man in Los Angeles tormented by a series of racial incidents.

Though unrelentingly harsh in its depiction of race relations, the book was well received. Himes moved to New York and in 1947 finished *Lonely Crusade*, another novel, this time about a black union organizer who is betrayed by everyone he relies upon. *Lonely Crusade* was too harsh for the critics, however, who attacked it ruthlessly, for Himes's unrelenting portrayal of the effects of racial oppression on black Americans made both black and white readers profoundly uneasy. "If this plumbing for the truth reveals within the Negro personality homicidal mania," he said in a 1948 speech, "a pathetic sense of inferiority . . . arrogance, Uncle Tomism, hate and fear and self-hate, this then is the effect of oppression on the human personality. These are the daily horrors, the daily realities, the daily experiences of an oppressed minority."

In 1948, Himes briefly became a writer-in-residence at the Yaddo artists' retreat in Saratoga Springs, New York, but he was depressed by the negative reaction to *Lonely Crusade* and had difficulty writing while there. He managed to complete two autobiographical novels, *Cast the First Stone* and *The Third Generation*, but could not find publishers for them until the early 1950s. His marriage began to deteriorate, and Himes started to drink and use drugs so heavily that he experienced frequent extended blackouts.

In 1953, Himes decided that he could escape all his troubles by leaving the United States. In April of that year, following the path taken by his friend, the ex-

patriate writer Richard Wright, Himes sailed for
Paris. Wright helped him find a room across from the
Café Tournon, a popular meeting place for black
intellectuals. Himes met James Baldwin and other
black writers, but the constant discussions about race
depressed him, and in July 1953, he moved to London.
He was now living with Alva Trent, a Dutch woman
he had met on the way to Europe. In January 1955,
Himes and Trent returned to the United States briefly
and settled in Greenwich Village in New York City.
Himes had been writing novels and short stories
throughout this period, but they had been rejected by
publishers as too violent and melodramatic, and he
was now reduced to washing dishes and mopping
floors in Horn & Hardart Automats to support himself. In December 1955, he returned to Paris alone,
determined to find a new and more successful direction for his fiction.

"I [still] had the creative urge," he later said about
that period in his life, "but the old, used forms for the
black American writer did not fit my creations. I
wanted to break through the barriers that labeled me
as a protest writer. I knew the life of an American black
needed another image than just the victim of racism.
We were more than just victims. We did not suffer,
we were extroverts. We were unique individuals,
funny but not clowns, solemn but not serious, hurt but
not suffering . . . we had a tremendous love of life."

At the request of the French publisher Gallimard,
Himes abandoned his role as a black protest writer and
turned to detective stories. He studied the works of

Dashiell Hammett and Raymond Chandler and began to produce a series of novels and stories based on the exploits of two fictional black detectives in Harlem, Grave Digger Jones and Coffin Ed Johnson. The violent, melodramatic style that had frightened the critics of his earlier works seemed to work perfectly in his crime fiction. In 1957, one of his first efforts, *The Five-Cornered Square*, was chosen by the French as the best detective novel of the year. In 1964, he completed *Cotton Comes to Harlem*, another detective novel that was in part a satire of the "Back to Africa" movement of the black nationalist leader Marcus Garvey, a notion that Himes regarded, in the past and in the present, as absurd. "The American black man has to make it or lose it in America; he has no choice," he said.

Himes was enjoying renewed popularity in France, but in the United States his books were usually published in cheap paperback editions with altered titles and mangled texts. In 1965, in France, where he was, he said, "the best-known black in Paris," he married Leslie Packard, a columnist for the Paris edition of the New York *Herald Tribune*.

In 1967, Himes completed *Blind Man with a Pistol*, an unusual detective story that condemned the cruelties and absurdities of life in Harlem and drew no simple conclusions. In 1970, Samuel Goldwyn, Jr., released the film version of *Cotton Comes to Harlem*, and Himes's reputation in the United States finally began to grow. In 1972 and 1974, Himes published two volumes of autobiography, *The Quality of Hurt* and *My Life of Absurdity*. By the 1980s, he was suffering from Parkinson's disease, and on November 12, 1984, at the age of 75, he died in Moraira, Spain.

There had been many ironies in Himes's life. He had gone from petty criminal to prison convict to an internationally recognized author of crime fiction that was often based on his personal experiences. As a protest writer, his unflinching portrayal of the violence in the lives of black Americans had angered critics, but the same world of violence had proved acceptable within the context of detective fiction. He had left the United States seeking peace of mind and acceptance of his work, but he could never turn away from the source of his stories—the black ghettos of America—and he always believed that the future of blacks lay in the struggle for equality at home, not in running away to Africa or Europe.

America's preeminent black poet and a leading figure of the Harlem Renaissance, James Langston Hughes was born on February 1, 1902, in Joplin, Missouri. His parents' marriage was not a happy one, and they separated when Langston was very young. He spent much of his youth in Lawrence, Kansas, in the care of his grandmother, a strong-willed, religious woman who had been married to one of the men who died with John Brown at Harpers Ferry. As a child of a broken home, Langston grew up feeling a strong sense of isolation and loneliness. Unlike his grandmother, he found no consolation in religion.

In 1916, Hughes entered Central High School in Cleveland, Ohio. There, he began to find pleasure in books and literature. He developed an interest in poetry and wrote poems for the school magazine, copying the broad cadences and free verse of his favorite poets, Walt Whitman and Carl Sandburg. But from the beginning, his poems revealed an individual genius with bursts of song from black spirituals, blues and jazz rhythms, and a language enriched by regional black dialects.

After graduation, Hughes dreamed of attending Columbia University in New York City. When he was summoned to Toluca, Mexico, by his father, he went, hoping to get the money for his college education. James Hughes, however, wanted his son to become a mining engineer and refused him the money. Hughes then stayed in Mexico, working as a teacher and continuing to write poetry. In 1920, he sent several poems, including "The Negro Speaks of Rivers," to two of Harlem's most well known magazines, the arts journal *Brownie's Book* and *Crisis*, the magazine of the National Association for the Advancement of Colored People (NAACP), edited by W. E. B. Du Bois. The poems were published and, seeing his son's success, Hughes's father relented and agreed to finance his first year at Columbia.

Hughes arrived in New York in September 1921. He did not enjoy his year at Columbia, however. His classes bored him, and there were very few black students at the university. He preferred the city's entertainments—Harlem jazz clubs, Broadway plays by such playwrights as Eugene O'Neill and George Bernard Shaw, and new productions by left-wing theater groups. When his first year at Columbia was finished, he left school and moved to Harlem. He met Du Bois and the younger black intellectuals grouped around the NAACP and was encouraged to continue with his poetry. In early 1923, he wrote "The Weary Blues," a brilliant evocation of black speech and music, a pioneering effort in the creation of a new poetic voice for African Americans.

As more of his poems appeared in Du Bois's *Crisis*, Hughes began to attract a growing readership, but he was restless. In the summer of 1923, he took a job as a seaman aboard an old freighter, the *West Hesseltine*, and sailed to Africa. He marveled at the vitality and diversity of African tribal culture, but he also saw how the continent was exploited and impoverished by the European colonial powers. In late 1923, he shipped out again aboard the *McKeesport*, this time bound for Europe. He made his way to Paris, where he got a job as a dishwasher at Le Grand Duc, a popular nightclub. After hours, jazz musicians would come into the club for late-night jam sessions. The Parisians seemed free of prejudice against blacks, and everywhere there was artistic experimentation and excitement. In 1924, Hughes moved on to Italy, where he was stranded in Genoa without enough money to return home. Depressed and homesick, he wrote one of his most famous poems, "I, Too, Sing America," echoing the words of Walt Whitman and insisting that the black man be free to "sit at the table" with other Americans. Finally, Hughes found a ship to take him home. He had arrived in Paris with seven dollars in his pocket and returned to the United States with 25 cents. He jokingly said that his grand tour of Europe had cost him "exactly six dollars and seventy-five cents."

By the time Hughes returned home in late 1924, the publication of his poems in leading black journals had established him as a major artist of the Harlem Renaissance. But Hughes chose not to stay in Harlem. Instead, he moved to Washington, D.C., in 1925 to reunite with his mother. During this time, he wrote "Railroad Avenue" and "The Cat and the Saxophone," two poems that imposed violent jazz rhythms on verse. His works were now appearing in *Vanity Fair*, and Alfred Knopf agreed to publish his first collection of poems under the title *The Weary Blues*. In late 1925, while working as a busboy in a downtown Washington hotel, he slipped several of his works to the poet Vachel Lindsay, who had come in for dinner before giving a poetry reading. Later at the poetry reading, Lindsay announced that he had "discovered" a talented new black poet and read Hughes's poems along with his own. The incident helped Hughes find a larger audience outside of the black community.

In 1926, Hughes enrolled at Lincoln University, an all-black college near Philadelphia, Pennsylvania. When he was not studying, Hughes would travel up to Harlem to meet with a small circle of black artists whom the writer Zora Neale Hurston had named the Niggerati. In 1927, Knopf published his second collection of poetry under the title *Fine Clothes for the Jew*. He met Charlotte Mason, a wealthy New York widow, who helped to support him for three years. He graduated from Lincoln University in 1929, the year the Great Depression hit the country. In 1930, he published *Not Without Laughter*, an autobiographical novel about his childhood.

During the 1930s, Hughes became more radical politically, writing poems that protested racial and social injustice, and supporting many of the causes of the Communist party. He toured the South giving poetry readings, and in 1932 he traveled to the former Soviet Union. He returned to the United States and settled in Carmel, California, an artists' colony where a friend had offered him a rent-free cottage in which he could write. He joined the local branch of the John Reed Club, a group of left-wing artists, and became involved in supporting strikes by farm workers and longshoremen. In 1934, he published a collection of stories entitled *The Ways of White Folks*. But as his views became more radical, his audience outside the black community declined, and many of his works were turned down by publishers.

In late 1934, after a brief trip to Mexico to settle the estate of his deceased father, Hughes returned to

New York to work on several plays. *Mulatto*, *Troubled Island*, and *Joy to My Soul* were produced on Broadway in the late 1930s. In 1937, Hughes returned to Paris, where he was drawn into the Alliance of Antifascist Intellectuals, an organization that was formed to save Republican Spain from the right-wing rebellion of Francisco Franco. Hughes traveled to Spain and toured the battlefronts of the Spanish civil war as a reporter for the Baltimore *Afro-American* and the Associated Press. He came into close contact with other antifascist artists such as André Malraux, Ernest Hemingway, Lillian Hellman, and Dorothy Parker.

Hughes returned to New York in 1938 and produced the play *Don't You Want To Be Free?* for the Harlem Suitcase Theater, which he had cofounded with Louise Thompson. He tried writing for Hollywood but found the experience humiliating. No matter what he wrote, the film industry twisted it to fit its primitive stereotypes of black people. By 1942, he was back in Harlem, working for the Writers War Board with W. C. Handy, producing patriotic songs. In 1947, he became a poet-in-residence at Atlanta University, and in 1949 he was offered the position of poet-teacher at the University of Chicago. In Chicago, he began to publish a series of short stories based on the character of Jess B. Semple, a kind of black Everyman who reacts to racism with infinite patience, humor, and quiet determination. The Semple stories were probably the most widely read of Hughes's works during his lifetime. In 1951, he published *Montage of a Dream Deferred*, a third collection of poetry that used modernist techniques to paint portraits of everyday life in Harlem.

In 1953, Hughes was interrogated by the House Un-American Activities Committee about his radical political associations, and invitations for poetry readings and lectures dwindled. But Hughes was growing tired of politics. Lending his name to controversial causes had cost him a decent livelihood, which was hard enough for a poet to earn under any circumstances. When, in 1959, he put together a new anthology of his *Selected Poems*, he did not include many of his angrier attacks on social injustice. In the last decades of his life he tried to produce several Broadway musicals based on gospel music, but they were only modestly successful with the public. He helped to promote the works of younger black writers such as James Baldwin, Gwendolyn Brooks, Alice Walker, and Imamu Amiri Baraka.

In the early 1960s, Hughes traveled to Europe and Africa as a cultural spokesman for the John F. Kennedy and Lyndon B. Johnson administrations. By 1967, however, his health began to fail, and he died on May 22 in a New York City hospital. Langston Hughes's creation of a distinctive poetic voice for black Americans made him one of the most important figures in modern American literature.

RICHARD WRIGHT

Poet, playwright, political activist, and the first novelist to portray the harsh realities of black life in white America, Richard Nathaniel Wright was born on September 4, 1908, near Natchez, Mississippi. He was the son of sharecroppers who grew cotton on a small plot rented from a local landowner. Tenant farmers like the Wrights were often in debt to the landowners and lived as indentured servants on their farms, which perpetuated the plantation system long after the disappearance of legal slavery. To escape this fate, the Wrights moved to Memphis, Tennessee, when Richard was four years old, but his father could not find work in the city and abandoned the family in 1914.

Wright's early life was one of poverty, and he often did not have enough to eat. His mother's health was poor, and when she could not manage he was sent to an orphanage or to stay with his grandmother in Jackson, Mississippi. At the Smith-Robertson Public School in Jackson, Wright began to take an interest in literature. He published his first short story, "The Voodoo of Hell's Half Acre," in 1923 in the *Southern Register*, a local black weekly newspaper. But he was a rebellious student, rejecting his family's religious fundamentalism and defying teachers and counselors who urged him to accept his fate as a poor southern black boy. He wanted nothing less than to get out of the South and to get away from the oppressive weight of racism and segregation.

In 1925, Wright returned to Memphis. He worked at odd jobs, saving what money he could, dreaming of leaving the South. In the city's old bookshops he picked up used copies of magazines, including H. L. Mencken's *American Mercury*. Mencken was a sharp-witted satirist of American institutions who had attacked racial prejudice, and Wright was amazed that there were white men who felt this way. Mencken also talked about writers who were unknown to Wright—

Mark Twain, Joseph Conrad, Fyodor Dostoyevsky, and Leo Tolstoy—and Wright was fascinated. Blacks were not permitted to take books out of the local library, so Wright asked a young white friend for the use of his library card and began to read both the classics and the new American writers—Theodore Dreiser, Sherwood Anderson, Sinclair Lewis, and Mencken himself—who were savagely attacking social injustice and prejudice. Wright yearned to use words as weapons, as these writers were using them. Finally, in 1927, he saved enough money to leave the South, and the Wright family moved to Chicago, Illinois.

In Chicago, Wright got a job with the post office, but with the coming of the Great Depression in 1929 his hours of work were reduced, and he often had to stand on breadlines to get enough to eat. In 1931, he managed to publish a second short story, a murder mystery called "Superstition," in a local magazine, but this did little to improve his finances. Experiencing firsthand the plight of poor black and white workers during the depression, Wright's thinking became radicalized, and in 1932 he joined the Communist party and its special organization for left-wing writers and intellectuals, the John Reed Club. He began to publish protest poems in the party's literary magazines—*Left Front*, *New Masses*, *The Anvil*, and *International Literature*—expressing his belief that only socialism could eliminate racism from American society.

In 1935, Wright went to work for the Federal Writers' Project, a New Deal program designed to provide employment for writers. In 1936, one of his short stories, "Big Boy Leaves Home," was published in *The New Caravan* and favorably reviewed by the leading critics of the day. Struggling to develop his literary skills, Wright came into increasing conflict with the Communist party, which wanted him to produce formula works based on the party's views on black liberation. The party had dissolved the John Reed clubs because they were too intellectually independent, and though Wright retained his commitment to socialism, his relationship with the party grew increasingly strained. In 1937, at the age of 29, he decided to move to New York City, where he hoped to promote his writing career.

Wright moved into a furnished room in a Harlem hotel. Though he continued to annoy Communist party leaders by speaking in favor of creative freedom for writers, he was made editor of the party's new literary magazine, *New Challenge*. He also wrote articles for the *Daily Worker*. In New York, he met Ernest Hemingway, Lillian Hellman, and Archibald MacLeish, and he befriended two other aspiring black writers—Langston Hughes and Ralph Ellison. In 1938, his short story "Fire and Cloud" won a $500 Federal Writers' Project prize. In the same year, Harper & Brothers published *Uncle Tom's Children*, a collection of Wright's stories about the effects of racism on Mississippi blacks. The book was well received and brought Wright national attention.

By 1939, Wright was living in Brooklyn, New York, and had stopped writing for Communist publications to concentrate on the novel that would make him famous, *Native Son*. Published in 1940, it told the harrowing story of Bigger Thomas, an angry black youth trapped in an urban ghetto who is driven to commit murder and is sentenced to die in the electric chair as a result. Few novels had ever portrayed the pain of ghetto life with such uncompromising honesty, and *Native Son* was a stunning success. In 1941, Wright collaborated with Paul Green on a stage version of the novel, which was produced on Broadway by John Houseman and Orson Welles of the Mercury Theater group, with Canada Lee in the role of Bigger Thomas. Later that same year, Wright published *Twelve Million Black Voices: A Folk History of the Negro in the United States*, a photo-essay on black life from the Civil War to the present.

In 1942, Wright ended his association with the Communist party, which had continually hounded him to alter his writings and speeches to suit party doctrine. Ironically, as Wright's relationship with the party was ending, J. Edgar Hoover of the Federal Bureau of Investigation (FBI) and members of the House Un-American Activities Committee were beginning to investigate him as a political subversive, and these investigations would plague him for the rest of his life. In 1945, Wright published *Black Boy: A Record of Childhood and Youth*, an account of his early years in the South. Within three months, the book sold a half million copies. But in spite of his large readership, Wright was growing increasingly disillusioned. He was harassed by critics on the left and the right and placed under continual surveillance by government agencies. Praised as a courageous spokesman for black Americans, he still could not sit next to whites on a bus or a train or in a restaurant. In 1947, he left the United States to live in voluntary exile in Paris, France.

Wright thrived in Paris, meeting writers such as Jean-Paul Sartre, Albert Camus, and André Gide. The Parisians seemed free of racial prejudice and treated Wright with the same respect they showed their own intellectuals. He became involved in the Pan-African movement that sought to promote African culture and fight colonialism. In 1953, he published his second novel, *The Outsider*. Another portrait of black life in America, *The Outsider* was introspective and philosophical in tone, like Ralph Ellison's recently published *Invisible Man*. It was not as well received as his earlier works, and some critics suggested that he had been living outside the United States for too long to write about black life there.

In 1954, Wright published *Black Power: A Record of Reactions in a Land of Pathos*, an account of his trip through West Africa, and *Savage Holiday*, his third novel. In 1956, there followed *The Color Curtain*, a report on his participation in the 1955 conference of Third World nations in Bandung, Indonesia, and *Pagan Spain*, a book about life under the Spanish dictator Francisco Franco. In 1957, Wright published *White Man, Listen!*, a collection of essays that called upon the industrialized world to offer economic assistance to the nations of Africa. In 1958, he published his fourth novel, *The Long Dream*, but again critics accused him of being out of touch, of writing about the South as if it were still the 1920s and there was not a growing civil rights movement fighting to change things.

In his last years, Wright continued to produce short stories and plays, and he helped to promote the works of younger black writers such as James Baldwin and Imamu Amiri Baraka. He experimented with new forms, writing a large number of poems in the style of Japanese haiku. In 1960, he contracted a very severe intestinal virus and died in Paris on November 28 at the age of 52. No black writer before Richard Wright had done as much to expose the effects of racism in American life and to prod the conscience of the nation.

JAZZ STARS

LOUIS ARMSTRONG

One of the most acclaimed
American musicians, the man who introduced the
element of solo improvisation to jazz, thereby paving
the way for its transformation from popular entertainment to serious art form, Louis Armstrong was born
in 1899 in a house on Jane Alley in the Storyville
section of New Orleans, Louisiana. His father, Willie
Armstrong, who stoked a coal furnace for a turpentine

manufacturer, deserted the family after Louis's birth, and he was raised by his mother, Mary Ann "Mayann" Miles Armstrong, and his paternal grandmother, Josephine Armstrong.

Nicknamed the Battlefield, the black section of Storyville was a notorious haunt of gamblers, hustlers, petty criminals, and prostitutes. Armstrong's home lacked running water, and he often had no shoes to wear. But for all Storyville's poverty, there was one thing there to inspire little Louis Armstrong—music. Storyville was the most musical section of a most musical city; its musicians played in dance halls, cafés, casinos, brothels, on street corners, and at funerals.

The music of Storyville was jazz, a uniquely American creation that combined many musical ideas. To the bright sounds of the marching band, jazz added driving African rhythms and the syncopations used by ragtime composers like Scott Joplin. Some of its melodies were witty and aggressive; others had a mournful quality derived from the spirituals of the black church. Jazz was exciting, funny, loud, and joyful and expressed many of the emotions that black people found necessary to mask in their day-to-day dealings with whites. When Louis Armstrong was growing up, the black musicians of Storyville were perfecting a unique New Orleans style of jazz that they called Dixieland.

As a boy, Armstrong sang in the streets for pennies from tourists, and his heroes were the great cornet players Buddy Bolden, Bunk Johnson, and Joseph "King" Oliver. At the age of 13, he was arrested for firing a pistol in the street and was sent to the Colored Waifs' Home, a reform school run by black social workers, where he joined the brass band and learned to play the cornet. After two years, he was released, and he returned to Storyville. By day he worked shoveling coal; by night he played with small bands in local saloons. He began to follow King Oliver around town, showing up wherever Oliver played with Kid Ory's Sunshine Orchestra. King Oliver encouraged Armstrong, and occasionally the eager young musician was even asked to sit in and play.

During World War I, military traffic through the port of New Orleans increased. With thousands of its sailors daily roaming the streets of the city, the navy insisted that the city close its houses of prostitution. As night spots shut down, the opportunities for musicians dwindled, and they began to leave for other cities. When Oliver left for Chicago, Armstrong replaced him as Kid Ory's cornetist. In 1918, he married Daisy Parker, a former prostitute, and began to play with Fate Marable's orchestra, which worked on the big paddle boats that ran up and down the Mississippi River.

It was aboard these elegant floating casinos and dance halls that Armstrong learned to read music. And although he was required to play formal arrangements of dance music, it was on the riverboats that Armstrong first revealed his genius for improvisation. In the middle of a live performance, during a cornet solo or while supporting other instruments, he would spontaneously compose new variations, and the melodies, harmonies, and rhythms always "fit" what the other players were doing.

In 1922, with his marriage rapidly failing, Armstrong left New Orleans for Chicago and a spot with King Oliver's Creole Jazz Band. For two years, Armstrong played with his mentor and idol's band, always in the great cornetist's shadow, but after his marriage to the group's piano player, Lil Hardin, in 1924, she encouraged him to strike out on his own. Armstrong took his wife's advice and lit out for New York to work for Fletcher Henderson's Black Swan Troubadours at the Roseland dance hall.

New Yorkers were hungry for good jazz. The city was then experiencing the glorious effects of the so-called Harlem Renaissance, and nowhere else in America were black writers, artists, and musicians making such an impact on culture. In such a heady atmosphere, Armstrong continued to grow artistically and to perfect his improvisational method, and he began to cut records, most notably five sides recorded in 1925 with Bessie Smith, the enormously popular "empress of the blues." But despite his success—"I went mad with the rest of the town," a colleague said about hearing Armstrong play for the first time—Armstrong soon grew restless with the Henderson group and returned to Chicago.

Over the next three years, Armstrong, as the head of a new band that he called Louis Armstrong and His Hot Five (soon expanded to the Hot Seven)—the other original members were clarinetist Johnny Dodds, trombonist Kid Ory, banjoist Johnny St. Cyr, drummer Baby Dodds, and pianist Lil Hardin—made more than 50 recordings that forever changed the course of American music. The group's first hit, "Heebie Jeebies," was followed in short course by electrifying new versions of "Muskrat Ramble," "St. James Infirmary," and the now legendary "West End Blues," which featured Earl "Fatha" Hines on piano. Armstrong's emotive tone on his instrument (he was now playing the trumpet rather than the cornet), his improvisational techniques, and his raspy "scat" singing, in which he replaced the lyrics of a song with nonsense syllables, made jazz musicians and listeners all over the country take notice. He was fast becoming a star.

In 1928, Prohibition came to Chicago, and as speakeasies and saloons shut down, musicians were thrown out of work. Armstrong returned to New York, playing at the Savoy Ballroom in Harlem and then working in the orchestra for the Broadway revue *Hot Chocolates*, composed by Thomas "Fats" Waller. Broadway gave Armstrong a taste of fame and fortune. He stopped performing with small jazz ensembles and put together larger bands that showcased his own playing. In 1932, he toured London and Paris, where American jazz was becoming popular. Onstage, he referred to himself as "Satchelmouth" because of his wide, trademark grin; a British journalist heard him wrong and coined the nickname "Satchmo," which soon caught on.

Though his personal life during this time was tumultuous (he would divorce Lil and marry twice more), and his business affairs were often in disarray (the artist was often the victim of unscrupulous promoters and managers), Armstrong was now entering the period of his greatest popularity. A crowd-pleasing showman as well as a profoundly serious artist, Armstrong by the end of the 1930s played regularly at the best jazz clubs in New York and Chicago, made appearances in Hollywood films, and reached millions of listeners with his recordings. During World War II, he toured the battlefields of Europe, entertaining American troops.

After the war, a new style of less melodic, more rhythmically and harmonically complex jazz called bebop captured the critical vanguard and the ears of younger listeners—"those cats play all the wrong notes," Armstrong complained of pioneer beboppers such as Charlie Parker, Dizzy Gillespie, and Thelonious Monk—but Armstrong, whose improvisations had paved the way for the even more ambitious forays of bebop's soloists, remained personally popular. With such masterful instrumentalists of his own generation as Earl Hines, clarinetist Barney Bigard, and trombonist Jack Teagarden, he put together a new small group, Louis Armstrong and the All Stars, with whom he toured incessantly, both in the United States and abroad.

Though critics argued that his best work was behind him, Armstrong achieved a new level of popular success in the late 1950s with his hit recordings of "Blueberry Hill" and "Mack the Knife." In 1964, he achieved the singular feat of knocking the Beatles from their number-one perch on the nation's pop chart with his vocal rendition of the title song from the Broadway smash *Hello, Dolly!*

While his fame remained undiminished, by the end of the 1960s Armstrong's health, compromised by his perennially grueling performance schedule, began to fail. In 1969, he spent three months in a New York hospital with heart and kidney problems. Persistent bronchitis made both singing and trumpet playing painful, and he began to spend an increasing amount of time with his wife, Lucille Wilson, in their Queens apartment. On July 6, 1971, at the age of 72, he died of kidney failure.

The world mourned his passing. One of the most popular musicians of his time as well as a serious artist and musical pioneer, Armstrong created an audience for jazz outside the black communities and beyond the borders of the United States. His influence remains immeasurable. "Nobody was bigger than Louis," Barney Bigard wrote about his friend—words that are as true today as ever.

COUNT BASIE

One of America's pre-eminent jazz pianists and bandleaders for more than 50 years, William Basie was born in Red Bank, New Jersey, on August 21, 1904. His father, Harvey Basie, was a groundskeeper on a nearby estate, and his mother, Lilly Ann, earned a little extra money for the family by taking in clothes for washing and ironing. The family was poor, but comfortable.

Both of Basie's parents played musical instruments, and they encouraged their son's interest in music at an early age. Basie started with the drums, but at the age of 15 he switched to the piano and began to play the ragtime tunes composers Scott Joplin and Tom Turpin had made popular in the 1890s.

In the days of silent films, movie theaters employed live piano players to accompany the action on-screen. Basie got his first break one night when the piano player at a local theater got sick and he was asked to fill in. He did so well that the theater manager offered him the chance to perform onstage with a band.

Seizing the opportunity, Basie and three friends formed a jazz quartet and were soon widely in demand as performers at dances, parties, and local clubs. He was quickly so successful as a professional musician that he dropped out of high school, a decision that he later said he regretted. After playing for a short time with Harry Richardson's Sunny Kings of Syncopation at the Hongkong Inn in Asbury Park, in 1924 he was lured to New York City by the flourishing music scene in the black community of Harlem.

Basie's skillful playing impressed a Harlem bandleader, and he got a job backing up a vocalist with the *Hippity Hop* traveling vaudeville show that kept him touring the country for over a year. Back in Harlem in 1925, he played regularly at famous night spots like Leroy's and the Rhythm Club, where after hours other local musicians would drop by to hold jam sessions and cutting contests in which they competed with each other to sharpen their chops. Under the influence of the stride piano style of James P. Johnson and the wild improvisations of Thomas "Fats" Waller, perhaps the two foremost jazz pianists of the day, Basie's playing became looser and more mellow.

Left stranded and broke in Kansas City in 1927 when the band with which he was touring broke up, Basie landed in a hospital for four months with a case of spinal meningitis. After his release, he tried to make ends meet by once again playing piano for silent films in a local movie house; to make his name known among local musicians, he circulated business cards on which he called himself the Count, imitating the noble nicknames of jazzmen like King Oliver and Duke Ellington.

In 1928, Basie went on tour with Walter Page and his Blue Devils, an outfit out of Oklahoma City that produced a smooth, synchronized, big-band sound using a strong rhythm section that would exert a great influence on Basie's style. In 1929, he returned to Kansas City's thriving jazz scene and began to play with the Bennie Moten Orchestra, with whom he toured the Southwest and performed on his first recordings. When Moten died tragically in 1935 as a result of a botched tonsillectomy, Basie formed his own band, the Barons of Rhythm, which performed regularly at Kansas City's Reno Club and soon attracted the favorable attention of record producer John Hammond.

As a result, in 1936 the Barons of Rhythm secured a recording contract. Basie now gave his group a new name—Count Basie and His Orchestra—and enlarged it from 9 to 15 musicians, including a rhythm section, four trumpets, and three trombones, a lineup that allowed him to begin creating the disciplined, velvety, big-band sound that would become the hallmark of the Basie style.

Although the orchestra's first performances, at such venues as Chicago's Grand Terrace Ballroom and Roseland in New York City, were somewhat ragged and were not especially well received, the group soon jelled and began producing the smooth, tight, yet swinging sound that Basie desired. In 1937, Count Basie and His Orchestra opened at Harlem's prestigious Apollo Theater with its new vocalist, Billie Holiday, who stayed with the band for a year. Success at the Apollo opened doors, and soon the group was appearing all over the East Coast, in Baltimore, Philadelphia, and Washington, steadily building a national reputation.

In performance and on the more than 50 recordings that the orchestra made for Decca Records, which include such timeless American classics as "Pennies from Heaven," "Roseland Shuffle," "Jumpin' at the Woodside," and "One O'Clock Jump," Basie's piano did not dominate the band but laid out a simple melodic line that pulled the other instruments together and gave his soloists space to shine in. His embellishments and improvisations were gentle and supportive and served to highlight the contributions of such virtuoso instrumentalists and musicians as smooth trumpeter Buck Clayton, innovative saxophonists Lester Young and Herschel Evans, rhythm guitarist Freddie Green, and powerhouse vocalist Jimmy Rushing; most often he used the piano as a rhythm instrument to back up the more flamboyant forays of the reeds and horns. Basie's was a style that often caused him to be underappreciated as an instrumentalist, though seldom by fellow musicians. "Basie don't play nothing," said one such colleague, "but it sure sounds good."

By the end of 1937, jazz fans were lining up in the streets to hear the new Kansas City sound, and Basie was rapidly becoming as popular as the famed Duke Ellington and the leaders of other celebrated big bands. Engagements in New York City at Harlem's Savoy Ballroom and other venues were commercially and critically successful, and in January 1938, Basie and four members of his band were invited onstage for a jam session by Benny Goodman, the phenomenally popular clarinetist and "king of swing," at his legendary Carnegie Hall concert. In the 1940s, the Count Basie Orchestra toured the country several times and was featured in several Hollywood films. The decade was good to Basie personally as well as professionally; in 1942, he married Catherine Morgan, a vaudeville dancer. The couple would be parents to four children, three of them adopted.

By the late 1940s, the Count Basie Orchestra, like many other big bands, began to experience problems. The rationing of gasoline during World War II made touring more difficult. Old musicians left the group and new ones joined, eliminating the natural camaraderie that had contributed so much to the band's unique harmonious sound. Arrangements had to be written down and taught formally to the band members, causing much of the spontaneity and improvisational quality of the group's best music to be lost. The public's musical tastes were changing; the era of swing and the big bands was coming to an end.

In 1950, Basie broke up his orchestra. For the next two years, he toured with smaller bands of six to eight musicians. These new enterprises were popular and successful, but Basie missed the big-band sound. In 1952, he and saxophonist Marshall Royal formed a new Count Basie Orchestra. Most of the musicians were new, and the music itself was fresh and even more polished than the earlier arrangements. Basie explained the difference by saying that he had "put mink coats on the chords."

Basie's second band was enormously popular, and in 1954 it made the first of several European tours. Vocalist Joe Williams's rendition of "Every Day I Have the Blues" pushed it to the top of the charts in 1955, and there were performances and recording sessions with Duke Ellington, Sarah Vaughan, Ella Fitzgerald, Tony Bennett, Frank Sinatra, and Sammy Davis, Jr. By the 1960s, Basie was as popular as ever, and he was asked to perform at the inaugurations of presidents John F. Kennedy and Lyndon Johnson. In 1969, when American astronauts first set foot on the moon, the song they chose to broadcast back to earth was "Fly Me to the Moon," featuring Frank Sinatra and the Count Basie Orchestra.

Despite his advancing age, Basie continued to perform as often as possible, constantly touring the United States and in 1971 taking his band to the Far

East; the pace soon took its toll on his health. In 1976, he suffered a heart attack; though he returned to performing after a six-month layoff, by 1980 he was so crippled by arthritis that he used a motor scooter to reach the stage.

Count Basie died of cancer on April 26, 1984, soon after completing his autobiography, *Good Morning Blues*. At his funeral at the Abyssinian Baptist Church in Harlem, Joe Williams sang a spiritual composed by Duke Ellington, Basie's only real rival, in terms of influence and historical importance, as a leader of big bands. His beloved orchestra lived on; under Thad Jones and Frank Foster it has continued to thrill listeners with its jazz mastery, reminding them of what Basie and many others always believed about his band—"that they were the best on the planet earth."

A saxophonist whose legend grows with every passing year, John Coltrane was born in Hamlet, North Carolina, on September 23, 1926, into a proud and well-respected family. His maternal grandfather, William Blair, was a prominent preacher; his father, John, Sr., was a skilled tailor and a gifted amateur musician. John, Jr., grew into a strong, athletic young man who had a gentle and thoughtful nature. At the age of 12 he joined a community band in the town of High Point, where the family had moved shortly after his birth, and took up the clarinet. As he learned more about music, he became interested in the saxophone and hoped to someday follow in the footsteps of the jazz greats Lester Young and Johnny Hodges.

The Coltrane family began to fragment when John was in his teens. His grandfather and father both died within a short space of time, a double loss that appears to have had long-lasting effects on John. After the outbreak of World War II in 1941, John's mother, Alice, moved north to Philadelphia in order to take advantage of the high wages being offered for war-related factory work. In 1943, when he graduated from high school, John joined his mother. Alice Coltrane supported her son's decision to pursue a musical career instead of attending college. During the day he worked in a sugar refinery, and at night he studied saxophone at the Ornstein School of Music. In 1945, he was drafted and spent the final year of the war in Hawaii, playing clarinet in a U.S. Navy band.

When he returned from the service in 1946, Coltrane resumed his music studies. He was living with his mother and his aunt, and both women encouraged him to devote all his time to music. Typically, he practiced late into the night, diligently going over the finger positions on his horn without blowing so as to avoid disturbing the neighbors. He also began to play in a number of rhythm-and-blues bands, and at this time he switched from the alto saxophone to the deeper-toned tenor saxophone, on which he was eventually to make his reputation.

During the late 1940s and early 1950s, Coltrane continued to develop his musical skills, studying and practicing relentlessly in the conviction that he was destined to become a great musician. He played and recorded with a number of leading musicians, including Dizzy Gillespie and Johnny Hodges, one of his boyhood idols. In 1955, his life changed in two significant ways: he married Juanita Grubbs, known as Naima, and he joined musical forces with the young trumpeter Miles Davis.

Davis, who was the same age as Coltrane, was regarded as the most exciting figure in jazz, the heir apparent to the brilliant saxophonist Charlie Parker, who had recently died. Coltrane was introduced to Davis by the drummer "Philly" Joe Jones; when Davis put together a group consisting of Jones, pianist Red Garland, and bassist Paul Chambers, he invited Coltrane to join. Now considered one of the great ensembles in the history of jazz, the group made its first recording, *The New Miles Davis Quintet*, in 1956, and followed up with several more. Coltrane did solid work on these recordings, but some critics felt that he was not at the same level as the other players.

Coltrane received a great deal of notice by working with Davis, but his mind was not always on his music. Always quiet and sensitive, he now became moody and withdrawn, and he was deeply involved with both heroin and alcohol. Davis, an intense and strong-willed individual, came to the conclusion that Coltrane was unreliable and asked him to leave the group in 1957, replacing him with another gifted saxophonist, Sonny Rollins.

After Coltrane's break with Davis, his family feared that he was on the verge of a mental and physical collapse, and they considered putting him into the hospital. Fortunately, Coltrane woke up one morning and announced that he was giving up drugs, liquor, and tobacco. For the better part of a week he remained in his room, consuming nothing but water. He emerged a changed man, and although he was known to smoke in later years, he never again touched drugs or alcohol.

Shortly after his recovery, Coltrane was invited to play with the pianist Thelonious Monk. Free of his emotional problems, he was able to absorb a great deal of musical knowledge from Monk, who was both a brilliant innovator and a prolific composer. At this time, Coltrane perfected his technique on the saxophone. Whereas most jazz musicians were able to improvise two or three related chords in place of the original chords in a song, Coltrane now found that he was able to insert *four*. In order to do this, he had to play as many as 1,000 notes a minute, a tremendous feat attainable only through years of practice. This technical mastery, in combination with his profound grasp of music theory, enabled Coltrane to create the cascades of sound that distinguished his breathtakingly dynamic and poetic solos.

After his stint with Monk, Coltrane rejoined the Miles Davis group, which was now a sextet, and played brilliantly on a number of acclaimed recordings, including *Kind of Blue*, regarded by many jazz fans as the finest jazz album ever made. In 1960, the group embarked on a highly successful European tour; at a March 22 concert in Stockholm, Sweden, Coltrane's playing reached heights achieved by few musicians in any field. When he returned to the United States, he knew that he was ready to go out on his own.

In 1960, Coltrane assembled a quartet that included pianist McCoy Tyner, drummer Elvin Jones, and bassist Steve Davis (later supplanted by Jimmy Garrison). Late in the year, the group released its first recording, *My Favorite Things*. Coltrane's work on the title track represents yet another musical experiment. Here he plays soprano saxophone and delves into a technique known as polytonality, common in 20th-century classical music but unusual in jazz. For all its novelty, the result was also appealing to the public: *My Favorite Things* enjoyed substantial sales and made Coltrane a major force in the jazz world.

Coltrane followed up his success with a series of now-classic albums, including *Crescent*, *Impressions*, *Meditations*, and *A Love Supreme*. *A Love Supreme*, released in 1964, had a special appeal for the young generation of Americans that was drawing its main inspiration from rock 'n' roll and taking a keen interest in non-Western cultures. In addition to its musical excitement, the album celebrated the spiritual principles of the Eastern religions, which Coltrane had found increasingly attractive since his personal resurrection in 1957. *A Love Supreme* sold more than 250,000 copies and made Coltrane a genuine cult figure, a musician whom many fans considered to be endowed with mystical powers.

While he was earning widespread adulation, Coltrane was enjoying a happy family life. His marriage to Naima had ended, but in 1963 he met the pianist Alice McLeod, whom he married two years later. When he was not playing, Coltrane spent most of his time in his spacious Long Island home, enjoying his children, practicing, gardening, and reading books on spiritual subjects.

However, Coltrane was not content to bask in his celebrity, nor did his commercial success cause him to grow artistically complacent. Even while making his most successful recordings, he had been experimenting with the style known as free jazz, pioneered by fellow saxophonist Ornette Coleman. In free jazz, musicians ignored the traditional chord changes and punctuated their solos with seemingly disconnected notes—in the case of saxophonists, startling shrieks and growls that disconcerted some listeners while intriguing others. Coltrane released his first free-jazz album, *Ascension*, in 1965 and continued to work in that style for the next two years.

By 1967, no one was sure what direction Coltrane's music would take. He was known to be in seclusion, preparing material that he felt was not yet ready for public exposure. Before long, it also became apparent that Coltrane was seriously ill. He had for some time been suffering from pain in his abdomen, and the doctors eventually diagnosed his ailment as cancer of the liver. Coltrane remained at home as long as possible, but on July 16 he checked himself into the hospital. He died the following day, two months short of his 41st birthday. Speaking to an interviewer a few years earlier, he expressed a thought that poignantly sums up his musical legacy: "I think the main thing a musician would like to do is to give a picture to the listener of the many wonderful things he knows of and senses in the universe." Succeeding generations of listeners—and musicians—are still reaping fresh insights from John Coltrane's vision.

DUKE ELLINGTON

Pianist, bandleader, and
America's most prolific and accomplished jazz composer, Edward Kennedy Ellington was born on April
29, 1899, in Washington, D.C. His father, James
Edward Ellington, was a charming and dashing man
who worked as a butler, a caterer, and later as a
blueprint maker for the navy. His mother, Daisy Ellington, pampered young Edward, whom she always

referred to as her "jewel." Both parents loved music and played the piano, but as a youngster their only son preferred baseball to music lessons. That ended one day when Daisy saw her jewel accidentally get hit on the head with a baseball bat. She decided then and there that piano lessons were a much safer activity for her beloved boy.

Ellington's lessons—the only formal music instruction he would ever receive—lasted only a short time. At first, he was still more interested in playing baseball, but after hearing a young pianist named Harvey Brooks play, he decided that he, too, would master the instrument, and he gave up sports for music. "I learned that when you were playing the piano there was always a pretty girl standing down near the bass clef end of the piano. I ain't been no athlete since," he once said in explaining his decision.

Ellington began to practice on his own, and he was soon playing his own compositions at friends' parties. Because he had grown into a handsome, snappily dressed, suave young man, a friend nicknamed him Duke. He attached himself to a local piano player, Oliver "Doc" Perry, and learned the tricks of all the popular styles—ragtime, stride, and jazz. A talented painter as well, Ellington made a fateful decision after graduating high school and turned down a scholarship to Pratt Institute in Brooklyn, New York, in order to continue playing music. He spent several years working for Louis Thomas, a nightclub owner who booked him to play at dances and dinner parties, and in 1918, he married Edna Thompson, his high school sweetheart. Soon he began to organize and book bands on his own.

In 1919, Ellington went to hear the greatest of the stride pianists, James P. Johnson, perform at Convention Hall in Washington. Eager to see if the local favorite could outplay the celebrated Johnson, friends pushed Ellington onstage for a "cutting contest." Impressed with Ellington's playing, Johnson became a lifelong friend and teacher. "What I absorbed on that occasion," Ellington said, "might have constituted a whole semester in a conservatory."

By the early 1920s, Ellington had assembled a superior group of musicians dedicated to good music and to Ellington himself, but Washington was not a big music town, and opportunities were limited. In 1923, Ellington, along with saxophonist Otto "Toby" Hardwick and drummer Sonny Greer, went to New York to break into the music scene in the predominantly black community of Harlem, which was then enjoying its famed Harlem Renaissance—an explosion of new ideas and talent in the fields of music, literature, and the other arts. "We were awed by the never-ending roll of great talents there," Ellington said. "Harlem to our minds did indeed have the world's most glamorous atmosphere. We had to go there." They formed Duke Ellington and the Washingtonians and began to draw big crowds at Barron's Exclusive Club. After moving his group to the Kentucky Club, Ellington met Irving Mills, a struggling music publisher who became his business partner for the next 15 years. Mills insisted that Ellington retain the rights to his songs and compositions and that he record only his own works so that he would earn more of the income from a hit record. Ellington and Mills would make each other rich, and income from Ellington's more than 2,000 original jazz compositions would support his band members when times were hard.

By the mid-1920s, the Washingtonians had added Bubber Miley on trumpet, Barney Bigard on clarinet, Joe "Tricky Sam" Nanton on trombone, and Harry Carney on baritone sax. They quickly evolved from a dance band into a jazz band, perfecting a unique, deeply rhythmic kind of jazz known as jungle style. Their big break came in 1927, when Mills booked the Washingtonians into Harlem's most famous night spot, the Cotton Club. Under the new name of Duke Ellington and His Orchestra, the band was a smash. They were soon making live radio broadcasts from the Cotton Club and becoming well known across the country for such hit songs as "Creole Love Call," "East St. Louis Toodle-oo," and "Black and Tan Fantasy."

By the early 1930s, Ellington was a nationally known bandleader and symbol of the Harlem Renaissance, and the "Ellington sound" was recognized by jazz fans all across the country. But Ellington's private ambition was to compose innovative new jazz pieces as serious instrumental music. He abandoned the "jungle style" and began to create more sophisticated compositions with complex, symphonylike orchestrations. His 1930 hits "Mood Indigo" and "Creole

Rhapsody" demonstrated the change, but the orchestra still sustained itself with Ellington's more traditional songs at clubs and dance halls. Trombonist Lawrence Brown, trumpet player Cootie Williams, bass player Jimmy Blanton, saxophonists Johnny Hodges and Ben Webster, and vocalist Ivie Anderson joined the orchestra, and with its expanded size it began to take on a big-band sound and some of the elements of the new style of swing, which used the piano, guitar, bass, and drums as a special rhythm section to hold the beat for dancers. Ellington's hits of this period included "In a Sentimental Mood," "Solitude," and "Echoes of Harlem."

In collaboration with composer and arranger Billy Strayhorn, Ellington enjoyed the most creative period of his career in the early 1940s. He scored hits with "Sophisticated Lady," "I Got It Bad (And That Ain't Good)," and "Concerto for Cootie." In 1941, Ellington established his own music publishing company—a most unusual achievement for a black artist in those days—and his orchestra recorded what would become its signature tune, "Take the A Train," as well as his music for the Hollywood revue *Jump for Joy*, a celebration of black life in America.

On January 23, 1943, Duke Ellington and His Orchestra became the first black jazz band to perform at New York's Carnegie Hall, an appearance that became an annual event through the early 1950s. By the late 1940s, however, big-band jazz seemed to be dying. A new generation of musicians—among them Dizzy Gillespie, Thelonious Monk, and Charlie

Parker—was inventing a sophisticated new kind of jazz, called bebop, that was intended more for listening than dancing. The crowds the big bands counted on turned to the music of the popular crooners.

Ellington managed to keep his orchestra together, but several key musicians left, including Sonny Greer and Lawrence Brown, and the band's playing during the early 1950s seemed uninspired. But in 1956, Ellington signed a contract with Columbia Records and rerecorded some earlier pieces with new arrangements for a band that now included a younger group of musicians. The rejuvenated sound of the Ellington orchestra caught on. In the same year, Ellington performed to great acclaim at the Newport Jazz Festival, introducing his music to a younger audience, and he was soon as popular as ever. In 1958 and 1959, the orchestra toured Europe. There were bold new compositions as well, like *A Drum Is a Woman* and *Such Sweet Thunder*, and recording sessions with avant-garde artists such as John Coltrane. In 1963, the orchestra toured Africa, Asia, and the Middle East at the request of the State Department. In 1965, Ellington wrote the Sacred Concerts to celebrate the opening of Grace Cathedral in San Francisco; in 1968, he won two Grammy Awards from the National Academy of Recording Arts and Sciences. In the 1970s, there were more world tours and exciting new compositions like New Orleans Suite, *Afro-Eurasian Eclipse*, and *The River*.

In 1973, Ellington discovered that he had terminal cancer. He finished his autobiography, *Music Is My*

Mistress, and died on May 24, 1974, at the age of 75. His son, Mercer Ellington, took over the orchestra and has kept it alive to the present day. Ellington still has millions of fans, his greatest recordings are re-issued yearly, and each new generation of jazz musicians rediscovers his music. A giant among jazz personalities, a brilliant pianist, creator, and leader of the greatest American jazz band, today more than ever Ellington stands alone as the foremost jazz composer.

ELLA FITZGERALD

Known to her fans as the First Lady of Song, Ella Fitzgerald was born in Newport News, Virginia, on April 25, 1918. Her father died shortly after she was born, and her mother soon took her to live in Yonkers, New York. Though times were always hard, Tempie Fitzgerald, who loved music, did everything she could to encourage her daughter's budding talent.

Ella studied music as a child, but her first love was dancing rather than singing. In 1934, at the age of 16, she entered a talent contest at the Harlem Opera House, where the audiences were known to have little patience for bumblers. When it was her turn to go onstage and dance, the teenager was almost paralyzed by fear and stood trembling before the audience. Desperate to avoid being hooted off the stage, she began to sing "Judy," a song she had often heard on the radio—by the time she was done, the audience was cheering, and she was clutching a $25 prize.

Fitzgerald now knew that she had the ability to succeed as a singer, but work was hard to find in the midst of the economic depression gripping the country. To make matters worse, her mother died, leaving her in the care of an aunt. Fitzgerald's big break came when she was introduced to Chick Webb, the diminutive drummer who led one of the leading swing bands of the day. Webb was impressed by Fitzgerald's voice, and despite her youth and inexperience he hired her as a singer. Webb and his wife, Sallye, also became Fitzgerald's legal guardians, taking her into their home and treating her like a daughter.

Fitzgerald played many dates with Webb's band at the Savoy Ballroom in Harlem and made her first record, "Love and Kisses," in 1935. She was now being taken very seriously by jazz fans, who marveled at her vocal range and her seemingly effortless mastery of pitch and harmony: by 1937, she had won the *Down Beat* magazine poll as Best Female Vocalist of the year.

The record that made Fitzgerald nationally known at the age of 20 was "A-Tisket, A-Tasket," a swinging rendition of the old nursery rhyme that Fitzgerald worked out with one of Webb's music arrangers, Al Feldman. The toe-tapping disk became a smash hit in 1938, topping the charts for 17 weeks in a row. Fitzgerald and Webb followed up on the record's success with appearances at posh New York hotels and Broadway theaters, in some cases breaking racial barriers by being the first black musicians to perform in these venues. In 1939, however, the warmhearted and talented Webb died of pneumonia, leaving Fitzgerald on her own once again.

Unsure of her future, Fitzgerald was surprised and gratified when Webb's former manager, Moe Gale, insisted that the band be kept together and renamed Ella Fitzgerald and Her Orchestra. Though a number of the band members actually ran the show, the change of title was a tribute to Fitzgerald's stature in the music world. For two years the band traveled throughout the United States, playing to wildly enthusiastic audiences.

When the United States entered World War II in December 1941, the big-band era effectively died; many musicians joined the armed forces, and gasoline rationing made large-scale touring impossible. The demise of the big band brought vocalists into the limelight; though recording activity was suspended due to a lengthy musicians' strike, Fitzgerald traveled to Hollywood to make a movie and appeared with the popular quartet known as the Four Keys. When recording resumed, she found herself much in demand, but she was asked to perform the sentimental ballads in vogue during the war years, when so many couples were separated.

Fitzgerald's talent could not be so confined for long. Yearning to return to jazz, she found herself drawn to bebop, the new style of playing that featured quicker tempos and sudden shifts of rhythm and harmony. Joining the band led by Dizzy Gillespie, the trumpet player who was one of bebop's pioneers, Fitzgerald worked out the vocal equivalent of bop instrumentals by singing scat, a technique originally developed by the early jazz titan Louis Armstrong. Instead of singing the words to a song, Fitzgerald would use her voice like a trumpet or a saxophone, improvising a rapid string of syllables that would propel the music in surprising and exhilarating directions. In 1947, she recorded two scat songs, "Oh Lady Be Good" and "How High the Moon." Both records became hits, establishing a style that was ever after identified with Fitzgerald.

Nineteen forty-eight was a pivotal year for Fitzgerald. First she married bassist Ray Brown and settled down with him in Queens, New York. In the same year, she met Norman Granz, a young music promoter who was eager to be a part of her career. Because Granz was known both for his commitment to jazz and for his willingness to champion the rights of black musicians, Fitzgerald agreed to work with him.

Granz immediately booked Fitzgerald into his "Jazz at the Philharmonic" tour, which had begun in 1944 and included such jazz greats as Lester Young, Oscar Peterson, and Roy Eldridge. Fitzgerald loved the tour and took all the hardships of the traveling musician's life in stride—even when Granz's insistence on integrated audiences caused trouble in the segregated South. "Jazz at the Philharmonic" took Fitzgerald all over the United States, as well as to Europe and Japan, where she gained legions of new fans. As Granz watched her perform year after year, he became convinced that despite her repeated triumphs, Fitzgerald had not yet tapped her full potential. He was so convinced of this that he offered to be her manager for a year without receiving any pay. Fitzgerald decided to give him a chance.

When Granz became Fitzgerald's manager in 1954, the first thing he did was to negotiate a release from her recording contract with Decca Records. He then signed her up with Verve, his own label. The extended-play record was just coming into vogue at this time, and Granz convinced Fitzgerald to record an album of Broadway show tunes, a project never before tackled by a singer with her gifts. *The Cole Porter Songbook*, released in 1956, was a revelation to listeners, who snapped up more than 100,000 copies, a phenomenal figure for that time. Within the next few years, Fitzgerald recorded albums dedicated to all the great American songwriters: Jerome Kern, George and Ira Gershwin, Harold Arlen, Irving Berlin, Duke Ellington, Johnny Mercer, and Rogers and

Hart. Each one a classic in its own right, together these albums endure as a treasury of American popular music. True to Granz's expectations, they earned Fitgerald healthy royalties and made her a household name throughout the country.

During the 1960s, when rock 'n' roll replaced more traditional forms of music at the top of the charts, Fitzgerald began to work less than she had in previous years. She had resettled in Beverly Hills, California, and was content to spend more time at home with her young son, Ray, Jr. (Her marriage to Ray Brown had ended after five years.) In the 1970s, interest in jazz began to revive, and Fitzgerald was in great demand for concert dates and even television commercials. As the extent of her achievements became more and more evident, a number of leading universities and colleges, including Yale and Dartmouth, awarded her honorary degrees in music, and the University of Maryland named its performing arts center after her.

Fitzgerald's health began to deteriorate during the 1980s, and at one point she had to undergo open-heart surgery. But she has bounced back from every illness, and her annual appearances at the JVC Jazz Festival in New York City are anticipated by music fans as one of the highlights of the year. In 1993, the Schomburg Center for Research in Black Culture held a celebration at New York's Carnegie Hall in honor of Fitzgerald's 75th birthday. Luminaries from all the arts gathered to express their love and admiration for Fitzgerald and to commemorate one more milestone in a life filled with breathtaking accomplishments. To name just a few, Fitzgerald had been named the top female jazz singer for 18 years in a row in the *Down Beat* poll and for 13 years in a row in the *Playboy* poll; she had won more Grammy awards than any other female vocalist in history; she had been previously feted at Washington's Kennedy Center, an honor accorded only to legendary entertainers; she had received the Whitney Young Award from the National Urban League for her contributions to African-American life; and the president of the United States had presented her with the National Medal of the Arts. Summing up the spirit and dedication that brought her to these heights, Fitzgerald once declared, "The only thing better than singing is more singing."

DIZZY GILLESPIE

One of the greatest innovators in American musical history, John Birks Gillespie was born on October 21, 1917, in Cheraw, South Carolina. His father worked as a bricklayer to support his nine children, but in his spare time he played piano for a number of bands that traveled up and down the eastern seaboard. Growing up in a home filled with musical instruments, young John fell in love with music and dreamed of someday playing in a big-time band.

When John was 10 years old his father died, and the youngster's grief drove him to become a troublemaker who was constantly in fights at school. Fortunately for him, a dedicated music teacher named Alice Wilson took an interest in him and convinced him to take up the trombone. By the time he was 12, John was playing both the trombone and the trumpet and was working hard to make himself a truly skilled musician.

When Gillespie was 16, his mother moved the family north to Philadelphia in search of a better life. Gillespie soon found that he could earn money with his trumpet and decided to make music his career. Like most jazz musicians during the 1930s, Gillespie began his career playing swing music in big bands. His idol was the leading jazz trumpeter of the day, Roy Eldridge. Eldridge was admired for his ability to play at great speed, with unexpected swoops and turns, and Gillespie began to copy his style. He did it so well that radio broadcast listeners often could not tell which of the two trumpeters they were hearing.

Because of his ability to play like Eldridge, Gillespie landed a job in Teddy Hill's band, which played regularly at the Savoy Ballroom in New York City's Harlem. During this time, he developed a flair for outlandish outfits that often featured a baggy suit, loud tie, wide-brimmed hat or beret, and a long cigarette holder. He loved to wisecrack and play practical jokes on his fellow musicians; during shows he would often put his feet up on the music stand and perform other high-spirited pranks. Legend has it that one of his fellow band members began to call him Dizzy, and the name stuck for the rest of his life.

Clowning aside, Dizzy Gillespie could play. By the late 1930s, he was being included in recording sessions with some of the finest musicians in jazz, including Coleman Hawkins, Lionel Hampton, and Ben Webster.

When Gillespie joined Cab Calloway's band in 1939, he came into contact with musicians who were experimenting with new styles. The most important of them was the saxophonist Charlie Parker, whom Gillespie met in Kansas City while on tour with the Calloway band. Parker, Gillespie, and other musicians, such as pianist Thelonious Monk and drummer Kenny Clarke, would often get together and improvise music that was faster, more inventive, and more complex than the swing music played by the big bands.

The turning point in Gillespie's career came when he lost his regular job after a fight with Calloway. Gillespie now found that he could make a living on his own. He soon began to play and record with the leading lights in the world of jazz. By 1945, when he and Charlie Parker had completed such now-classic recordings as "Salt Peanuts," "Ko Ko," "Billie's Bounce," and "Woody 'n' You," he was at the forefront of the new jazz movement known as bebop, which was to remain the dominant influence on jazz for years to come.

Gillespie always gave Parker full credit as the co-inventor of bebop, but Parker was an unruly genius who often missed performances and recording dates, making it necessary for Gillespie to provide the actual leadership and stabilizing force. It was Gillespie who dealt with the record producers and club owners, making sure that all the business arrangements were scrupulously carried out. Unlike Parker and many other jazz musicians, Gillespie stayed away from drugs and alcohol and was careful with his money. He gave much of the credit for his levelheadedness to his wife, Lorraine, a former dancer, whom he married in 1940 and lived with happily for the rest of his life.

In 1946, Gillespie created the Dizzy Gillespie Orchestra and once again changed the history of jazz. He recruited two leading Cuban musicians, trumpeter Mario Bauza and drummer Chano Pozo, who brought conga and bongo drums into jazz for the first time. From this mix of black American bebop and Latin rhythms came a new music known as Afro-Cuban jazz. The numbers recorded by Gillespie's band—most notably "Manteca" and "Cubana Be, Cubana Bop"—exerted a lasting influence on both traditional jazz and Latin music.

The hallmark of bebop was the small combo, and Gillespie's greatest contribution in the eyes of many jazz fans was the remarkable quintet he formed in 1946 with Parker, pianist Bud Powell, drummer Max

Roach, and bassist Ray Brown. The quartet had an often stormy career, but in 1953 its members were reunited (with Charles Mingus sitting in on bass) for a concert at Massey Hall in Toronto, Canada. Playing before a wildly enthusiastic audience, Gillespie and his group turned in a sizzling performance that has since been hailed as "the greatest jazz concert ever."

By this time, Gillespie was not only a trumpeter without peer but also one of the leading figures in American entertainment. Like his fellow jazz great Louis Armstrong, he was beloved by the public as much for his exuberant personality as for his musical ability. Gillespie reveled in his role as a master showman. When someone accidentally bent his trumpet, he decided that he liked it better that way and had all his trumpets made in the same pattern from then on. The image of Gillespie blowing his horn, with his cheeks puffed out and the bell of his trumpet sticking up at a wild and jaunty angle, became one of the most distinctive sights in show business.

In 1956, Gillespie brought jazz to an international audience when the U.S. State Department provided him with the funds to conduct a world tour as a musical goodwill ambassador. Gillespie was the first bandleader asked to undertake such a mission. He put together a group of musicians that represented a racial, ethnic, and religious cross section of the United States and delighted foreign audiences with classic music making and high spirits. (In the course of the tour he was photographed riding camels, charming snakes with his trumpet, and wearing the native costumes of various countries.) During this stage of his career, he also served on the faculty of the Lenox School of Jazz in Massachusetts and made brilliant recordings with such jazz greats as Stan Getz and Sonny Rollins.

Unlike so many musicians of his generation, who either burned out at an early age or fell into neglect when styles changed, Gillespie never lost his verve or his public appeal. Throughout the 1960s and 1970s, he led a variety of big bands and small ensembles, which he took on extended tours. He also revived his recording career, and his new recordings won Grammy awards in 1975 and 1980.

During the 1980s, Gillespie assumed the role of an elder statesman in the jazz world, appearing as a guest artist with a variety of bands. His energy was undiminished: in 1989, at the age of 72, he gave 300 performances in 27 different countries. His stature was such that 14 universities awarded him honorary degrees; the French government decorated him with the Legion of Honor; and his own nation honored him with the National Medal of the Arts.

In the fall of 1992, the Blue Note in New York City engaged Gillespie for a monthlong appearance in honor of his 75th birthday. During the month, the greats of the jazz world joined Gillespie on the bandstand, paying tribute to him as a man and an artist, most of them unaware that he was afflicted with cancer of the pancreas. On January 6, 1993, Dizzy Gillespie died in Englewood, New Jersey, leaving behind a creative legacy seldom equaled by any American artist.

BILLIE HOLIDAY

Hailed by critics as the greatest jazz singer who ever lived, Billie Holiday was born Eleanora Fagan in Baltimore, Maryland, on April 7, 1915. Her parents married after she was born and divorced when she was very young. Her father, Clarence Holiday, a traveling musician, soon disappeared from her life. When Eleanora's mother, Sadie Fagan, went north to work as a maid, Eleanora was left in the care of a cousin who often mistreated her. At the age of six, Eleanora went to work, scrubbing the steps of houses and doing chores in a brothel; there she heard the records of such early jazz greats as Louis Armstrong and Bessie Smith, and she forgot her troubles for a while by singing along with the music. She also began to call herself Billie after Billie Dove, a popular actress of the day.

When Billie was 10, a grown man tried to rape her; he was sent to jail, but the judge also ordered that Billie be confined in a reform school for her own protection. She endured two dreadful years in the institution before her mother managed to get her released. She then headed north to join her mother in Harlem, New York City's most important black neighborhood.

Life proved to be just as difficult in New York. Billie's mother worked long hours and had little time to look after her; by the time she was 13, Billie was working as a prostitute. After being arrested, she decided to find another way to survive, but with the arrival of the Great Depression in 1930, jobs became scarce. Before long, Billie and her mother had no money for their rent and were faced with eviction; searching desperately for some way to earn money, Billie entered a basement club named Pod's and Jerry's and asked for work as a dancer. The owner quickly saw that she was not a skilled dancer and was about to send her away. But the club's pianist felt sorry for her and gave her the chance to sing a popular song of the day, "Trav'lin' All Alone." As she sang, a hush fell over the crowded club, and some of the customers began to weep; when she was done, people threw money at her feet. Her career was launched.

Holiday was fortunate enough to arrive on the scene when jazz was taking hold of Harlem, and there were ample opportunities to perform in clubs and theaters. In these forums Holiday developed her unique singing style, improvising variations on familiar songs just as the leading jazz instrumentalists did. In 1933, Holiday came to the attention of the influential critic and producer John Hammond, who wrote about her in magazines and arranged for her first recording date.

Holiday's first real breakthrough occurred in 1935, when she had a successful engagement at Harlem's prestigious Apollo Theater. At this time, she also began to record in earnest, doing several sessions for the Brunswick label along with such star performers as pianist Teddy Wilson, clarinetist Benny Goodman, and saxophonist Ben Webster. The records established Holiday's reputation in the music world. She was soon able to buy a restaurant for her mother, and the two of them lived comfortably in an apartment upstairs.

Holiday also tried her hand at touring with the popular bands led by Count Basie and Artie Shaw, but she could not adjust to life on the road. Conditions were especially hard in the segregated South, where black musicians were barred from the better hotels and restaurants. Holiday soon decided that she was better off taking her chances in New York. She was now in demand as a recording artist; between 1936 and 1942, when a musicians' strike called a halt to recording, Holiday made a steady stream of disks for the Commodore label. As in her first recordings, she was backed by all the best players in jazz and was captured at the height of her form. The Commodore sides, wrote a later jazz historian, "constitute one of the major bodies of work in jazz."

In 1938, Holiday found the perfect showcase for her talents at Café Society, an integrated nightclub opened in Greenwich Village by Barney Josephson. In a nine-month engagement at the new club, Holiday became a full-fledged star. Combining her sophisticated vocal technique with raw emotional honesty, she made everything she sang—even the most shopworn standards—sound brand-new to her listeners. It was at Café Society that she first performed "Strange Fruit," a haunting, somber protest against the lynching of blacks in the South. When Holiday recorded the controversial song in 1939, she gained recognition not only as a singer but as a public figure.

During the 1940s, Holiday, now known to her fans simply as Lady Day, reached the peak of her popularity. She found steady work in the clubs sprouting up along West 52nd Street: the Onyx, the Spotlite, Kelly's Stable, and the Famous Door were among the night spots that signed her to sing before packed houses, paying her as much as $1,000 a week. At this time, Holiday began wearing a white gardenia in her hair, an elegant touch that soon became her trademark.

She also made two of her best-known recordings, "Gloomy Sunday" and "God Bless the Child."

Sadly, fame did not erase the memories of Holiday's painful childhood or ensure her a happy personal life. She had often been unfortunate in her choice of men, and this pattern continued when she married Jimmy Monroe in 1941. Monroe was an opium smoker, and Holiday soon shared his addiction to the potent narcotic. When the marriage began to come apart after little more than a year, Holiday turned to heroin. Before long, her drug habit was consuming half her earnings. "I was making a thousand a week," she later said, "but I had as much freedom as a field hand in Virginia a hundred years before."

For a time, Holiday's career continued to soar. She was voted Best Vocalist in an *Esquire* magazine poll in 1943 and two years later made her first concert appearance at New York's Town Hall. But she continued to use heroin, and the death of her mother in 1945 deprived her of the one person she could rely on for understanding and encouragement. More and more, she showed up late for performances or missed them altogether; she began to wear long white gloves onstage to hide the needle marks on her arms.

In May 1947, Holiday was arrested by federal narcotics agents on a drug possession charge. She threw herself on the mercy of the court, hoping that the judge would send her to a clinic for treatment. Instead, she was sentenced to a federal prison in West Virginia, where she underwent a harrowing drug withdrawal and endured nine and a half months of isolation and misery.

Those who knew Holiday well believed that she never recovered from the pain of her imprisonment. However, barely two weeks after her release, she enjoyed one of her greatest triumphs. Knowing how much her fans had missed her, Holiday's agent, Joe Glaser, booked her into New York's legendary Carnegie Hall. On March 27, 1948, a standing-room-only audience gave Holiday a tumultuous welcome. Her talents undiminished by her prison ordeal, she rewarded her cheering fans with one of her most brilliant performances.

Unfortunately, the concert did not completely revive Holiday's fortunes. Because of her prison record, she could not get a permit to sing in clubs; she earned a living during the 1950s with theater performances, but she eventually began using heroin again. Still she fought on, making a series of recordings for the Verve label and enjoying a highly successful 1954 tour of Europe.

In 1956, following another arrest, Holiday kicked her drug habit again. But she began to drink heavily, and her stage appearances were sometimes marred by drunkenness. Theater managers became wary of dealing with her, and audiences often came to see her out of curiosity, wondering if she would make it through her set. Once surrounded by admirers and hangers-on, Holiday now spent most of her time alone in a small apartment on Manhattan's West Side, drinking and watching television. In the spring of 1959, beset by heart and liver ailments, she finally collapsed. With hospital care her condition improved temporarily, but on July 17, Billie Holiday died at the age of 44. Thousands of fans attended her funeral, knowing that there would never be another singer like her.

CHARLIE PARKER

Perhaps the single most in-
fluential figure in modern jazz, Charles Parker, Jr.,
was born in Kansas City, Kansas, on August 29, 1920.
His father, Charles, Sr., once a vaudeville performer,
worked as a railroad chef, spending long periods of
time away from home. Finally, when young Charlie

was eight, his father left for good. An only child, Charlie grew up under the influence of his mother, Addie, a strong and devoted woman who kept things together by working long hours cleaning other people's houses.

Addie Parker urged her son to work hard in school, and his good grades encouraged her to believe he might become a doctor. However, when he reached high school, Charlie discovered the alto saxophone. Mastering the instrument soon became the passion of his life.

Along with a few school friends, Charlie formed a band called the Deans of Swing and played at dances and parties. His musical activities soon affected his schoolwork; when he was left back a grade, he decided to drop out and devote himself to music. Before his musical career was fully under way, he became a married man. Just short of his 16th birthday, he wed his high school sweetheart, Rebecca Ruffin, and the newlyweds moved into Addie Parker's house.

An early turning point in Parker's life came shortly after his marriage, in 1936, when he took part in a jam session at Kansas City's Reno Club, a mecca for top-flight jazz musicians. Hoping to make an impression, Parker took a solo during one of the club's famous jam sessions and faltered badly. After being hooted off the stage by the veterans, he left the club with an angry determination to redeem himself. With the help of a friend, he spent months studying music theory, working out chords and harmonies over and over on his horn. Finally, he was ready to begin his career in earnest.

Unfortunately, at this time Parker also began to develop the personal problems that were to make so much of his life a misery. He had been exposed to marijuana and alcohol at an early age, and by the age of 17 he had taken up heroin. To the dismay of his wife and mother, he began to pawn household items to support his drug habit, and his moods would swing suddenly from happiness and charm to anger and menace. Not even the birth of a son, Francis Leon, was enough to stabilize his personal life.

His musical life, however, began to flourish. After a stint in Buster Smith's band and a brief stay in Chicago, Parker set out for New York City. But he had a difficult time finding work and had to take a job as a dishwasher in a Harlem night spot. He did, however, have a chance to hear some of the great jazz innovators, such as the pianist Art Tatum, and to sit in on jam sessions with practiced players. During one of these sessions, he hit upon a unique method of improvising chord changes and developed a style that would soon create a revolution in jazz.

Before that happened, Parker returned to Kansas City in 1939 for his father's funeral. While there, he accepted an offer to join the Jay McShann Orchestra as first saxophonist. Around this time he also acquired the nickname Yardbird—later shortened to Bird—supposedly because of his extreme fondness for chicken.

His work with the McShann group earned Parker the admiration of his fellow musicians. But audiences were not yet ready for Parker's innovative solos, which seemed coarse and unmusical when compared with the mellow swing music that was the rage throughout the 1930s. Nevertheless, he continued to tour with McShann until 1942, when he decided once again to seek his fortune in New York.

After some difficulty, Parker found a spot in the Earl Hines Orchestra, but his unruly personal life began to get in the way of his music. His heroin addiction was now out of control. In addition, he had divorced his first wife, Rebecca, married the dancer Geraldine Scott, and then split up with Scott only a year later. His frequent absences soon led to his dismissal from Hines's band. After a brief stint with Billy Eckstine's band in 1944, Parker decided to devote his energies to smaller groups, where his creativity could be unleashed.

Parker now found a home on New York's West 52nd Street, where jazz clubs crowded both sides of the block between Fifth and Sixth avenues. At a club named the Three Deuces, he teamed up with Dizzy Gillespie, Ray Brown, Bud Powell, and Max Roach. With Parker and Gillespie leading the way, the quintet pioneered the bebop revolution throughout 1944 and 1945. Spurning the conventions of swing, they improvised fast-paced, free-ranging variations on familiar tunes that left their audiences breathless.

After Gillespie moved on to form his own big band, Parker remained on 52nd Street to lead his own combo, commanding a growing corps of devoted fans. At the time, he also made a series of recordings with Gillespie that became jazz classics, among them "Ko Ko," "Billie's Bounce," and "Now's the Time." When the 52nd Street scene began to decline, Parker's group made a historic visit to Los Angeles, where they introduced bebop to West Coast audiences.

When the rest of the group returned to New York, Parker chose to remain in California. He found work, but his heroin addiction was worse than ever; he could not have survived without the help of a handful of devoted friends, such as the talented young trumpeter Miles Davis and the bassist Charles Mingus, who looked after Parker's business affairs and let him stay in their homes. Despite his personal woes, his art was reaching its peak; the recordings he made for Dial Records in the spring and summer of 1946 are among the classics of bebop. By the end of the year, however, Parker had suffered a nervous breakdown and was committed to Camarillo State Hospital.

The care he received at Camarillo restored Parker to mental and physical health. He emerged from the hospital in early 1947, cut some more recordings for Dial, and then went back to New York. There he found the bop revolution in full swing. As one of the new music's great practicioners, Parker enjoyed unprecedented popularity, steady employment both in clubs and in the recording studio, and a good income. He also found some tranquillity in a third marriage, to Doris Sydnor, though this relationship, like the first two, was not to last.

In 1949, Parker made his first trip to Europe and achieved a triumph at the Paris Jazz Festival. Back home he experimented with different forms, including a string orchestra and a Latin jazz band, though his best forum was still the small combo. Among the high points of this period in Parker's life were a new romantic attachment—with Chan Richardson—that would last the rest of his life, as well as the opening of the club Birdland, named in Parker's honor. There was no name in jazz that had more luster.

But by 1951, Parker's indulgence in heroin and alcohol had become even more excessive. Because of his association with known drug dealers, New York State revoked his cabaret card, making it impossible for him to perform in nightclubs, and he was forced to go out on the road to make a living. His music suffered greatly from the lack of a stable group, and the routine of travel began to wear him down. Even when his cabaret card was restored in 1953, he found it hard to regain his former income; when his daughter, Pree, died of a heart condition at the age of two, Parker bitterly blamed himself for not being able to afford better care for the child.

In 1954, at odds with his musical colleagues and seriously depressed, Parker attempted suicide. He recovered, but his continuing unhappiness caused him to leave his wife and live like a vagabond, often sleeping on the subways or in the street. On March 12, 1955, while trying to recuperate from an illness in a friend's apartment, Parker suffered a fatal heart attack. The doctor who examined Parker's ravaged body estimated his age at 53. In fact, he was barely 35. His life was brief and tormented, but the legacy of his genius still inspires fans and musicians alike.

PERFORMING ARTISTS

ALVIN AILEY

Choreographer and director Alvin Ailey, Jr., was born on January 5, 1931, in Rogers, Texas. He was the only child of Alvin Ailey, a laborer, and his wife, Lula. When Alvin junior was very young, his parents separated, and he was raised by his mother. In 1942, Mrs. Ailey and her son moved to Los Angeles.

Alvin was active in school sports and also took tap dancing lessons. Another early influence was the ritual of the Báptist church, which fascinated Alvin, and he was also drawn to that form of African American music known as the blues. In 1948, following his graduation from high school, Alvin enrolled briefly at the University of California, Los Angeles (UCLA), then transferred to Los Angeles City College, where he remained until 1951.

Two years earlier, in 1949, Ailey had been introduced to the work of Lester Horton, an African American modern-dance choreographer, and began attending weekend classes offered by Horton. By 1951, Ailey was serving on the stage crew of the Lester Horton Dance Theater and also dancing with Horton's company. Yet he was still not fully committed to a career in dancing and made plans to become a teacher. He moved to San Francisco and enrolled at San Francisco State College as a student of Romance languages. The lure of dancing proved too strong, however, and by early 1953 Ailey was dancing in a nightclub act in San Francisco. In May of that year, he returned to Los Angeles and rejoined the Lester Horton Dance Theater.

Six months later, in November 1953, Horton died, and a committee was formed to keep the company together. Ailey began choreographing dances for the group and two of them, *Mourning Morning* and *According to St. Francis*, were performed at the world-famous Jacob's Pillow Dance Festival in the summer of 1954. That same year Ailey danced in the film *Carmen Jones* and was invited to appear in the Broadway production of *House of Flowers*, a musical written by Truman Capote, which opened in December 1954.

Following his move to New York City, Ailey studied dance with many well-known choreographers, including Martha Graham. He appeared in other musicals, including *The Carefree Tree* (1955) and Harry Belafonte's *Sing, Man, Sing* (1956). In 1957, he became the leading dancer in *Jamaica*, a musical that starred Lena Horne.

In March 1958, Ailey and fellow dancer-choreographer Ernest Parham assembled a group of dancers, most of them from the cast of *Jamaica*, and presented a program at the 92nd Street YMHA in New York City. For this presentation, Ailey choreographed three pieces: *Ode and Homage* (to Lester Horton), *Blues Suite*, and five dances with Latin themes that were later retitled *Cinco Latinos*. Ailey was widely praised for both his choreography and his dancing and soon afterward he formed the Alvin Ailey American Dance Theater, a troupe of both black and white dancers that gave its first full-scale concert in December 1958 at the YMHA.

As Ailey's reputation grew, he continued to dance and to choreograph new works. *Revelations*, widely considered his masterwork, premiered at the YMHA in January 1960. According to the program notes, *Revelations* explored the "motivations and emotions of American Negro religious music." It was an instant hit and was later included in every presentation by the Alvin Ailey Dance Theater.

In the fall of 1960, Ailey presented his first program at the Clark Center for the Performing Arts, which was part of New York City's West Side YWCA. The Clark Center soon became the headquarters of the Alvin Ailey Dance Theater. Rehearsals were conducted there, and dance classes were offered. At his Clark Center performances, Ailey began including the works of other choreographers in his repertory, a practice that was generally not followed by other modern-dance companies. Ailey revived Lester Horton's *The Beloved* and presented the New York premiere of choreographer Joan Butler's *Portrait of Billie*, a dance about jazz singer Billie Holiday.

In 1960–61, Ailey also introduced a new work of his own, *Knoxville: Summer of 1915*, choreographed to music by Samuel Barber, and a duet, *Roots of the Blues*, which he danced with Carmen de Lavallade. The duet premiered at the Boston Arts Festival in June 1961 and was presented later that summer in concert at Lewisohn Stadium in New York City. In December of that year, Ailey introduced another work that was soon widely acclaimed: *Hermit Songs*, again set to music by Samuel Barber, and featuring Ailey in a solo role.

In February 1962, Ailey and codirector Carmen de Lavallade led the company on a tour of the Far East sponsored by the U.S. State Department. The group visited 10 countries and presented a number of what had now become modern-dance classics, including *Been Here and Gone*, Ailey's suite of African American folk dances, and Glen Tetley's *Mountain Way Chant*, based on Navajo Indian rituals. The tour marked the first time an African American company had performed in Southeast Asia, and audiences responded enthusiastically, especially in Australia. The company's warm reception established their reputation as a group with universal appeal and paved the way for future international tours.

During the summer of 1962, the Alvin Ailey Dance Theater performed at the American Dance Festival in New London, Connecticut. Ailey also created new dances for the Robert Joffrey Ballet, including the famous *Feast of Ashes*, which later became part of the repertory of the Harkness Ballet. In September, the Ailey company appeared twice at a dance festival held in New York's Central Park.

During the next few years, Ailey taught dance classes at the Clark Center and toured with his company throughout the United States, appearing mostly on college and university campuses. In 1963, Ailey introduced *Labyrinth*, based on the myth of Theseus and the Minotaur; the work was subsequently revised and became his well-known ballet *Ariadne*. Also in 1963, Ailey and his company appeared at the Century of Negro Progress exhibit in Chicago, where their fellow performers included Duke Ellington. That fall the Alvin Ailey Dance Theater traveled to Brazil, where they performed at the Music and Dance Festival in Rio de Janeiro.

In the fall of 1964, the Ailey company embarked on its first tour of London and the continent of Europe. Enthusiastic audiences cheered every performance—

in Hamburg the group received an unprecedented 61 curtain calls—and critics raved. In December, the company revisited Australia, and in the spring of 1965 returned to London for more appearances. By the end of that year, Ailey was no longer performing, but he continued to direct the group and to choreograph new dances. In the early 1960s, he also appeared as an actor in several off-Broadway plays.

In 1966, Ailey traveled with his dance company to Dakar, Senegal, where they appeared at the World Festival of the Negro Arts—the first racially integrated group to do so. Later that spring they appeared with the Harkness Ballet in Barcelona and Paris. In addition to work for his own company that year, Ailey choreographed the dances for *Antony and Cleopatra*, the opera by Samuel Barber that opened the new Metropolitan Opera House in New York City in September 1966.

During the following two decades, Ailey maintained his troupe's prominence as the most popular modern-dance group in the world. His later works included *Masekela Language* (1969), *Cry* (1971), and *Night Creature* (1974), one of several homages to Duke Ellington. Ailey died in New York City on December 1, 1989.

MARIAN ANDERSON

Singer Marian Anderson was born in Philadelphia, Pennsylvania, sometime around 1900. She always claimed that her birth date was February 1902, but toward the end of her life newly discovered family documents indicated that she had been born on February 27, 1897. Her father, John Anderson, sold ice and coal at the Reading Terminal Market in downtown Philadelphia. Marian began singing in public at the age of six, when she joined the choir at the Union Baptist Church, which her family attended.

Marian Anderson's father died when she was 10 years old, and the family moved in with her paternal grandparents. Her mother supported Marian and her two younger sisters by working as a cleaning woman in a department store. When Marian was 14, the famous black tenor Roland Hayes performed at the Union Baptist Church and Marian was asked by the choir director to appear on the same program. Hayes was astonished by the quality of the young woman's voice and encouraged her to get further training.

Encouraged by Hayes's opinion of her voice, Marian realized that she might be able to help support her family by singing professionally, but she still needed additional training. At the age of 15 she tried to enroll in a small music school in Philadelphia but was rejected because of her race. Despite her lack of formal singing lessons, her reputation grew and she was hired to sing at church socials and benefits in the black community.

When Anderson was a junior in high school, a family friend introduced her to a black voice teacher named Mary Patterson, who agreed to give her free lessons. Anderson progressed rapidly, and when she graduated from high school, the principal, Dr. Lucy Wilson, arranged for her to audition with an Italian vocal coach named Giuseppe Boghetti. After Boghetti agreed to accept her as a pupil, Dr. Wilson and the

Union Baptist Church arranged a benefit concert to raise money for voice lessons. Roland Hayes performed and the event raised more than $600, enough for a year of lessons. Although Boghetti remained her teacher for many years, he never charged her for lessons after the first year.

Through her studies with Boghetti, Anderson expanded her repertoire and was now performing more frequently, sometimes two or three times in the same evening. She soon found an accompanist named Billy King, and he became her manager. Anderson and King became well known in Philadelphia and were much in demand; within two years they were being paid $100 for each performance. In 1920, Anderson embarked on her first tour, performing with King at black colleges throughout the South before returning to Philadelphia for more concerts.

In 1923, Anderson competed in a vocal contest sponsored by the Philharmonic Society of Philadelphia and became the first black singer to win. Her prize was an invitation to perform with the Philadelphia Orchestra in a concert that was broadcast over the radio. Later that same year she sang in a standing-room-only concert in New York City's Harlem, followed by several other appearances in the city.

In April 1924, Anderson gave a major recital at New York's Town Hall before a largely white audience. Applause was polite but restrained, and critics panned her performance, especially her "wooden" rendering of songs in German. A dejected Anderson returned to

Philadelphia and several months passed before she resumed her singing.

In 1925, after intensive study with Boghetti, Anderson entered a competition sponsored by the National Music League in New York City. Following an arduous selection process, Anderson was declared the winner. Her prize was an appearance with the New York Philharmonic that summer at Lewisohn Stadium, an enormous open-air theater in the city.

The concert was a resounding success and critics praised Anderson for her remarkable voice. Invitations for her to perform came pouring in from around the country. That fall she toured Canada and California with King, and other engagements followed as her fees rose to as much as $500 per concert. While King continued as her accompanist, she acquired a new manager, Arthur Judson, the head of a prestigious concert bureau in New York.

Despite her successes during the next few years, Anderson believed that she needed training abroad to improve her singing and language skills. In the summer of 1929, she traveled to England, where she studied voice for several months and performed at London's Wigmore Hall. Two years later, supported by a grant from the Julius Rosenwald Fund, Anderson sailed for Germany. Boarding with a family in Berlin to improve her German, she took voice lessons and gave a recital at the Bachsaal, a celebrated music hall in the city. Before returning to America in 1932, Anderson gave a series of concerts in Scandinavia that were well received.

In 1933, Anderson traveled again to Europe with the assistance of another grant from the Rosenwald Fund. She made a second tour of Scandinavia, giving 108 concerts in other European cities, including Paris, Geneva, Brussels, Vienna, and Salzburg, which had been arranged for her by the Judson agency. In Paris, she was heard by the noted American impresario Sol Hurok, who offered her a new contract upon her return to the United States. In the audience at her Salzburg concert was the renowned conductor Arturo Toscanini, who came backstage afterward and told her that "Yours is a voice one hears once in a hundred years."

Anderson came back to the United States in December 1935 with a new accompanist, the Finnish pianist Kosti Vehanen. On December 30, she returned to New York City's Town Hall to present a concert arranged for her by Sol Hurok. This time the audience and critics alike were wildly enthusiastic—despite the fact that Anderson performed with a broken ankle. She had injured herself in a fall on board ship a week earlier, but her cast was carefully concealed by her long gown.

Anderson returned to Europe in March 1936 for further concerts, again accompanied by Vehanen. The highlight of the tour was a series of engagements in the Soviet Union, one of which was attended by dictator Joseph Stalin. During the next few years, Anderson and Vehanen toured in the United States, Europe, and South America. She was now internationally acclaimed, and many honors were bestowed upon her. In 1936, she became the first black singer to perform at the White House, at the invitation of President and Mrs. Franklin D. Roosevelt. In 1938, she received an honorary doctorate in music from Howard University in Washington, D.C., the first of dozens of honorary degrees that she would be awarded during her lifetime. In January 1939, Anderson was named the recipient of the Spingarn Medal, an honor conferred annually by the National Association for the Advancement of Colored People (NAACP) for "the highest or noblest achievement by an American Negro."

The year 1939 also brought Marian Anderson an experience that made headlines around the world. When Sol Hurok tried to book Anderson for a concert at Constitution Hall in Washington, D.C., he learned that the owners of the hall, a patriotic organization called the Daughters of the American Revolution, excluded black performers from appearing there. An outraged Hurok informed the press about the ban and support for Anderson poured in from around the country. Many famous Americans publicly criticized the DAR's policy, and First Lady Eleanor Roosevelt resigned from the organization in protest.

The Roosevelts and Secretary of the Interior Harold Ickes came to the rescue by inviting Anderson to give a free public recital on the steps of the Lincoln Memorial on Easter Sunday, April 9, 1939. Anderson, who had remained calm and dignified throughout the uproar and refused to comment publicly on the DAR's decision, accepted the government's offer and gave a memorable concert that was attended by 75,000 people. Four years later, when the DAR invited her to sing at a benefit concert at Constitution Hall, she graciously agreed to perform.

Anderson, now an international superstar, continued to give concerts throughout the world, accompanied by a new pianist, a German refugee named Franz Rupp, after Vehanen returned to Finland in 1940. During World War II, she made frequent tours of military bases, entertaining troops. In 1943, she married Orpheus Fisher, an architect whom she had first met in 1922. They bought a farm near Danbury, Connecticut, and Fisher built his wife a separate studio where she could practice undisturbed.

In 1955, Anderson reached another milestone in her career when she became the first black singer to perform with the Metropolitan Opera in New York City, singing the role of the sorceress Ulrica in Verdi's *A Masked Ball.* Her acclaimed performance opened the door for other black singers at the Metropolitan Opera, including Leontyne Price. In January 1957, she sang "The Star-Spangled Banner" at President Dwight D. Eisenhower's inauguration and later that year made a worldwide goodwill tour at the request of the U.S. State Department. In 1958–59, she served as a member of the U.S. delegation to the United Nations, and in January 1961, she sang at the inauguration of President John F. Kennedy. Three years later she was awarded the Presidential Medal of Freedom by President Lyndon B. Johnson.

Anderson, accompanied by Franz Rupp, gave her final concert on April 19, 1965—Easter Sunday—at Carnegie Hall. This was the climax of a farewell tour that had begun the previous October at Constitution Hall in Washington, D.C. In retirement, she continued her involvement in the artistic life of the country, participating in numerous musical and charitable organizations and receiving countless honors, including a lifetime achievement award from the Kennedy Center for the Performing Arts in Washington, D.C., in 1978.

In 1992, Anderson moved from her Connecticut home to Portland, Oregon, to live with her nephew, James De Priest, the conductor of the Oregon Symphony. She died in Portland on April 8, 1993.

JOSEPHINE BAKER

Singer and dancer Josephine Baker was born Josephine McDonald in St. Louis, Missouri, on June 3, 1906, the oldest of three children. Her father was an itinerant musician who was seldom at home, and her mother supported the family by taking in laundry. Josephine was an imaginative child who enjoyed dressing up in adult clothes and giving "plays" in the family's basement.

Between the ages of 8 and 10 she stayed out of school in order to earn money as a kitchen helper, maid, and baby-sitter. She later recalled that she was not especially happy in elementary school anyway, since she was constantly being reprimanded by her teachers for making faces.

By the time she was a teenager, Josephine had moved to Philadelphia, where she lived for a while with her grandmother. She had been married briefly at the age of 13 in St. Louis and two years later married Willie Baker, a Pullman porter. Josephine frequently attended local vaudeville shows and began dancing in a chorus line. At the age of 16 she joined a traveling troupe of dancers and by 1923 was dancing in New York City in a musical comedy called *Shuffle*. Her improvisation and mimicry drew such applause that she was hired to do another show, *Chocolate Dandies*, on Broadway. When that closed, Baker joined the floor show at the Plantation Club at $125 a week.

In 1925, Baker, who was now separated from her second husband, was offered a major dancing role in an American-sponsored French show, *La Revue Nègre*, at twice her Plantation Club salary. The production opened at the Theâtre des Champs-Elysées in Paris that fall and introduced what the French called *le jazz hot* to Europe. Baker was an instant success and was soon hired away by the celebrated Folies Bergère, Paris's most famous music hall. Here she was billed as "Dark Star" and created a sensation by dancing on a mirror, clothed only in a bunch of rubber bananas strung around her waist. Banana-clad Josephine dolls were soon being sold on the streets of Paris to thousands of children and tourists.

In December 1926, while still performing at the Folies Bergère, Baker founded her own nightclub, Chez Josephine, on the rue Pigalle; it was later moved to the rue Fontaine and finally to rue François I. By this time Baker was wealthy and famous, and had acquired a reputation as a charming eccentric who often walked her pet leopards down the Champs-Elysées, the main thoroughfare of Paris. She received thousands of fan letters, many of them proposing marriage. From 1928 to 1930, she toured the world and performed in 25 countries.

In 1930, Baker's manager and close friend, Pepito Abatino, persuaded her to talk and sing during her performances. The director of the Casino de Paris, Henri Varna, created a new show for Baker, and she left the Folies Bergère briefly to make her formal debut that fall as a singing and dancing comedienne at the Casino. Critics and audiences raved at Baker's transformation from an exotic dancer into "a complete artist, the perfect master of her tools."

Returning to the Folies Bergère, Baker found her name in neon lights on the marquee and giant color photographs of her flanking the entrance. Throughout the 1930s, she continued as the star attraction at the Folies while appearing in movies and light opera. Her film debut occurred in the summer of 1934 when she appeared as the title character in *Zouzou*, the story of a laundress who becomes a music hall star. In December 1934, she began a six-month run at the Théâtre Marigny as the star of *La Creole*, an operetta about a Jamaican girl that was based on music by Jacques Offenbach. Baker made several more films during the 1930s. In 1937, following a divorce from Willie Baker, she married for a third time; her new husband was a millionaire businessman named Jean Lyon. That same year Baker became a French citizen. She and Lyon separated several years later.

When German troops invaded Belgium in May 1940, Baker became a Red Cross volunteer, helping fleeing Belgian refugees. The next month, following the German takeover of France, Baker joined the underground intelligence network and carried secret messages from the Italian embassy to a French army captain named Jacques Abtey. In October, Baker, accompanied by Abtey, began a journey that took her on secret missions to London, Spain, Portugal, and finally to Rio de Janeiro, Brazil, where she performed in several shows. Returning to Marseilles in December 1940, she appeared in a revival of *La Creole*. Early the following year she traveled to Algiers, North Africa, and remained there to recuperate from severe bronchitis.

Beginning in early 1942, Baker traveled throughout North Africa and the Middle East entertaining troops. She was officially designated as a sublieutenant in the women's auxiliary of the Free French forces, and after the war ended she was honored by the French government with the Legion of Honor and the Rosette of the Resistance.

Following the liberation of Paris in August 1944, Baker returned to the French capital and starred in a revue at the Théâtre aux Armées. In the postwar years Baker alternated appearances at the Folies Bergère with frequent world tours. She appeared occasionally on French television and also recorded several well-known songs from her repertoire, including "Pretty Little Baby" and "J'Ai Deux Amours." In 1947, she married her fourth and last husband, Jo Bouillon, a French orchestra leader.

During these years, Baker also became increasingly involved with the development of her 300-acre country estate in southwest France, where she kept numerous pet animals.

The centerpiece of the estate was a medieval chateau named Les Milandes, which she had begun renting in the 1930s and eventually purchased outright. In the early 1950s, Baker began adopting orphaned babies of various nationalities and raising them at the estate.

In 1956, Baker announced her retirement from show business and became a full-time resident of Les Milandes to preside over what she called her rainbow family, which eventually numbered 12 children. However, the cost of running Les Milandes forced her to return to the Paris stage three years later in *Paris, Mes Amours*, a musical based on her own life. The following year she took the show on a world tour.

Beginning in the 1930s, Baker had returned several times to the United States to perform before American audiences. Following a visit in the early 1950s, during which she was the target of racial snubs,

Baker was openly critical of America's treatment of blacks. In August 1963, she traveled to Washington, D.C., to participate in the March on Washington, the civil rights demonstration that featured Martin Luther King, Jr., delivering his famous "I have a dream" speech. Two months later Baker came to New York City and gave a benefit performance for the civil rights movement at Carnegie Hall.

In early 1964, Baker presented shows at the Brooks Atkinson and Henry Miller theaters in New York City. After her return to Les Milandes that spring, she spent much of her time trying to keep her "experiment in brotherhood" from falling into financial ruin. The strain on her health was enormous, and in July she suffered a severe heart attack, followed by a second one three months later. As she recuperated during the next few years, Baker still sought to save Les Milandes, but she lost her fight in May 1968, when the property was auctioned off to pay longstanding debts.

That summer, Baker and her children moved to Monaco, where Princess Grace and the Red Cross helped her find a large villa near Monte Carlo. Baker resumed her international tours, often taking some or all of her children with her. In June 1973, she returned to New York City to give a series of sold-out concerts at Carnegie Hall. A few months later she suffered another heart attack and a stroke while on tour in Denmark. She was soon performing again, however, the need for financial security overcoming her desire to retire.

On April 8, 1975, Josephine Baker opened at the Bobino Theater in Paris with a new revue, entitled *Josephine*. The show was an instant hit, and Baker was once again the toast of Paris. She realized that it might be such a financial success that she could at last retire. Two days later those dreams were ended when Baker suffered a cerebral hemorrhage at her hotel and slipped into a deep coma. She died on April 12 and was buried three days later in a nationally televised ceremony at the Church of the Madeleine in Paris.

BILL COSBY

Actor Bill Cosby was born William Henry Cosby, Jr., on July 12, 1937, in Philadelphia. He grew up in an all-black housing project in that city's Germantown district. William Cosby, Sr., was a mess steward for the U.S. Navy and was away from home for months at a time. Mrs. Cosby, who worked as a cleaning woman, tried hard to protect Bill and his two younger brothers from their ghetto environment. She often read to them from the Bible and from the works of Mark Twain. Young Bill contributed to the meager family income by shining shoes and delivering groceries.

Bill Cosby's talents as a comedian were recognized at an early age. Inspired by TV comic Sid Caesar, young Cosby often entertained his classmates with made-up routines, and his sixth-grade teacher wrote on his report card that Bill was "an alert boy who would rather clown than study." Fortunately, the boy's brightness was also apparent and when he scored high on an IQ test in eighth grade he was assigned to a class for gifted students the following year at Germantown High School.

In high school Cosby excelled in athletics. He was captain of the track and football teams and also played basketball and baseball. His academic performance was unsatisfactory, however, and when he was told that he had to repeat 10th grade, he dropped out of school. Cosby worked for a while as a shoe repairman, then entered the U.S. Navy in 1956. During his four years in the navy, Cosby was trained as a physical therapist and worked at Bethesda Naval Hospital in Maryland. He also earned a high school equivalency diploma before his release in 1960.

Cosby enrolled at Temple University in Philadelphia in 1961 with the help of a track-and-field scholarship. He majored in physical education while participating on the university's track and football teams. During his sophomore year, Cosby began his career as a professional comedian when he was hired by a local coffeehouse to tend bar and tell jokes to customers for $5 a night. Later he was hired as a comedian at another night spot, the Underground, for $25 a night.

In the spring of 1962, Cosby took a leave of absence from Temple to entertain at the Gaslight Café, a coffeehouse in New York's Greenwich Village. Among his fellow performers was Woody Allen, then beginning his career as a stand-up comedian. Soon afterward Cosby severed his connection with Temple to become a full-time comic. As his reputation grew, he was invited to perform at leading clubs across the country and by 1963 he had become nationally known.

Almost from the beginning of his new career, Cosby had decided not to focus on racial material in order to reach a broad audience with his humor. "I want to play John Q. Public," he told an interviewer in 1963. His routines included anecdotes about everyday life, and he often made himself the butt of his own jokes, which he accented with humorous faces, sounds, and impersonations.

Following an appearance on Johnny Carson's *Tonight Show* in 1965, Cosby was asked by television producer Sheldon Leonard to do a screen test for a part in a new NBC-TV adventure series, *I Spy*. The test was successful, and Cosby was hired for the role of Alexander Scott, playing opposite Robert Culp as Kelly Robertson. Cosby thus became the first black actor to perform in a starring role in a nationally broadcast television series.

I Spy, with its realistic scenes and sly humor, was a popular show and ran for three years, from September 1965 to September 1968. It featured Culp and Cosby as a team of secret agents traveling undercover as a tennis player (Culp) and his trainer-companion (Cosby). Cosby won three consecutive Emmy awards for his performance in the show, in 1966, 1967, and 1968. Critics have since noted that Cosby's role was one of the most significant in the history of blacks on television, since it made a hero out of a mature, black secret service agent who was defending the United States around the world. Other black players often appeared in the series in nonstereotyped roles, including Cicely Tyson, Leslie Uggams, and Eartha Kitt.

Cosby returned to NBC-TV in the fall of 1969 with *The Bill Cosby Show*. The show was set in a high school located in a lower-middle-class neighborhood of Los Angeles and starred Cosby as a physical education teacher with a sense of humor who enjoyed helping others. The show ran for two seasons, until August 1971. That same year, Cosby made his first Hollywood film, costarring with Robert Culp in *Hickey and Boggs*, a movie about two private detectives in Los Angeles.

In February 1972, Cosby starred in *To All My Friends on Shore*, a made-for-television drama on CBS that he also wrote, scored, and produced. *The New Bill Cosby Show*, an hour-long comedy and variety program on CBS, premiered the following September. Cosby's guests included Sidney Poitier, Harry Belafonte, Peter Sellers, Lily Tomlin, and Tim Conway. Critics did not like the show, however, and it was dropped after one season.

During the 1972–73 season, Cosby also premiered another television program on CBS, a Saturday morning cartoon series called *Fat Albert and the Cosby Kids*. Cosby was the host and executive producer of the show, which featured a cast of humorous characters based on Cosby's boyhood friends. Cosby appeared at the beginning and end of each episode, which both entertained and offered a lesson in dealing with a specific childhood challenge—situations like losing a tooth, getting caught in telling a lie, or not being chosen for a team. *Fat Albert* was immensely popular, won numerous awards, and remained in production for 12 years; since 1984 it has been shown in reruns.

During the 1970s, Cosby was a frequent guest on the popular children's programs *Sesame Street* and *Electric Company*. In that decade, he also became a familiar television advertising personality, appearing in ads for a number of popular products. In 1974, Cosby appeared in another movie, *Uptown Saturday Night*, a comedy in which he costarred with Sidney Poitier, Harry Belafonte, Flip Wilson, and Richard Pryor. The following year Cosby and Poitier teamed up in another comedy, *Let's Do It Again*.

For several months in the fall of 1976, Cosby starred in *Cos*, a one-hour variety show for children on ABC-TV, but the show was unpopular and it soon went off the air. That same year, his fourth film, *Mother, Jugs and Speed*, was released, but it was not popular with either critics or audiences. Also in 1976, Cosby was awarded a doctorate in education by the University of Massachusetts, which gave him college credits for "life experience" and allowed him to fulfill practice teaching requirements by working as an instructor in prisons and appearing on *Sesame Street* and *Electric Company*.

In 1977, Cosby and Sidney Poitier were reunited in another film, *A Piece of the Action*, which also starred James Earl Jones. Although Cosby was praised for his performance, the movie itself received mixed reviews. Two years later, Cosby was part of an all-star cast that appeared in *California Suite*, a movie based on plays by Neil Simon. The film was a critical and popular success, although some reviewers criticized Cosby and costar Richard Pryor for engaging in a brawl scene, complaining that the fight was degrading to blacks and had racist overtones.

During the 1980s, Cosby appeared in several films, including *The Devil and Max Devlin* (1981), *Bill Cosby—Himself* (1983), and *Ghost Dad* (1989). In the fall of 1984, his new television program, *The Cosby Show*, premiered on NBC-TV. A situation comedy about a New York obstetrician, his lawyer wife, and their five children, the show was an immediate hit and ran for eight years.

In addition to a career as an actor and comic, Cosby is also well known as an author. His half-dozen books include *Fatherhood*, a collection of anecdotes and observations about being a father. (Cosby and his wife, Camille, whom he married in 1964, are the parents of five children.) *Fatherhood*, published in 1986, was a best-seller for more than a year and sold nearly 3 million hardcover copies. Cosby has also made a number of recordings of songs and comedy routines.

Bill Cosby has earned more money than any other entertainer in the world and makes tens of millions of dollars annually from his various endeavors. He and his family are eager to put that money to good use and have made substantial charitable contributions. In 1988, Cosby and his wife made headlines when they donated $20 million to Spelman College, a noted institution for black women in Atlanta. This is the largest contribution ever made to a black college.

KATHERINE DUNHAM

Dancer and choreographer Katherine Dunham was born in Chicago, Illinois, on June 22, 1909, the daughter of Albert Dunham, a tailor, and his wife, Fanny. Katherine and her older brother, Albert junior, lived with their parents in suburban Glen Ellyn for several years. Following the death of Fanny Dunham in 1914, the family moved to a tenement on the South Side of Chicago. Albert

Dunham remarried several years later and opened a dry cleaning shop in Joliet, Illinois. Katherine grew up in Joliet, attending local schools with her brother.

Katherine began to take piano lessons at the age of 11, and by the time she entered high school she had become both a gifted athlete and a talented amateur dancer. She excelled in basketball and track and was active in the school's dancing group, the Terpsichorean Club. The first hint of her talent as an entertainer came in 1924, when she organized a cabaret performance to benefit Brown's Chapel, the local African Methodist Episcopal church. Performing a Ukrainian folk dance before an audience of 400, she was the star of the show.

In 1926, following her graduation from high school, Dunham enrolled in a local junior college. Her brother, Albert junior, was now attending the University of Chicago. When she graduated two years later, her brother helped her gain admission to the university and find a job at a nearby public library. On campus, Dunham took dancing lessons in addition to academic courses, and her ballet teacher encouraged her to pursue a career as a dancer.

In 1930, with the help of friends, Dunham opened a dance studio on Chicago's South Side. Soon she had assembled a troupe of dancers, which she named the Ballet Nègre. In 1931, the troupe appeared at Chicago's annual Beaux Arts Ball, where they performed a routine called "Negro Rhapsody." The performance was not a success, however, and students drifted away from the studio, which soon closed.

One day Dunham attended a university lecture by a cultural anthropologist who discussed the influence of African culture on contemporary America. She was surprised to learn that many dances had originated in Africa and began studying African culture. Encouraged by her ballet teacher, she also began incorporating African dance movements into her own routines.

In 1934, Dunham danced the lead role in *La Guiablesse*, a new ballet based on a Caribbean folktale, which was presented at the Chicago Opera House. In the audience at the first performance, which received enthusiastic reviews, was an executive of the Rosenwald Fund, a philanthropic organization. Dunham was encouraged to apply for a grant from the fund, which she received early in 1935 for the study of African dance in the Caribbean.

After several months of preparation, including studies with noted anthropology professor Melville J. Herskovits, Dunham headed for the West Indies. She spent several months in a Jamaican village named Accompong, where she studied a group called the Maroons. These were descendants of 17th-century African slaves brought to Jamaica by the Spanish. Dunham then traveled to Haiti, the world's first black republic, and immediately fell in love with the country. As she learned traditional dances of the Haitians, she became fascinated by Voodoo, the folk religion of the country, and was initiated into its practices.

Shortly after her return to the United States in the summer of 1936, Dunham received her bachelor's degree in anthropology from the University of Chicago. Although she was encouraged to do graduate work in anthropology, Dunham decided to pursue a career in dance. She resumed work with an ensemble of dancers under the tutelage of her old ballet teacher, Ludmila Speranzeva. News of her talent spread, and in early 1937 Dunham and her troupe performed for the first time in New York City, where audiences were captivated by her newly choreographed West Indian dances.

Back in Chicago, Dunham became active in the Negro Federal Theater Project and presented two dances that she had choreographed, *Ballet Fèdère* and *Biguine*. These dances marked the beginning of Dunham's career as a major force in black American dance. Dunham's work with the Federal Theater introduced her to John Pratt, a white Canadian set and costume designer. The two were married in 1939; many years later, in 1952, the couple adopted an orphan from Martinique whom they named Marie Christine.

With Pratt as her partner, Dunham established the Dunham Dance Company with a resident troupe of dancers that performed a broad repertoire. In the fall of 1939, the group moved to New York City, and Dunham immediately began choreographing a new show, *Tropics and Le Jazz Hot: From Haiti to Harlem*. The show debuted in the rented Windsor Theater on February 18, 1940, and made dance history. The audience went wild, and Dunham was hailed by critics as "the first pioneer of the Negro dance."

The success of Dunham's first New York show attracted the attention of the famous choreographer George Balanchine, who offered her the opportunity to collaborate with him on a new, all-black Broadway musical, *Cabin in the Sky*. The show was a big hit and played for five months to standing-room-only audiences in New York before going on a cross-country tour. When they reached Hollywood, the Dunham Dance Company made a movie short, *Carnival of Rhythm*, for Warner Brothers. This was the beginning of a successful film career for Dunham, who appeared in five more movies during the 1940s.

In 1941, Dunham created a new show called *Tropical Review*, which she took on tour for several years. By 1944, when the tour ended, Dunham realized that she could not go on dancing forever. Age and severe arthritis were taking their toll. In New York City in 1945, she opened the Katherine Dunham School of Dance, which she hoped would give "the Negro dance student the courage really to study, and a reason to do so." During its 10-year existence the school trained an entire generation of black dancers, including Eartha Kitt and Arthur Mitchell. Many famous actors also came to Dunham's school to learn techniques of body movement.

In 1946, Dunham published *Journey to Accompong*, an account of her trip to Jamaica more than a decade earlier. Later that year she and her husband put together a new show, *Bal Nègre*, with Pratt as set and costume designer and Dunham as choreographer and dancer. The review, which featured black dances from the Caribbean, Africa, Latin America, and the United States, was another hit for Dunham. Buoyed by this success, Dunham prepared for her first world tour.

The two-year tour began in Mexico in January 1948, where the Dunham Dance Company performed for six months to enthusiastic audiences. That summer they moved on to the major cities of Europe, where more acclaim greeted Dunham's dancing. Upon returning to New York City in 1950, the troupe introduced a new show, *Caribbean Rhapsody*. They then traveled to Latin America, where they spent several months in Brazil, Argentina, and Jamaica. After the tour, Dunham and her husband traveled to Haiti, where they lived for a while at a villa called Habitacion Leclerq.

During the 1950s, Dunham and her company continued their dance tours in the United States and abroad. In 1955, she introduced a new production, *Carnaval*, and later that year made her first tour of Australia and the Far East.

Increasingly bothered by physical ailments, Dunham realized by the fall of 1957, as the group concluded its Asian tour, that she could no longer continue her present pace. Dissolving the company, Dunham stayed behind in Japan to rest and began writing an autobiography. She completed the book following her return to the United States in 1958, and it was published a year later as *A Touch of Innocence*. Her third book, an account of her experiences in Haiti entitled *Island Possessed*, was published in 1969.

In 1961, Dunham and her husband tried to establish a resort at Habitation Leclerq, their Haitian home, but the attempt was unsuccessful and the couple were forced to leave Haiti for financial reasons. In 1962, they put together a new show, *Bamboche*, which enjoyed a brief success in New York City. Later that year Dunham was hired as the first black choreographer by the Metropolitan Opera House, but her dances for *Aïda* were rebuffed by critics and she was not invited to work on other productions there.

In 1965, Dunham was named artist-in-residence at Southern Illinois University, and she and her husband moved to the university's home city of Carbondale. That same year she traveled to Africa to help run the First World Festival of Negro Arts in Dakar, Senegal, and also choreographed works in Rome, Paris, and New York. Two years later, with the help of government and private grants, Dunham established the Performance Arts Training Center, a school for impoverished black youth in East St. Louis, Illinois, which she continues to direct.

Dunham lived in East St. Louis with her husband of 47 years, John Pratt, until his death in 1986. She has received numerous honors for her work, including the Albert Schweitzer Music Award in 1979, the Kennedy Center Honors in 1983, an honorary doctorate from Lincoln University in 1984, and the Scripps American Dance Festival Award in 1986.

LENA HORNE

Singer and actress Lena Horne was born on June 30, 1917, in Brooklyn, New York. Her family had been prominent for many years in civic and cultural affairs. When Lena was three years old, her father, a civil servant as well as a numbers runner and gambler, left home. While her mother, an actress, toured the East Coast, Lena was raised by various relatives in the South. One of them,

Dr. Frank Smith Horne, an uncle who lived in Georgia, was an educator who later became an adviser on race relations to President Franklin D. Roosevelt.

When Lena was 12, she returned to Brooklyn. She lived first with her grandmother and then with her mother and stepfather, and attended local schools. At 16, Horne left high school to help support her mother. She was hired as a chorus girl at the Cotton Club, a famous nightclub in Harlem, and during the next two years appeared there with well-known African American entertainers. In 1934, she made her debut on Broadway in the play *Dance with Your Gods*. A year later she left the Cotton Club to become a singer with Noble Sissle's orchestra and toured the East and Midwest. Using the name Helena Horne, she became the orchestra's temporary leader after Sissle was injured in an accident.

In January 1937, Horne married Louis J. Jones, a friend of her father's who was active in Democratic party politics in Pittsburgh. The couple had two children—Gail, born in 1937, and Teddy, born in 1940. Horne had intended to give up show business when she married, but her husband had a difficult time finding a job during the depression and she was forced to continue working. She sang at private parties in Pittsburgh and in 1938 made her screen debut in an all-black film, *The Duke Is Tops*. The following year she was one of the stars of a Broadway revue, *Blackbirds of 1939*.

Horne's husband resented her career, and the couple separated in 1940; they were divorced four years later. Horne returned to New York City in the fall of 1940 and was hired as a vocalist with Charlie Barnet's orchestra, becoming one of the first black performers to sing with an all-white band. She went on to make two hit recordings with Barnet, "Good for Nothing Joel" and "Haunted Town." In March 1941, she became a soloist at the Café Society Downtown Club in Greenwich Village, again billed as Helena Horne.

Three weeks after Horne opened at the club, the manager, Barney Josephson, sponsored a concert for her at Carnegie Hall. During her year at Café Society, which she later described as one of the happiest years of her life, Horne made recordings with a number of well-known jazz musicians, including Teddy Wilson (who then led the Café Society orchestra), Artie Shaw, and Henry Levine's Dixieland Jazz Group. She also made her first solo recordings for RCA Victor, including "I Gotta Right To Sing the Blues" and "Moanin' Low."

In February 1942, Horne left New York and moved to Los Angeles, where she joined Katherine Dunham's dancers and other black performers in a show at Little Troc, a Hollywood nightclub. She quickly became the most popular member of the show, and a scout from Metro-Goldwyn-Mayer arranged for her to have a screen test. Her singing so impressed executive Louis B. Mayer that he offered her a contract. Although Horne was not sure that she wanted to act in movies, friends urged her to accept the offer. Among them were Walter White, executive secretary of the National Association for the Advancement of Colored People (NAACP), and the bandleader Count Basie; both White and Basie believed that Horne could pave the way for other black actors in films.

Horne made her MGM debut in 1942 in the movie *Panama Hattie*, a musical by Cole Porter. The following year she costarred in the all-black musical *Cabin in the Sky*. Also in 1943, she was top star in another black musical, *Stormy Weather*. Horne had already sung the title song in her nightclub act and had recorded it, and it became the song most closely associated with her during her long career.

Cabin in the Sky and *Stormy Weather* established Horne as a film star, but she and the movie studios could not agree on subsequent roles for her. She refused to play stereotyped black characters, and as a light-complexioned African American she was neither "black" nor "white." As a kind of compromise, her subsequent film roles featured her in entertaining musical numbers that were inserted into movies but were unrelated to the main plot.

Despite this restriction in her roles, Horne was still a popular actress and was the favorite pinup girl of black soldiers during World War II. Horne made a major contribution to the war effort, touring army bases around the country to entertain troops. She was dismayed to find her audiences segregated, however, and was particularly upset when she came onstage during a performance at Fort Riley, Kansas, and discovered that German prisoners of war had been given better seats than black troops.

During the 1940s, Horne continued to work in nightclubs in addition to her film roles and armed forces shows. As the first black performer to appear at the Savoy Plaza Hotel and the Copacabana in New York City, she set box office records. Soon she was performing at top clubs in cities across the country, and she also appeared in London and Paris, where she quickly became a favorite. In 1948, *Life* magazine called her "the season's top nightclub attraction," and by 1952 she was earning as much as $12,500 a week.

Shortly after this, however, Horne's career began to decline. Over the years she had become involved in a number of political and social organizations, and some of them had been identified as having communist sympathies. In the early 1950s, there was strong anti-communist feeling in the United States, and Horne was blacklisted for her alleged connections to communism. Her friendship with the singer Paul Robeson, an open supporter of the Soviet Union, also contributed to her being blacklisted.

Horne fought back, denying that she was anything but a loyal American. By 1956, she was once again performing for audiences, making a guest appearance in the movie *Meet Me in Las Vegas* and appearing on popular TV shows hosted by Ed Sullivan, Steve Allen, and Perry Como. Horne also recorded new songs for RCA Victor. One of her first LPs (long-playing records) for RCA, *Lena Horne at the Waldorf-Astoria*, became the largest-selling album by a female performer in the company's history. In 1957, Horne starred in the Broadway musical *Jamaica;* although critics were lukewarm about the show they lauded her performance, and *Jamaica* lasted for 555 performances.

During the 1960s, Horne was one of the most prominent black celebrities who supported the civil rights movement. She traveled throughout the South, singing and speaking at rallies, and she added songs with civil rights themes to her repertoire. She also participated in meetings of black leaders with government officials. During these years Horne starred in several television specials and also published her autobiography, *Lena* (1965).

In 1970–71, Horne lost several of those closest to her. First her father died, and then her son succumbed to a kidney ailment. In 1971, her second husband, Lennie Hayton, also died. She had married Hayton, a musical director at MGM, in 1944, and he had become her conductor and arranger.

In the face of these multiple tragedies, Horne lost interest in her work for a while. Gradually she resumed her tours of theaters and nightclubs throughout the country, appearing with fellow stars Alan King, Tony Bennett, and Count Basie. In 1974, she appeared as Glinda the Good Witch in the film *The Wiz*, an all-black version of *The Wizard of Oz*.

Horne's one-woman show, *Lena Horne: The Lady and Her Music*, was an instant hit when it opened in New York in 1981. Nearly all of its 333 performances sold out, and Horne received a number of awards, including the Handel Medallion, New York City's highest cultural award, and the Emergence Award from the Dance Theatre of Harlem. She was also honored by the Duke Ellington School of the Arts in Washington, D.C., which established a scholarship in her name. Horne later took the show on tour across the United States and to London, where audiences were uniformly enthusiastic.

Horne has received other awards for her work as a performer and civil rights activist. In 1979, she was awarded an honorary doctor of laws degree from Howard University in Washington, D.C. Three years later she received the Spingarn Medal, given annually by the NAACP in recognition of high achievement by a black American. In December 1984, Horne was one of five recipients of the annual Kennedy Center Honors in Washington, D.C. She has also received the Governor's Arts Award from New York State and the Paul Robeson Award from Actors' Equity.

SIDNEY POITIER

Actor Sidney Poitier was born on February 20, 1927, in Miami, Florida. His parents, farmers in the Bahamas, had come to Miami to sell their crop of tomatoes, and their seventh child was born there prematurely. Several weeks later the three Poitiers returned to their home on Cat Island, where Sidney spent the first ten years of his life.

In 1937, worsening economic conditions led the Poitiers to move to Nassau, the capital city of the Bahamas. Their lives did not improve, however, and they lived in extreme poverty. The only bright spot in Sidney's life was the movies, which he had discovered soon after his arrival in Nassau. He often skipped school, and by his early teens, pranks and more serious misbehavior were causing his parents concern. In January 1943, they sent him to Miami to live with his oldest brother, Cyril, and his wife.

In Miami, Sidney Poitier experienced severe racial discrimination for the first time. He also discovered that there were few employment opportunities for him, since he had little education. After a few months of working at a series of menial jobs in the racially tense atmosphere of the South, Poitier decided to leave. Working his way north, he reached New York City in the summer of 1943.

Poitier was immediately captivated by New York, although his first months there were far from comfortable. He worked for a while as a dishwasher and often slept outdoors. As winter approached, Poitier experienced cold weather for the first time. With no warm clothing and no place to stay, he decided to join the U.S. Army. Lying about his age, he was inducted in November 1943 and served for a year as an orderly in a mental hospital in Northport, New York.

Dismissed from the service in December 1944, a more mature Poitier returned to New York City determined to make a career for himself. With severance pay from the army, Poitier rented a room in Harlem and found a job as a dishwasher. One day in 1945, he read an article in the *Amsterdam News*, a black newspaper, about the American Negro Theatre, which was looking for new actors. On a whim, Poitier decided to audition but was turned aside by the group's manager, Frederick O'Neal, because of his thick West Indian accent and also because he was barely literate.

Poitier responded by embarking upon a self-improvement program. He bought a radio and every evening spent hours imitating voices that he heard on broadcasts. He also improved his literacy skills by reading a newspaper carefully every day. In April 1946, Poitier returned to the American Negro Theatre for another audition. This time he was given a three-month trial admission to the school run by the group.

Poitier worked as a packer in a shirt factory during the day while he attended acting classes at night. At the end of the trial period, Poitier was asked to leave because of insufficient progress, but he won a three-month extension by agreeing to serve without pay as the theater janitor. The determined Poitier slowly made progress, and he became the under-study for a young actor in the troupe named Harry Belafonte in a play called *Days of Our Youth*. One night when Belafonte was ill, Poitier assumed his role during a rehearsal. In the audience was James Light, a prominent director, who was so impressed by Poitier that he offered him a part in an all-black

Broadway production of the ancient Greek comedy *Lysistrata*.

Although the production was a failure, critics praised Poitier for his performance, and the American Negro Theatre offered him a job as an understudy in their touring show, *Anna Lucasta*. Poitier toured with the show for three years, and by the time it ended in 1949 he had learned to act and to work with a drama company. Back in New York, he won an audition for a major role in the film *No Way Out*, in which he played a young doctor who was the victim of racial prejudice. Critics praised Poitier for his performance in the film, which was released in 1950.

Poitier's next project was the film version of Alan Paton's novel *Cry, the Beloved Country*, a story of racial segregation in South Africa. The movie was made in that country, and Poitier, forced because of his color to stay near the black shantytowns of Johannesburg, got a close look at the pain and suffering of racial oppression. Released in 1951, Poitier's second film was also a critical success.

That same year Poitier married Juanita Hardy, a model and dancer, and a year later their first daughter was born. Poitier and his wife had three more daughters before their divorce in the 1970s. Poitier married his second wife, an actress named Joanna Shimkus, in 1976; they are the parents of two daughters.

Despite the success of his first two films, Poitier found it difficult to find other parts during the early 1950s. Finally, he was offered a leading role in the

1955 movie *Blackboard Jungle,* in which he played a rebellious teenager. The film was a great commercial success and Poitier was acclaimed for his performance. He made other films in quick succession, including *Edge of the City, Something of Value, Mark of the Hawk,* and *Band of Angels,* and also appeared in a television drama for the first time. His next film, *The Defiant Ones,* released in 1958, earned Poitier his first Academy Award nomination for Best Actor.

In 1959, Poitier starred as Porgy in the movie version of George Gershwin's musical *Porgy and Bess,* lip-synching the songs. Poitier was criticized for making this film, which many blacks felt was denigrating to their race. The following year, however, he received cheers from both blacks and whites for his performance in the Broadway production of *A Raisin in the Sun,* a play about a poor black family in Chicago. In 1961, he also starred in the film version. During the early 1960s, Poitier made four other movies: *All the Young Men,* in which he played a sergeant in the Korean War; *Paris Blues,* about jazz musicians; *Pressure Point,* in which he played a prison psychiatrist; and *Lilies of the Field,* about a young drifter who befriends a group of nuns in the American Southwest.

Lilies of the Field won Poitier an Oscar as Best Actor in the spring of 1964—the first time a black man had won the award. Following this victory, Poitier made five more films in quick succession—*The Bedford Incident, The Long Ships, The Slender Thread, Duel at Diablo,* and *A Patch of Blue*—which were moderately successful. Poitier had a major hit in the 1967 film *To Sir with Love*, in which he played a schoolteacher in the London slums. That year a Gallup Poll named him the most popular movie star in America.

Poitier made two more hit films in 1967: *Guess Who's Coming to Dinner?* in which he plays the fiancé of a white woman, and *In the Heat of the Night*, costarring Poitier as a detective arrested for murder in a small southern town. Both movies were nominated for an Academy Award as Best Picture of the Year, and *In the Heat of the Night* received the Oscar.

By this time, Poitier had decided to create his own projects rather than waiting for roles to be offered to him. His first attempt in this direction was a low-budget film called *For Love of Ivy* (1968), about the strivings of a young black woman; Poitier developed the idea for the script, helped finance the picture, and costarred. During the early 1970s, however, his career fell into what he later termed a "twilight zone." So-called black-exploitation movies were on the rise, featuring street life, and there was little demand for the gentler "crossover films," those appealing to both black and white audiences, that Poitier had acted in and sometimes directed during these years.

Poitier's career took an upturn in 1975 with the box office success of *Uptown Saturday Night*, a comedy he directed and in which he costarred with Bill Cosby, Harry Belafonte, and Richard Pryor. A sequel, *Let's Do It Again*, was released the following year and was also a commercial success, as was *A Piece of the Action*, another comedy released in 1977.

During the next decade Poitier was absent from the screen as an actor, although he directed several successful pictures, including *Fast Forward* (1985). In 1987, he returned to film acting in *Little Nikita* and has appeared in several other films in recent years. Poitier's autobiography, *This Life*, was published in 1980.

PAUL ROBESON

Singer and actor Paul Leroy Robeson was born on April 9, 1898, in Princeton, New Jersey, where his father, William, was the pastor of a black church. Paul was the youngest of eight children. His mother, Anna Robeson, was a schoolteacher of African, Indian, and English ancestry. William Robeson had escaped from slavery at the age of fifteen, fought in the Union Army during the Civil War, and then worked his way through Lincoln University, where he trained to become a minister.

When Paul Robeson was six years old, his mother died from burns suffered in a household accident. By this time, Paul was the only child still living at home, and he and his father moved to Westfield, New Jersey, where they lived for a while. Then William Robeson was appointed pastor of the St. Thomas African Methodist Episcopal Zion Church in Somerville, another New Jersey town, and father and son resettled there.

Paul Robeson attended local schools in Somerville and was an excellent student. During his senior year in high school, he scored highest in a competitive examination for a four-year scholarship to Rutgers College (later Rutgers University). In the fall of 1915, several months after his high school graduation, he entered Rutgers, becoming the first member of his family to attend a white college. At Rutgers he was the only black student then enrolled, and only the third black student in the college's 149-year history.

Despite his uniqueness, Robeson was a popular student at Rutgers. Standing six feet three inches and weighing 240 pounds, Robeson was a handsome and imposing figure with a deep voice, and he impressed everyone who met him. He won the freshman prize for oratory and the sophomore and junior prizes for extemporaneous speaking. He also excelled in athletics and earned an impressive 12 varsity letters in four sports—football, baseball, basketball, and track. He was named an All-American end in 1917 and 1918 and won the admiration of white teammates who had earlier threatened to quit the football team if he was allowed to play.

Robeson participated in a number of other college activities while compiling an outstanding academic record and working throughout his four years at Rutgers at a series of menial jobs to pay for expenses. He was elected to Phi Beta Kappa, the academic honor society, in his junior year, and the following year was named to another honor society, Cap and Skull. He was selected to give the commencement address at his graduation in 1919.

Robeson then moved to Harlem, a black neighborhood in New York City, and in 1920 was admitted to the Columbia University Law School. He paid for his studies by playing professional football on weekends. During his first year at Columbia, a new friend named Eslanda Goode encouraged him to launch a career as an actor. Robeson first appeared in an amateur production at the Harlem YMCA and made his professional debut at the Lafayette Theatre in 1921. That same year he married Goode, a graduate student in chemistry at Columbia.

Robeson continued his law studies while he appeared on Broadway and also toured England briefly. In 1923, he received his law degree from Columbia, was admitted to the bar, and was hired by a law firm headed by a well-known Rutgers graduate. Robeson quickly realized that there would be few opportunities for him in an all-white firm, and the lure of the theater proved irresistible. By 1924, he had abandoned a career as a lawyer and joined the Provincetown Players, an experimental acting troupe based in Greenwich Village. The well-known playwright Eugene O'Neill was associated with the troupe, and in May 1924 Robeson starred in two O'Neill plays presented at the Provincetown (Massachusetts) Playhouse: *The Emperor Jones* and *All God's Chillun Got Wings.* Reviewers were enthusiastic, and Robeson became particularly celebrated for his portrayal of Brutus Jones, the black dictator of a West Indian island in *The Emperor Jones.*

In 1925, Robeson and a friend, composer and pianist Lawrence Brown, presented a concert of Negro spirituals and folk songs in New York City. Robeson's performance impressed audience and critics alike, and during 1925–26, Robeson and Brown toured the United States, Great Britain, and Europe. Robeson had an aptitude for languages—he eventually mastered more than twenty—and he learned the folk songs of many nations in their original tongues.

During the next 15 years, Robeson gave numerous concerts at home and abroad. He also performed as a singer and actor on the radio and stage and in films, and made more than 300 recordings. His most notable roles included Joe in *Show Boat,* singing "Ole Man River," and the lead in *Othello.* Robeson first played Othello in London in 1930; 13 years later he starred in a highly acclaimed Broadway production of Shakespeare's play and made theater history as the first black lead with a white supporting cast. In 1959, Robeson was again hailed when he starred in a performance of Othello in Shakespeare's home village, Stratford-on-Avon, England.

Robeson also appeared in celebrated film versions of *The Emperor Jones* (1933) and *Show Boat* (1936), and was praised for his work in other movies during the 1930s and early 1940s. During World War II, he withdrew from film acting, however, explaining that "The industry is not prepared to permit me to portray the life or express the living interests, hopes, and aspirations of the struggling people from whom I come."

During his first visit to the Soviet Union in 1934, Robeson had been impressed by the communist system and what he believed was its lack of social and racial discrimination. He became fluent in the Russian language and was a frequent visitor to the USSR, where he became a popular performer. At one point Robeson declared that he loved Russia more than any other country and sent his only child, Paul junior, to school there.

Robeson became a prominent supporter of many left-wing causes at home and abroad, including those in Great Britain, Spain, and West Africa, and in the 1930s he spent much of his time abroad. When he returned with his family to the United States in 1939, he observed that the country's racial climate seemed to have improved. During World War II, Robeson continued his support of antifascist groups, often giving benefit concerts to raise money for refugees.

After the war, as tensions increased between the United States and the Soviet Union, Robeson's popularity in his home country declined. He was accused of being a communist and was denounced in newspapers and magazines as a supporter of the USSR. He was no longer in demand as a concert performer and actor, and his recordings were withdrawn from stores. Pressure was even placed upon Rutgers University to withdraw Robeson's name from alumni rolls and athletic records and to rescind an honorary degree that the college had given him.

In the face of these attacks, Robeson reaffirmed his support for the socialist practices of the Soviet Union, "which in one generation has raised our people to the full dignity of mankind." In 1950, the U.S. State Department demanded that Robeson surrender his passport and denied him the right to travel abroad unless he signed a loyalty oath. For the next eight years, Robeson fought this ban through a series of lawsuits in federal courts. During this time he earned virtually no money; his only concert appearances were before small radical groups. His stature in America was further diminished in 1952, when the Soviet Union awarded him the Stalin Peace Prize.

By 1958, when Robeson won his battle with the State Department and recovered his passport, anticommunist feeling in the United States had lessened somewhat, and he gave what was billed as a "farewell concert" that year in New York City's Carnegie Hall. After making a short tour of the West Coast and recording an album, he left the United States and lived abroad for five years. In 1959, while traveling in Russia, he was hospitalized for circulatory and other ailments. He spent the next few years in and out of hospitals in Eastern Europe and England but never fully regained his health.

In 1963, Robeson and his wife returned to the United States. Robeson announced his retirement from the stage and all public affairs—he had not sung in public since 1961—and went into seclusion. Following the death of his wife in December 1965, Robeson moved to Philadelphia to live with a sister.

During the 1970s, many of Robeson's recordings were reissued and in 1973 he was honored on his 75th birthday by a gala at Carnegie Hall. Paying tribute to Robeson on this occasion were leading black entertainers and civil rights leaders, including Harry Belafonte, Sidney Poitier, and Coretta Scott King. Robeson was too ill to attend, but a tape-recorded message from him was played at the event. He died on January 23, 1976, in Philadelphia.

SPORTS HEROES

ARTHUR ASHE

Champion of the tennis courts and of social issues, Arthur Robert Ashe, Jr., was born in Richmond, Virginia, on July 10, 1943. His father, Arthur, Sr., was a guard in charge of Brook Field, Richmond's largest playground. His mother, Mattie, died of complications during her third pregnancy when Arthur was six years old, leaving her husband to raise Arthur and his younger brother, John.

A strict disciplinarian, Mr. Ashe taught his sons the importance of self-reliance and self-discipline, two traits that would later prove essential to Arthur. Arthur first picked up a tennis racket at the age of six on the courts at Brook Field. Though childhood illnesses had left him with a slight build, he learned how to perfect his stroke from Ronald Charity, a top-ranked black player who worked there as an instructor.

Arthur showed such promise on the court that at the age of 10, Dr. Robert Johnson, a member of the all-black American Tennis Association (ATA) who had trained Althea Gibson, offered to train him. When Arthur was 12 years old, he won the ATA National Championship for his age group, then continued to win tournament after tournament. Nevertheless, he was disappointed when the predominantly white U.S. Lawn Tennis Association (USLTA), the sport's most important governing body, rejected his application for a junior tournament in his hometown of Richmond even though the organization then ranked him fifth among all tennis players in his age group.

In 1960, Arthur became the ATA's youngest champion ever when he won both the junior and the men's singles titles. By this time, it was clear that because Arthur was becoming one of the great black tennis players in the ATA, it was time for him to leave Richmond, where segregation laws prohibited him from playing on indoor courts, thus restricting his court time to the summer and hindering his development.

That year, Ashe was sent to Sumner High School in St. Louis, Missouri, where he could play tennis indoors in the winter and compete in tournaments during the spring and summer. In November, he became the first black to win the National Juniors Indoor Tournament when he upset the top-seeded player in a four-and-a-half-hour marathon match. His equally committed dedication to his studies paid off also; that spring he graduated from Sumner first in his class. His grades and tennis skills allowed him to become the first black to receive a tennis scholarship to the University of California at Los Angeles (UCLA).

At UCLA, Ashe majored in business administration. While a student there, he represented the United States several times as a member of the Davis Cup team, participated for the first time in the All-England Championships at Wimbledon, and improved his standing in the world amateur rankings from 28th to 6th. In 1964 he was given the Johnston Award, which is voted annually to that individual who contributes the most to the game while exhibiting good sportsmanship and character. For Ashe, the award carried an additional significance: after years of discrimination, blacks were finally being accepted in the tennis world.

By 1965, Ashe was the top-ranked collegiate tennis player in America. He continued to be a driving force for the Davis Cup team, and he played well at both

Wimbledon and the U.S. National Championships at Forest Hills, New York, although he failed to win either title. His hometown proclaimed February 4, 1966, Arthur Ashe Day, and the city where he had once been prohibited from playing on all-white tennis courts honored him with a banquet and a ceremony at city hall.

After graduating from UCLA in June 1966, Ashe fulfilled his two-year ROTC commitment to the U.S. Army as assistant tennis coach at the U.S. Military Academy at West Point. Though his military obligation played havoc with his tournament schedule, he still rose to the number-two ranking among U.S. amateurs.

Nineteen sixty-eight proved to be a banner year for Ashe. After a strong showing at Wimbledon, Ashe became the first black man to win a Grand Slam tournament when he won the first U.S. Open at Forest Hills, thereby securing his top ranking among the world's amateurs. He followed up his victory in December by helping his teammates bring home the Davis Cup from Australia.

Upon his return to the United States, Ashe found himself in the spotlight. His picture appeared on the cover of numerous magazines, and he was courted by various companies to promote their products. It was not only his victories on the tennis courts that made him a celebrity but his involvement in social causes as well.

In 1969, Ashe and several other players created the International Tennis Players Association (ITPA) to protect the interests of tennis players. The ITPA evolved into the Association of Tennis Players (ATP) in 1972 and, with Ashe serving as vice-president, boycotted Wimbledon that year in protest over unfair treatment of a Yugoslavian member of the ATP.

Racism was another issue of importance to Ashe. In 1969, after he applied for and was refused a visa to South Africa to play tennis there, he enlisted the support of various groups; his efforts resulted in the expulsion of South Africa from the Davis Cup competition in 1970.

Because of his support of human rights issues, the U.S. government invited Ashe to speak before the African subcommittee of the House of Representatives Foreign Relations Committee. He was also invited to serve as a U.S. goodwill ambassador for a tour of Africa. When, in 1973, South Africa finally granted Ashe a visa and the opportunity to play in the South African Open, it marked the first time a black had ever competed in the event. Ashe made his appearance in the tournament even more memorable by teaming with Tom Okker to win the doubles title.

As Ashe became more involved in business and civil rights matters, his tennis game began to fall off somewhat. From 1971 to 1974, Ashe won only 11 of the 123 tournaments he entered. In 1975, at the age of 31, he came back to win the WCT championship in May, and he finally reached his goal by winning at Wimbledon, where he beat Jimmy Connors in five sets. His victories that year earned him the distinction of being ranked number one in the world—the first black male professional tennis player to attain that position.

Ashe married Jeanne Marie Moutoussamy, a professional photographer, on February 20, 1977, at the United Nations Chapel in New York City. He continued to participate in tournaments until July 1979, when his career was cut short by a heart attack. Though the tennis superstar later underwent quadruple bypass surgery to alleviate several blocked arteries, he continued to be active in the sports world as captain of the 1981 U.S. Davis Cup team and as a television commentator for the ABC and HBO networks. Ashe was also an active member of the USTA Player Development Committee, which he cofounded to promote junior tennis and to offer underpriviledged children the opportunity to play the sport.

Ashe was inducted into the Tennis Hall of Fame in Newport, Rhode Island, in 1985. In 1987, his wife, Jeanne, gave birth to their only child, a daughter, Camera Elizabeth. Ashe's other contributions included serving on the board of the American Heart Association and his authorship of several books. *A Hard Road to Glory*, his three-volume history of black American athletes, was especially well received and brought Ashe many requests to lecture at universities and colleges.

Ironically, the heart operations that saved Ashe's life ultimately robbed him of it as well. On April 8, 1992, Ashe held a press conference to announce that he had contracted acquired immune deficiency syndrome (AIDS) from a blood transfusion following heart surgery that contained the AIDS virus. Ashe revealed that he had felt compelled to make the announcement because the newspaper *USA TODAY* was about to publish the story.

Once again, Arthur Ashe found himself in the spotlight, championing another cause and fighting more discrimination. He spoke out both for his own right to privacy and that of similarly afflicted individuals, and he became active in the fight against AIDS and the ignorance and prejudice that surround the disease, forming a fund-raising foundation and joining the boards of the Harvard AIDS Institute and the UCLA AIDS Institute. Even after the announcement of his condition, Ashe continued the fight against racism and prejudice, and he was arrested and jailed in the summer of 1992 following a protest in front of the White House regarding U.S. policy on Haitian refugees.

Arthur Ashe, tennis champion, defender of human rights, and fighter against racism, contracted pneumonia, a frequent complication of AIDS, and died on February 6, 1993, in New York City. After lying in state in the governor's mansion in Richmond, Virginia, he was buried in his hometown following a funeral service in which he was praised not only for his achievements in the sport of tennis but also for his quiet dignity and unshaken beliefs.

CHUCK COOPER

Charles "Chuck" Cooper, the first African-American in the National Basketball Association (NBA), was 24 years old when he was drafted by the Boston Celtics on April 25, 1950. A solid six-foot-five-inch, 215-pound center, Cooper had been a first-team all-American at Duquesne University in Pittsburgh and had led his team to the semifinals of the prestigious National Invitational

Tournament (NIT). Nevertheless, all the owners and general managers present at the Chicago hotel where the NBA draft was held were shocked when the owner of the Celtics, Walter Brown, announced that he was making Cooper Boston's second-round pick. "Walter, don't you know he's a colored boy?" one of the other owners blurted out. To which Brown retorted, "I don't give a damn if he's striped, plaid, or polka-dot! Boston takes Chuck Cooper of Duquesne!"

Cooper's choice by the Celtics was the culmination of a long journey by black players that had begun soon after the first game of basketball was played on January 15, 1892, in Springfield, Massachusetts. By the beginning of the 20th century, black players were featured on a number of college basketball squads; the most notable of these performers was the versatile Paul Robeson of Rutgers, who went on to become a renowned singer and actor as well as a political activist. The pool of talented black players was augmented in the years following World War I, when the black colleges in the segregated South formed their own athletic conference, the Central Interscholastic Athletic Association (CIAA). Among the CIAA's members, Morgan State, Virginia Union, and Xavier of New Orleans emerged as dominant teams during the 1920s and 1930s, attracting players from the North as well as the South.

Black professional basketball teams also came into being in the early 1900s—most notably, the Incorporators and the Loendi Big Five—but the best of the black pro teams was created in 1923. In that year,

Robert L. "Bob" Douglas persuaded a fellow immigrant from the Caribbean, William Roche, to make his Harlem Renaissance Casino available for basketball games. The teams played with portable baskets, and after the game they cleared the floor so that the audience could dance to the music of a swing band. Douglas's team, the Harlem Renaissance, soon known simply as the Rens, was a dominant force from the start, ultimately compiling a record of 2,318 wins against only 381 losses. The Rens truly hit their stride during the 1930s, when they boasted such standout players as William "Pops" Gates, Fats Jenkins, Bill Yancey, and Charles "Tarzan" Cooper. Traveling from city to city on their own bus, the Rens steamrolled black and white teams alike. Opposing players and sports reporters acknowledged them as the best team in the world.

Though there were instances of black players being hired by white teams, an unofficial color line clearly existed in professional basketball. Aside from playing for the Rens, there was only one other way for black players to earn a decent living at the game—by playing for the Harlem Globetrotters. The Globetrotters, who evolved from a Chicago semipro team known as the Savoy Big Five, achieved prominence when they hired a white promoter, Abe Saperstein. With Saperstein making the contacts—and eventually running the team—the Trotters were able to get more bookings, for better money, than a team like the Rens, whose management was black.

The Globetrotters, who continued to make Chicago their home base, soon became known as much for their clowning on the court as for their considerable basketball prowess. Their ball-handling tricks and other antics made the Trotters less threatening to white spectators and took the sting out of the drubbings they administered to all-white teams. Even though Saperstein's legacy has become a controversial one, with some regarding him as a benefactor of black players and others as an exploiter, he made a long-lasting financial success of the Globetrotters and provided a showcase for such outstanding athletes as Goose Tatum and Marcus Haynes.

During the 1940s, basketball changed from a slow-paced, grinding type of game to a more up-tempo sport that featured such innovations as the jump shot and the fast break. Black players were often at the forefront of these changes, making the most of their superior jumping ability and quickness.

When the National Basketball Association came into being in 1949, the color line still prevailed, but it had become clear that segregation in sports was on its way out. Two years earlier, Jackie Robinson had broken the color line in major league baseball when he stepped on the field for the Brooklyn Dodgers. Nevertheless, when the Celtics picked Chuck Cooper in the NBA's second player draft, the move created shock waves, and not merely among NBA owners. Abe Saperstein, fearing that his Globetrotters would no longer have first pick of the nation's best black players, threatened to cancel all his team's engagements at the Boston Garden. But Boston owner Walter Brown refused to back down, and the NBA was open to the nation's great black hoopsters.

Two rival teams quickly followed Boston's example—so quickly, in fact, that although Chuck Cooper was the first black player taken in the draft, he was neither the first to sign an NBA contract nor the first to play in an NBA game. The distinction of signing the first NBA pact belonged to Nat "Sweetwater" Clifton, whose contract was purchased from the Globetrotters (after he and Saperstein had a falling out) by the New York Knickerbockers. And the first black player to actually enter a game during the 1950 season was Earl Lloyd, who started for the Washington Caps against the Rochester Royals on October 31.

None of the three players followed the example of Jackie Robinson by achieving stardom and Hall of Fame status. Cooper's first year for the Celtics, in which he averaged 9.3 points a game and contributed a total of 562 rebounds and 174 assists, was quite respectable—but it turned out to be the best he enjoyed with the team. Too short to play center in the pros, he now had to adjust to playing forward and occasionally guard. In 1951, Cooper's scoring average fell to 8.2; it dropped still further, to 6.5, the following year. In 1954, the Celtics traded him to the Milwaukee Hawks, and in 1955–56 he moved on to play for the Fort Wayne Pistons and the St. Louis Hawks. By 1956, Cooper's NBA career was over.

In looking back on his NBA days, Cooper felt that he was never given a fair chance to show what he could do. He claimed that his offensive potential was overlooked and that he was always asked to do the rebounding and tough defensive work while his white teammates did the shooting. He also believed that his injuries were taken less seriously than those of white players. Interestingly, Lloyd also felt that he had been stifled as a professional player, though he had a longer career than Cooper, playing until 1960. Even Clifton, whose seven-year career with the Knicks was distinguished by a 10.3 scoring average and a 1957 All-Star selection, later asserted that New York management had kept him under wraps.

After Cooper left the NBA, he spent a few seasons with the Harlem Magicians, a team organized by former Globetrotter Marcus Haynes. After retiring as a player, Cooper returned to Pittsburgh, where he had attended college, and enjoyed a successful business career until his death in February 1984. Sweetwater Clifton, by contrast, drove a cab in his native Chicago for 25 years, until his death in 1990. Lloyd was the only one of the trio who remained in the game, eventually serving as head coach of the Detroit Pistons during the 1970s.

Before the 1950s were over, the NBA was to be all but dominated by black stars such as Bill Russell, Wilt Chamberlain, Elgin Baylor, and Oscar Robertson. In 1966, the NBA became the first major professional league to feature a black head coach when Bill Russell took the helm of the Boston Celtics. By the 1990s, more than 70 percent of the league's players were black, and the hiring of black coaches and front-office personnel was taken for granted in the league. Though frustrated in his quest for NBA stardom, Chuck Cooper, along with fellow pioneers Earl Lloyd and Sweetwater Clifton, began the quiet revolution that has made professional basketball a model of equal opportunity in sports.

ALTHEA GIBSON

Tennis champion Althea Gibson was born on August 25, 1927, in Silver, South Carolina. Her sharecropper parents, Daniel and Annie Gibson, later moved the family to New York City in an attempt to escape the poverty and racial discrimination of the South.

A mischievous and rebellious child, Althea grew up in the predominantly black neighborhood of Harlem.

As she grew older, she was often in trouble, skipping school and getting into fights. She did, however, excel at athletics, and at the age of 13 she was discovered by a member of the community on a paddle-tennis court and taken to the Cosmopolitan Club, New York's most prestigious black tennis club, where she was given lessons.

Tennis had been introduced to the United States as a country club sport in the 1880s. Because most clubs were segregated, it had remained a predominantly white sport. In large part, the members of the Cosmopolitan Club encouraged Althea to play because they saw in her a chance to promote the participation of blacks in tennis.

A year after she started tennis lessons, Althea played in and won her first tournament, the New York State Open Championship, sponsored by the American Tennis Association (ATA), an association of black tennis players. Her victory proved to the members of the Cosmopolitan Club that Althea was a talent worth developing.

Althea continued to work on her game at the Cosmopolitan Club, and when she was 18 years old she was befriended by Sugar Ray Robinson, the celebrated boxer, who encouraged her to pursue her education and her tennis career. She was given this opportunity after two men who were interested in promoting black tennis players spotted her at an ATA competition and offered to give her the opportunity to finish high school and to continue her tennis lessons.

Terrified at first at the thought of leaving home, Althea eventually moved into the household of Dr. Hubert A. Eaton, a wealthy South Carolina doctor. While she concentrated on her studies and her tennis game, Althea was introduced to the legally sanctioned racial discrimination that was prevalent in the Deep South. She had to sit in the back of buses and was not allowed in areas marked "Whites Only." This discrimination was more overt than the discrimination she had experienced in New York.

In 1947, Gibson won all nine of the women's singles titles on the ATA circuit. Her victory at the U.S. National Championship was the beginning of her winning streak of 10 consecutive ATA National Championships. In the following years, as Althea continued to dominate black women's tennis, the ATA increased its efforts to break tennis's racial barrier. These efforts paid off in Althea's senior year of high school, with the acceptance of her entry to the Eastern Indoor Championships, an event sponsored by the U.S. Lawn Tennis Association (USLTA), which governed tennis events played by whites.

Althea played well in the tournament, advancing to the quarterfinals. The USLTA was impressed with her performance and invited her to the National Indoor Championship, in which she put in another strong showing but lost in the quarterfinal once again. During this time, Althea was also given an opportunity to achieve her other goal—the completion of her education—when Florida A & M

University offered her a full scholarship for the fall of 1949.

Although she continued to play at the USLTA indoor championships, Althea was not invited to any of its outdoor events because these were played at private, segregated country clubs. However, as she continued to play well and public interest in her increased, the USLTA's practices were brought into question. An important development in this regard came in 1950, when Alice Marble, who had dominated women's tennis in the 1930s, spoke out against racial discrimination in tennis.

Marble's article in *American Lawn Tennis* magazine shamed the USLTA into offering Althea invitations to play in their tournaments. The main event of the USLTA tour was the U.S. National Championships, held annually in Forest Hills, New York, and in August of 1950, Althea Gibson was invited to play in the tournament.

Though mobbed by curious reporters and onlookers, Gibson held her own at Forest Hills, losing in the second round to Louise Brough, the Wimbledon champion. Nonetheless, Gibson's appearance at the U.S. National Championships was a victory in itself; she had caused a media sensation and had torn down the barrier to blacks participating in USLTA events.

In 1951, Gibson broke another color barrier when she became the first black to play in the All-England Tennis Championships at Wimbledon, the most prestigious event in tennis. However, she was disappointed in her performance and was eliminated in the third round. Over the next few years, Gibson remained a strong player on the ATA and USLTA circuits, achieving the highest ranking of her career to date in 1953, when she was ranked the seventh-best woman player in the United States.

After reaching this pinnacle, her performance began to slip, and she gradually slipped out of the public's notice. After her graduation from college, Gibson took a position as a physical education instructor at Lincoln University, a black college in racially segregated Jefferson City, Missouri. Unhappy with her career, she submitted an application to the Women's Army Corps, but these plans were put aside when the U.S. State Department asked her to participate in a goodwill tennis tour of Southeast Asia.

The tour renewed Gibson's confidence and enthusiasm for tennis. She was greatly impressed by the Far East, and she was able to concentrate on her game. At the end of the tour, Gibson chose to go to Europe to prepare for the Wimbledon championship that spring.

Gibson thus began a whirlwind tennis tour in which she swept European tennis with victories from Cannes to Monte Carlo. In May 1956, she became the first black to win a major singles title with a victory at the French Championships. However, Wimbledon once again proved to be her nemesis, and she lost in her quarterfinals match. Even though she also lost the U.S. National Championships in the finals, she had leapt from thirteenth to second in the national rankings.

In 1957, Gibson realized the dream that had eluded her for so long when she won at Wimbledon, defeating fellow American Darlene Hard in the finals. Upon her return to New York, Gibson was greeted with a ticker-tape parade and luncheons in her honor. Despite her accomplishments, Gibson was uncomfortable with her new status as a symbol of black achievement. Many blacks criticized her for letting tennis take precedence over civil rights issues and attacked her reluctance to become an outspoken representative for black people.

Her victory at the 1957 U.S. National Tennis Championships clinched her standing as the best female tennis player in the world. The following year, she shocked the tennis world when, moments after her second victory at Forest Hills, Althea Gibson announced her retirement from amateur tennis. Her reason for retiring was purely financial. Despite her many titles, Gibson's economic situation was desperate, because in those days tennis was still ostensibly an amateur sport and players were not awarded money for their titles.

In the following years, Gibson attempted to pursue singing and acting careers with modest success, but her most successful venture came in 1959, when she toured with the Harlem Globetrotters in a tennis exhibition. Her financial troubles continued when she launched a disappointing exhibition tour of her own, which left her in debt when it ended. Her salvation came in the form of another game—golf.

Gibson had first played golf in the mid-1950s, but it was not until 1962 that she considered becoming a professional. Golf was another sport pervaded by racial prejudice, but Althea became the first black woman to enter the Ladies Professional Golf Association (LPGA) in 1964. Even though the country clubs where many of the LPGA tournaments were held were racially segregated, Gibson's entrance into the LPGA was smoother than her struggle in the world of tennis. LPGA members held considerable clout and could remove from their tournament list any country club that would not admit their members. Gibson had the full support of Leonard Wirtz, director of the LPGA, who would move tournaments to other clubs in response to discrimination against Althea.

Gibson set out to prove herself on the LPGA tour, gradually improving throughout 1964 and 1965. In 1965, Gibson felt her career was stable enough to concentrate on her personal life, and she married Will Darben, a man she had known for many years. Her golf game peaked in 1967, but by the end of 1971, she realized it was time for her to retire.

Her marriage also came to an end, and in 1975, Gibson found a new home when she became the manager of the Department of Recreation in East Orange, New Jersey, a city with a large black population. She was inducted into the South Carolina Hall of Fame in 1983 and the Florida Sports Hall of Fame in 1984. She currently maintains a quiet life in East Orange, New Jersey.

JACK JOHNSON

The first black man to win
the heavyweight boxing championship of the world,
John Arthur "Jack" Johnson was born in Galveston,
Texas, on March 31, 1878. Henry Johnson, Jack's
father, was a former slave from Maryland who had also
been an amateur boxer; at the time of Jack's birth,
Henry Johnson made a living as a woodworker and
school janitor. Jack's mother, Tina, called Tiny, was

a high-spirited woman who saw that her six children went to school and church; when necessary, she kept them in line with a two-by-four.

Tall and awkward as a child, Jack was inclined to be anything but a fighter. Indeed, the neighborhood bullies found him a tempting target until his mother grew tired of seeing him pushed around. She told him that if he did not begin fighting back, he would get an even worse beating from her. Jack decided to take his chances with the bullies and found that he could thrash them easily, making use of his extraordinary hand speed.

Despite his mother's efforts, Jack quickly lost interest in school. He dropped out after the sixth grade, working at a succession of odd jobs but always dreaming of somehow making his mark in life. He began to fight for sport along Galveston's rough-and-tumble waterfront and eventually gravitated into the local boxing clubs, where he honed his skills and had his first professional bouts. In 1899, he made a brief trip to Chicago but returned home after being badly outclassed in a bout and blowing his share of the purse at the racetrack.

After living through the dreadful hurricane that destroyed much of Galveston in the summer of 1900, Johnson left home for good the following year and made his way to California. At that time, none of the leading white prizefighters would agree to a match with a black opponent, so Johnson could not even dream of reaching the upper echelons of the sport. He fought other black heavyweights, some of whom were very skilled, and by 1903 he was recognized as the best of the group. He had also developed a taste for elegant, attention-getting clothes and fast motorcars.

In 1905, Johnson finally got a fight against a leading white contender, Marvin Hart, in San Francisco. Johnson pummeled Hart over 20 rounds, but the referee awarded the decision to the white fighter. A disgusted Johnson left California for Philadelphia, where he had the first of a series of bouts with Joe Jeannette, a top-notch black fighter. In 1906, he squared off against Sam Langford, the best of the black heavyweights, and won a 15-round decision. Still frustrated by boxing's color line, Johnson then issued a public challenge to the heavyweight champion, Jim Jeffries. Jeffries's reply: "When there are no white men left to fight, I will quit the business."

In May 1905, Jeffries followed up on his vow and hung up his gloves. He arranged a series of elimination bouts among the white contenders, and Jack Burns, a smallish Canadian, emerged from the lackluster group as the new champion. Burns's lack of popularity gave Johnson an opening. Having acquired a clever manager, Sam Fitzpatrick, Johnson began a public campaign to force Burns into a fight. After disposing of a number of white fighters—including former heavyweight champion Bob Fitzsimmons, Kid Cutler, and Fireman Jim Flynn—Johnson had the press calling on Burns to settle "the matter of fistic supremacy between the white race and the colored."

Burns avoided Johnson by going on a European tour in 1907–8. Johnson sailed after him, taking on a few opponents in England, and he and Burns eventually wound up in Australia, where they signed a contract that promised Johnson a $5,000 purse. (Burns's share was $30,000.) The fight took place before 20,000 spectators on Christmas Day, 1908, in Rushcutter's Bay, a suburb of Sydney. Burns, at five feet seven inches and 175 pounds, was no match for Johnson, a muscular six-footer who weighed more than 200 pounds. Johnson decked Burns with a terrific right uppercut in the first round and could have ended the fight right there. But he chose to carry his opponent for 14 rounds, dishing out fearful punishment while both the crowd and Burns hurled racial slurs at him. When the police finally stopped the contest, Johnson had the heavyweight crown at last.

Johnson played the role of champion to the hilt, buying jewelry, automobiles, and carousing with a succession of white women. A string of "great white hopes" emerged to reclaim the title, but Johnson dispatched them all easily, taking pleasure in the cat-calls of the hostile whites who came out to see him beaten.

Johnson's detractors lived in despair until 1909, when Jim Jeffries agreed to come out of retirement and try to regain the title. The Jeffries-Johnson match took place on July 4, 1910, in Reno, Nevada, and once again Johnson proved that he was the best heavyweight boxer in the world. He completely out-classed Jeffries under the hot desert sun, showing the former champion his entire repertoire before closing in for a 15th-round knockout.

The public reaction to Johnson's victory was a sad commentary on race relations in the United States. In city after city, blacks who took to the streets in celebration were set upon by mobs of whites; when the rioting subsided, 20 people lay dead, and hundreds more were injured. The situation was so alarming that federal authorities banned the distribution and showing of the fight film.

Johnson had earned $160,000—a phenomenal sum for that time—from the Jeffries fight, and he found that he could make as much as $2,500 a week traveling the vaudeville circuit. However, the money brought him neither public acceptance nor personal contentment. In 1911, Johnson married Etta Terry Duryea, a white woman he had been living with on and off for some time. The marriage was a disaster; the following year, Duryea, tired of being an outcast among both races, shot herself to death. Johnson quickly took up with Lucille Cameron, an 18-year-old prostitute. When Cameron's mother claimed that Johnson had abducted her daughter, the U.S. Justice Department decided to take action. Even though Johnson and Cameron were married in 1912, the government induced a former lover to testify against the champion and arrested him for violating the Mann Act, a law against transporting women across state lines for prostitution.

Johnson went on trial in Chicago in May 1913. The government's case was flimsy, but an all-white jury convicted Johnson just the same: his crime, in the eyes of society, was consorting with white women. When the judge sentenced Johnson to a year and a day in prison and released him on bail pending appeal, the champion decided to flee the country.

After sailing to Europe from Canada, Johnson enjoyed his exile for a time, until he ran out of money. Then he was forced to put on boxing and wrestling exhibitions in order to get by. In 1914, as World War I broke out in Europe, Johnson agreed to defend his championship in Havana, Cuba, against Jess Willard, a six-foot-six-inch, 250-pound giant from Kansas. Johnson took a leisurely route to Cuba and did little to get his 37-year-old body into fighting trim. The bout, scheduled to go 45 rounds, took place on April 15, 1915. After 20 rounds, it became clear that Johnson could not put the challenger away, and his lack of training began to show. In the 26th, Willard delivered a right to Johnson's jaw that sent the champion to the canvas, where he was counted out.

After the Willard fight, Johnson returned to Europe for a while and then gravitated to Mexico, where he was received as a guest of President Venustiano Carranza. Carranza's overthrow soon ended his welcome, and in 1920 Johnson crossed the border into the United States and surrendered to federal authorities. He served 10 months in the penitentiary at Leavenworth, Kansas; here, at least, the authorities treated him with respect and encouraged him to put on boxing exhibitions for the other inmates.

Upon his release in 1921, Johnson traveled to New York, where he was given a hero's reception in Harlem. He spoke of getting back into the ring and reclaiming his championship, but at the age of 43 he had to content himself with being a living legend. During the 1930s and 1940s, he was frequently called into the ring for a quick bow before important fights; the crowds, which had by now learned to idolize great black champions, such as Joe Louis and Sugar Ray Robinson, cheered him lustily.

On June 10, 1946, while Johnson was driving up from the South to attend the Joe Louis–Billy Conn heavyweight title match, he lost control of his car and crashed into a utility pole. He died a few hours later, at the age of 68. Despite the hard and often tragic circumstances of his life, he realized his ambition of making his mark in life—and made it possible for many other black fighters to realize their own dreams.

JESSE OWENS

The first black American to win an Olympic gold medal, James Cleveland Owens was born on September 12, 1913, in Oakville, Alabama. The youngest in a family of 10 children, James, nicknamed J.C., was a sickly child, prone to bouts of pneumonia and other ailments. His parents, Henry and Mary Emma, were former slaves who struggled to make a living by farming someone else's land. They could not afford decent medical care for young J.C., and they feared he would not survive long. Somehow he pulled through his many illnesses, and by the time he was six he was working the fields with his brothers and sisters and hiking the nine miles to Oakville's one-room schoolhouse.

When J.C. was 10 years old, the family moved north to Cleveland, Ohio, in search of a better life. The transition was difficult for the simple, religious folk from the rural South—but there was work for J.C.'s parents and older brothers, and soon the family enjoyed a level of comfort they had never dreamed of in Alabama. J.C. worked part-time in a cobbler's shop, and he also got to attend a real school. When he gave his name as J. C. Owens on his first day in class, the teacher misunderstood his Alabama drawl and wrote down "Jesse." He was too shy to correct her, and he remained Jesse Owens for the rest of his life.

By the time Jesse reached junior high school, he was a confirmed city boy, wise to the ways of the streets but unsure which direction he was going in. Then he met two people who changed his life. The first was Minnie Ruth Solomon, a young woman whose family had just come north from a farm in Alabama. Since he shared Ruth's background, Jesse was the ideal person to help her get used to Cleveland. Before long the two teenagers were in love, and though they were still too young to marry, the question was settled for both of them. The second important person who came into Jesse's life was Charles Riley, the track coach at Jesse's school. Jesse had not shown any special athletic promise at that point, but Riley saw some potential in him and invited him to try out for the track team.

After beefing up his diet (at Riley's expense) and going through a program to build up his body and his still-delicate lungs, Owens astonished the coach by running the 100-yard dash in 11 seconds, a remarkable time for a 15-year-old. Before long, Riley entered Owens in a variety of events, including the long jump and the high jump, and Owens excelled in them all.

If not for his mother, Owens would have had to leave school at this point, because the Great Depression of the 1930s had drastically reduced the family's income. But Mary Owens insisted that her son enroll at East Technical High School, where Charles Riley was soon hired as assistant track coach. Owens continued to progress under Riley's tutelage, often scoring more than half the team's points at track meets. Owens was named the captain of the team and was also elected student body president in the predominantly white school, a testament to his outgoing personality as well as his athletic brilliance.

In 1933, Owens entered Ohio State University, where he was given an unofficial scholarship, and came under the tutelage of track coach Larry Snyder. When Owens competed in his first Big Ten meet in early 1935, he immediately established his presence by winning three of the four events he entered. That May, at the Big Ten Championships, he astonished everyone by breaking five world records and tying another, a feat still unequaled in the annals of track and field.

Owens was propelled overnight into the role of a national sports star. Before he reaped the benefits of his new status, he took care of some unfinished business. Three years before, Ruth Solomon had given birth to a daughter. When her parents learned that Owens was the child's father, they refused to let Ruth see him again. The couple had been forced to live apart, although Owens sent money regularly for his daughter's support. Now that he had established himself, the Solomons relented; in July 1935, Jesse and Ruth Solomon were married in Cleveland.

The following year, Ohio State officials suspended Owens from the track team because of poor grades. He bore down and raised his average enough to be reinstated in time for the spring, when he ran 100 yards in a world-record time of 9.3 seconds. Dominating the sprints at the Olympic trials, Owens emerged as one of the mainstays of the American squad that journeyed to Berlin, Germany, for the 1936 Summer Olympics.

The Berlin Olympics were the most dramatic event of Owens's career, not only for the records he set but for the pride he brought to all Americans, especially blacks and other ethnic minorities. In 1936, Germany was ruled by Adolf Hitler and his Nazi party. The Nazis fostered the myth of a supposedly superior Aryan race, represented by blue-eyed, blond-haired men and women; they scorned and persecuted all other groups, including Jews and blacks. Hitler bragged that the 1936 Games would be a showcase of Aryan superiority.

Owens single-handedly shattered the Nazis' fantasies, winning his first gold medal with a time of 10.3 seconds in the 100-meter dash, thus tying the Olympic record he had set in a qualifying heat. Topping this feat, he went on to capture the long jump with a record-breaking leap of 26 feet 5 inches. Finally, Owens took his third medal with a record-shattering time of 20.7 in the 200-meter race. Despite the displeasure of their leaders, the German fans went wild over Owens, who became the star of the Games. In addition to his records, his close friendship with the German Luz Long, his biggest competitor in the long jump, exemplified the true Olympic ideals of sportsmanship and international understanding.

Owens returned home a celebrity, hailed in motorcades in New York, Cleveland, and Ohio's state capital, Columbus. He thought of returning to Ohio State, but the opportunity to cash in on his fame was too alluring to resist. His hopes of a movie contract did not pan out, but he was in demand for so many endorsements and banquets that he soon made a considerable sum of money, much of which he used to help his family. He realized, however, that a number of the things he was asked to do were beneath his dignity; perhaps the best-publicized among them was a race against a horse in Havana, Cuba. (With a 40-yard head start, Owens won.)

In the years that followed, Owens struggled continuously to turn his celebrity into a steady income for his family. In 1937, he went on tour as the leader of a 12-piece orchestra, then barnstormed with basketball and baseball teams, putting on running exhibitions when the opportunity presented itself. Unhappy about prolonged absences from his family, he soon found a job with the Cleveland recreation department and also opened a dry-cleaning business. Still, he struggled to make a living; then, in 1940, he suffered a double blow when his beloved mother died and the Internal Revenue Service got after him for back taxes, forcing him to close his business.

Regretting his failure to work harder as a student, Owens now determined to go back to Ohio State and earn his degree. Try as he would, it was too difficult for him to resume the role of a student, and he gave it up after a year. When the United States entered World War II in 1941, Owens was hired by the government to organize physical-fitness programs. Then he took an important and satisfying job with the Ford Motor Company in Detroit, looking after the social needs of the thousands of black workers on the Ford payroll.

Following the end of the war in 1945, Owens moved his family to Chicago and went into the public relations business, lending the luster of his still-famous name to a variety of companies. His business career was given an additional boost by the Associated Press in 1950, when they named him the greatest track-and-field athlete in history. Nevertheless, Owens was to watch with some sadness in the coming years as his records were broken by a new generation of athletes. His business success caused him to become rather conservative politically, and the black protest movement of the 1960s both surprised and annoyed him, causing him to say and write things that he later regretted.

Whatever his difficulties, Owens's spirits were never down for long. The one thing he could not overcome, however, was his health. His lungs, delicate in childhood, now succumbed to the ravages of a 30-year smoking habit. On March 31, 1980, Jesse Owens died of lung cancer in Tucson, Arizona. As an athlete and a man, he established standards that Americans still cherish, even after others have replaced him in the record books.

FRANK ROBINSON

Baseball's first black manager as well as one of its all-time great players, Frank Robinson was born in Beaumont, Texas, on August 31, 1935. When he was very young his mother moved the family to Oakland, California, where Frank grew up in a racially mixed neighborhood. In 1947, when Frank was 11 years old, Jackie Robinson became the first African-American to play major league baseball. At the time, Frank had no thought of playing in the major leagues himself, but he was a good all-around athlete who played baseball, basketball, and football with an intensity that became his hallmark in later years.

When Frank was a 14-year-old junior high school student, he attracted the attention of George Powles, the baseball coach at a nearby school. Powles recruited Robinson for his American Legion team, which went on to win a national championship. While playing for Powles's team, Robinson was noticed by Bobby Mattick, a scout for the Chicago White Sox. When Mattick went to work for the Cincinnati Reds, he remembered Frank and offered him a contract with the Reds' Class C minor league team in Ogden, Utah. Upon graduating from McClymonds High School in 1953, Frank signed his first professional contract, receiving a $3,500 bonus and a salary of $400 a month.

Robinson had a fine season for the Ogden club, batting .348 and smacking 17 home runs. But the season was not a happy one. In addition to being away from home for the first time, he had his first real experience with racial prejudice. Ogden was virtually an all-white community, and members of other races were made to feel unwelcome. No one would rent Robinson a room in a private home, and he had to share a hotel room with teammate Chico Terry, a dark-skinned Latino who spoke little English. It was a depressing time for Robinson, but he made up his mind that he would put up with anything in order to reach the majors.

Robinson's play at Ogden earned him a promotion to the Columbia, South Carolina, Reds in the South Atlantic (Sally) League. In the South, where segregation was still in force, he was subjected to even further indignities. Again, he made up his mind to ignore the distractions and pushed himself to excel. He batted .336 that year and looked so impressive during spring training in 1955 that the Reds named him their starting left fielder. However, Robinson had injured his shoulder playing winter ball and soon found that his ability to throw and swing the bat was severely hampered. He was sent back to Columbia, where he continued to struggle.

Finally, frustrated by his sore shoulder and by the racial taunts of the fans, Robinson was ready to quit baseball. Fortunately, Marv Williams, the only other black player on the team, convinced him to stick with it. Before long his shoulder improved; he tore up the Sally League for the rest of the season, and 1956 found him in left field for the Cincinnati club.

Robinson fulfilled all the Reds' expectations by batting .290, hitting 38 homers, and driving in 83 runs—named to the All-Star team in July, he was a unanimous choice for the National League Rookie of the Year Award. He quickly gained a reputation as a fierce competitor who would slide into bases with his spikes flashing and go out of his way to take out infielders. Opposing players often disliked him, but they also respected him, because he could take punishment as well as dish it out. During his first year, for example, Robinson was hit by pitches 20 times—his only response was to bear down harder and crowd the plate even more.

Each year, Robinson improved as a ballplayer, and by 1959 he was the highest-paid player on the Cincinnati squad. In 1961, he led the team to the National League pennant and was named the league's Most Valuable Player. But away from the playing field, he was treated like a second-class citizen: when he and his wife, Barbara, decided to buy a house, they found that because of the color of their skin they were unwelcome in any of Cincinnati's more affluent neighborhoods.

Though all the Reds players acknowledged Robinson as their leader, his relations with the team's management were often difficult. Each year, Robinson battled for the kind of contract he thought he deserved, and the Reds officials apparently grew tired of his combativeness. After the 1965 season, they traded him to the Baltimore Orioles of the American League.

In some of their public comments, the Reds implied that Robinson was over the hill at the age of 30. He quickly proved them wrong by batting .316, blasting 49 homers, and driving in 122 runs, leading the league in all three categories. More important, his fiery determination drove the Orioles all the way to the world championship. Robinson was named Most Valuable Player for both the regular season and the World Series, becoming the first (and still the only) player in baseball history to win the MVP Award in both leagues.

Robinson had one more ambition to fulfill—he wanted to become baseball's first black manager. He took his first step in 1968, when he was selected to manage the Santurce club in the Puerto Rican winter league. It was not the majors, but it gave Robinson the chance to show that he knew how to run a ball club. He also dispelled the myth, often advanced by opponents of change in baseball, that white players would refuse to take orders from a black manager.

Of course, Robinson was not quite ready to hang up his spikes. He led the Orioles to another world championship in 1970, hit his 500th home run in 1971, and then moved on to the Los Angeles Dodgers and the California Angels as his career began to wind down. Each winter he went back to manage in Puerto Rico, and by this time he was growing impatient when he was passed over for vacant managerial jobs. Finally, while Robinson was playing for the Cleveland Indians in 1975, the break came: the team dismissed its manager and placed Robinson at the helm.

Now that he had realized his ambition, Robinson found managing an often frustrating experience. As a superstar with the Reds and Orioles, he had played the game so hard that the other players had to follow his example. As a manager, however, he had to find other ways of motivating his team. He was puzzled and annoyed when he discovered that few of his players shared his all-out approach to the game. The Indians finished in fourth place in both 1975 and 1976, and when the team got off to a poor start in 1977, Robinson was fired.

Critics of baseball's hiring practices felt that Robinson had not been given a fair chance, and he agreed—but he refused to hang his head. Instead, Robinson managed in Mexico during the winter and went back to the Orioles as a coach. Meanwhile, two other well-qualified African-Americans were offered managerial jobs: Larry Doby with the White Sox and Maury Wills with the Seattle Mariners.

In 1981, the San Francisco Giants offered Robinson another chance to manage, and he repaid their confidence by guiding the team to a first-place finish the following year. For his efforts he was voted National League Manager of the Year. Also in 1982, he was inducted into the Baseball Hall of Fame along with baseball's all-time home-run king, Hank Aaron. After this peak, however, it was all downhill for the Giants. When the team finished last in 1984, Robinson found himself out of a job once again. He returned to the Orioles, first as a coach and then as a front-office official.

With the Orioles spinning their wheels early in the 1988 season, the team asked Robinson to take charge in the dugout. Making use of the experience he had gained in his previous jobs, he had the young team contending for the pennant the following season. Once again, he was named Manager of the Year. But the old maxim that managers are hired to be fired caught up with Robinson again in May 1991, when the Baltimore ownership attempted to charge up a slumping team by changing managers.

Robinson went back into the Baltimore front office—as an assistant general manager—without having fulfilled his ambition to be the first black manager to win a World Series. He will never realize that particular dream because Cito Gaston of the Toronto Blue Jays got there first in 1992. But Gaston's triumph also belonged to Robinson, because once again the former slugger, with his drive and determination, had showed others how to reach the heights.

JACKIE ROBINSON

The first black American to play major league baseball, Jack Roosevelt Robinson was born on January 31, 1919. The grandson of a slave, Jackie was the youngest of five children born to Mallie and Jerry Robinson, who lived a sharecropper's existence in Cairo, Georgia. When Jackie was six months old, his father abandoned the family, and Mallie Robinson moved with her children to Pasadena, California.

While their mother worked as a cleaning woman to support the family, the Robinson children went to school and played sports in their free time. One of the brothers, Mack, became a world-class sprinter and eventually competed in the 1936 Olympics in Berlin, Germany, finishing second to Jesse Owens, who won the gold medal.

As a youth, Jackie associated with a gang of local boys who committed minor offenses. With the intervention of concerned members of his community, Jackie left the gang and volunteered to teach Sunday school at his church. Jackie excelled in athletics at John Muir Technical High School, earning letters in football, basketball, baseball, and track.

His athletic prowess earned him a scholarship to the University of California at Los Angeles, which he entered in 1939. Though Jackie felt out of place at such a wealthy school, he certainly fit in on the playing field, and he became UCLA's first four-letter man. He was the top scorer in the basketball conference two years in a row, won the national championship in the long jump, and was named an all-American halfback in football.

Despite his success in athletics, Jackie left UCLA in the spring of 1941 because he believed an education would not help a black man get a job and he wanted to help relieve some of the financial burden his mother was carrying. He became an athletic director for the National Youth Administration, where he greatly enjoyed working with disadvantaged children.

His career was cut short when he was drafted by the U.S. Army in 1942 and sent to Fort Riley, Kansas, for basic training. Although Robinson was qualified to attend officer candidate school (OCS), he and other capable soldiers were passed over because they were black. Disappointed and disgusted, Robinson complained to Joe Louis, the heavyweight boxing champion, who was also at Fort Riley. Louis used his influence to get Robinson and the other black soldiers admitted to OCS, and in January 1943, Robinson became a second lieutenant.

His new stripes meant little difference in the amount of discrimination Robinson encountered in the army. His problems increased when he was transferred to Fort Hood, Texas, in 1944. He was almost court-martialed for his refusal to sit in the back of a bus he had been riding on, but he was found to be acting within his rights. However, the army labeled him a troublemaker and would not permit him to fight overseas, and he was granted an honorable discharge.

Robinson returned home more defiant than ever and joined the Kansas City Monarchs, a Negro League baseball team. Playing in the Negro Leagues was difficult; living conditions were terrible, players were discriminated against in hotels and restaurants, and talented ballplayers never received the recognition they deserved.

Branch Rickey, the president of the Brooklyn Dodgers, saved Robinson from this obscurity when he persuaded him to leave the Monarchs for the Montreal Royals, the Dodgers' minor league team. One of baseball's most innovative executives, Rickey had decided it was time to break baseball's color barrier, and he was looking for a special player to do the job. The first black man in major league baseball had to be an individual able to deal with the discrimination and abuse he would most certainly encounter, and he must be disciplined enough not to let anything affect his game.

After seeing him play with the Monarchs during the summer of 1945, Rickey decided that Jackie Robinson was the man he was looking for and offered the ballplayer a starting salary of $600 a month and a signing bonus of $3,500. Robinson received a bonus in his personal life when he married Rachel Isum—whom he had first met in 1940 while they were both students at UCLA—in the winter of 1946.

In April 1946, Robinson made his minor league debut with the Montreal Royals against the Jersey City Giants. The stands were packed with fans who saw Robinson hit a three-run home run and steal two bases, helping the Royals to victory over the Giants. Robinson continued his high level of play and became a popular sports figure in the Royals' hometown.

Outside Canada, people reacted quite differently to the rising young star. Racial slurs were thrown at him during games by fans and players alike, and he was pulled from games due to laws prohibiting interracial athletics. These incidents began to take their toll on the young player, and the pressure caused him to fall into a hitting slump. The Montreal fans, however, came to the ballpark to root for Robinson, and their support helped him shake out of his slump and lead his team to the league championship.

Rickey decided it was time to move Robinson to the major leagues, and on April 15, 1947, Jackie stepped up to the plate as a major league player for the first time. At first his performance was mediocre, and fans as well as Robinson's fellow players doubted whether he was ready for the big time.

During a game with the Philadelphia Phillies, Robinson was shocked by a constant stream of racial epithets from the Phillies' dugout. Robinson's calm and poise in the face of this onslaught won him the respect of his teammates as well as the New York sportswriters, who condemned the Phillies' players for their behavior.

Support from his teammates and the fans helped Robinson improve his performance on the field. Black fans in particular flocked to the ballpark to see Robinson play. Robinson helped his team win the National League championship that year, and although the Dodgers lost the World Series to their rivals, the New York Yankees, Robinson was honored with the title of Rookie of the Year.

Robinson's variety of skills soon made him one of the best players in the game. A fine hitter under any circumstances who batted over .300 lifetime, he became even more difficult to retire in clutch situations. In 1949, he led the league in batting. In the field, Robinson possessed the versatility and intelligence to play several different positions superbly; though primarily a second baseman, he played often at third base, first base, and the outfield as well.

But Robinson was at his absolute best on the base paths. Powerfully built, at nearly six feet tall and almost 200 pounds, he was one of the game's swiftest runners, and the sight of him dancing recklessly off base in his peculiar pigeon-toed gate, defying the opposition to hold him close, soon became one of the game's most thrilling sights. He twice led the league in stolen bases, exhibiting an exceedingly rare ability to swipe home as well as an aptitude for escaping rundowns.

Taken as a whole, Robinson's skills helped make the Dodgers a perennial National League powerhouse, and in 1949 he was voted the league's Most Valuable Player. As he settled into consistent excellence on the field, his home life also became more settled when he and his wife, Rachel, moved to a suburb in St. Albans, New York, with their son, Jackie, Jr., and their daughter, Sharon.

Robinson's happiness was marred by the retirement of Branch Rickey as president of the Dodgers. The new president, Walter O'Malley, resented Robinson for Jackie's continued loyalty to Rickey. The two had a strained relationship throughout Robinson's years on the team.

After his rookie year, Robinson became one of the most outspoken athletes of the time. While he was normally respectful and soft-spoken, he refused to remain silent when he thought he was being treated unfairly. Supported by Ford Frick, the baseball commissioner, Robinson felt free to speak out on any racial issues he felt needed to be addressed.

In 1955, the Dodgers finally beat the New York Yankees in the World Series, earning their only world championship. The following year was Robinson's last as a major league player and the last for the Dodgers in Brooklyn, as O'Malley decided to move the team west, to Los Angeles.

After his retirement, Robinson became the vice-president of community relations for the Chock Full O'Nuts coffee company. He enjoyed his work in building up the company's name and reputation within the community. He became more active in politics, business, and the civil rights movement and became a spokesman for the NAACP. In January 1962, he was inducted into the Baseball Hall of Fame.

Jackie Robinson died of a heart attack on October 24, 1972. His outstanding athletic ability, inner strength, and immense personal dignity had allowed him to triumph over racial prejudice; he remains a model to all those who fight to see their dreams and the dreams of others become reality.

BILL RUSSELL

The first black American to become coach of a National Basketball Association (NBA) team was born William Felton Russell on February 12, 1934, in Monroe, Louisiana.

Young Bill Russell was a member of a tightly knit family. His father, known as Mister Charlie, worked for a paper bag company and was respected within Monroe's black community for his willingness to stand firm for his beliefs. Mrs. Russell, the former Katie King, was as strong willed as her husband and very affectionate with Bill and his older brother, Charlie. Both parents stressed the importance of education and encouraged their two sons to concentrate on their schoolwork.

Life in the Deep South was not easy for blacks, especially strong-willed people like the Russells. After a gas-station attendant pointed a rifle at him for not being more respectful to whites, Mister Charlie decided to move his family to Oakland, California, where he and his wife took jobs in a shipyard. The family moved into an ostensibly integrated housing project—blacks lived in one section, whites in another—where Bill first learned to play basketball.

After his mother died from influenza in the fall of 1946, young Bill grew subdued and introverted, and he spent much of his time reading. His withdrawal grew more profound with his failure to make any sports teams at Hoover Junior High School. But at the age of 16, the boy experienced a surge of confidence, and he decided to try out for the junior varsity basketball team at McClymonds High School, where Charlie had been a star athlete.

Although Bill was awkward and largely unskilled, the team's coach, George Powles, worked with him and encouraged him to practice to improve his game. Though Bill excelled in drills that required only running and jumping, he had problems with ball handling. Still, as the result of much practice, by his junior year he had earned a spot on the varsity team.

Russell's game improved during his senior year, and even though he was still only a mediocre player, he was part of a winning basketball team. After graduating in January 1952, he was chosen for a team of high school all-stars that toured the Pacific Northwest. Now six feet five inches tall and 160 pounds, Russell learned much from watching his teammates. He mastered the art of rebounding and taught himself to excel on defense.

Upon his return to Oakland after the all-star tour, Russell became an apprentice sheet-metal worker at the San Francisco Naval Yard. In his spare time, he played in pickup basketball games in local schoolyards, and his game improved dramatically. Soon a scout who had seen him play arranged for him to receive a scholarship to the University of San Francisco (USF).

At USF, Russell took full advantage of the many opportunities open to him. His primary emphasis was his education, but he also found time to work on his game, receiving special help in that regard from his coach, Phil Woolpert, and his roommate and teammate K. C. Jones.

In a very short time, Russell became a very fine player indeed, the best "big man" in the country and the primary reason why USF was able to win national championships in 1955 and 1956. Though an adept player at the collegiate level who scored over 20 points a game, Russell was at best a merely adequate shooter who truly dominated games through rebounding and defense, especially the blocked shot, which as a component of his game was as much psychological tactic as physical feat. Russell might only block a few shots in any game, but his uncanny timing made opponents always aware of his presence on the court. Before him, the game's big men had generally been plodding, mechanical, earthbound players. Russell, by contrast, was frighteningly quick and a great jumper, an unprecedented combination of size and athleticism.

Russell also possessed a superb understanding of the dynamics of team basketball, an insight that would make him the winningest player ever to lace up a pair of sneakers. He followed his two national championships at USF with a stint as a member (with K. C. Jones) of the U.S. Olympic team that copped the gold medal at Melbourne, Australia, in autumn 1956. His winning streak continued after his return to the United States when, on December 9, 1956, he married Rose Swisher and then joined the Boston Celtics of the NBA. The rookie then carried the Celtics to their first championship.

Though Russell and the Celtics relinquished their crown the following year, when a sprained ankle kept him on the sidelines for the finals, with the 1958–59 season he and his teammates (who included his old friend K. C. Jones) began an unprecedented (and still unmatched) streak of eight consecutive NBA championships. That run came to an end in 1967, but the Celtics returned to the top in 1968 and remained there until Russell retired as a player following the 1968–69 season. In his 13 years in the NBA, Russell and the Celtics won the championship 11 times, a record of success unmatched by any individual or team. During those 13 years, Russell's surrounding cast changed several times, leaving him as the one constant in the Celtics' success. He was voted the NBA's Most Valuable Player (MVP) five times.

Off the court, Russell was an equally influential athlete. His public campaign against racism began with a personal slight: despite winning the league's MVP Award for the 1957–58 season, Russell was left off the NBA's all-league team as a result, he believed, of racial prejudice on the part of the selectors. (Though the NBA had been integrated in 1950—the Celtics had been the first team to sign a black player— the league was still, in the late 1950s, a predominantly white institution.)

Russell soon turned his attention to off-court racism. An outspoken advocate of the civil rights movement at a time when few prominent athletes were willing to take positions on social issues, Russell took part in the March on Washington in 1963 and participated in numerous civil rights demonstrations in the South. He also challenged the self-satisfaction of white fans who cheered his every move in the Boston Garden when he publicly proclaimed Boston to be the most racist city in America and delineated the examples of the prejudice he and his family had endured despite his somewhat privileged social status.

Despite his uncompromising positions, Russell was rewarded for 10 years of exceptional service to the Celtics in 1966, when he was asked to succeed the legendary Boston mastermind, Arnold "Red" Auerbach, as coach of the team. The appointment was testimony to Russell's fierce pride, unyielding will to win, and comprehensive knowledge of the game; even so, he realized that as the first black head coach in the history of the NBA, he would be regarded as having much to prove.

As a coach, Russell was most fortunate in one key regard: he could still call on his own services as a player. Still, his dual responsibilities—as a player, he had to concentrate on his own game, and as coach, he also had to concentrate on the job his teammates were doing—required some adjustment on the part of himself and his teammates. Despite 60 regular-season victories, in his first year at the helm the Celtics' long string of championships came to an end at the hands of the Philadelphia 76ers, led by Wilt Chamberlain, Russell's great rival over much of his career.

Russell and the Celtics were vindicated the following year when they beat the 76ers and reclaimed the NBA title. Off the court, Russell continued his fight against racial prejudice, but his many hours away from his family took a toll on his family life, and he and his wife separated in 1969. That year, the aging Celtics, despite a poor fourth-place finish in the regular season, regrouped in the playoffs, allowing Russell to claim his final championship. Worn out, he retired as both player and coach and moved to Los Angeles, where he landed several cameo roles on various television shows. He also did a number of very well received lecture tours of the United States.

He made his return to the game in the early 1970s as an analyst on national-television basketball broadcasts, a capacity in which he eventually served for three networks. During this time, he also began to be awarded various honors for his playing career.

Though the recognition made him uncomfortable—he had played for the pleasure of the game, he said, not for personal rewards—the honors continued nonetheless. In spite of his protests, his uniform was retired by the Boston Celtics in March 1972, and he was inducted into the Basketball Hall of Fame in 1974.

Despite initial hesitation, in 1973, Russell returned to the NBA as coach and general manager of the Seattle SuperSonics. Though Seattle initially experienced some success under his tutelage, Russell found it difficult to relate to the new generation of professional basketball players, and he left the franchise in 1977 to resume his broadcasting and lecturing careers. His second autobiography, *Second Wind*, was published in 1979, 13 years after his first autobiography, *Go Up for Glory*.

Though a coaching and executive stint with the Sacramento Kings in the late 1980s proved disastrously unsuccessful, Bill Russell's winning legacy remains the standard by which every new, would-be basketball champion is still measured.

Alvin Ailey

Haskings, James. *Black Dance in America.* New York: HarperCollins, 1990.

Mazo, Joseph H. *The Alvin Ailey American Dance Theater.* New York: Morrow, 1978.

Probosz, Kathilyn Solomon. *Alvin Ailey, Jr.* New York: Bantam Skylark, 1991.

Richard Allen

Frazier, Edward Franklin. *The Negro Church in America.* New York: Schocken Books, 1974.

Klots, Steve. *Richard Allen.* New York: Chelsea House, 1991.

Marian Anderson

Anderson, Marian. *My Lord, What a Morning.* New York: Viking, 1956.

Sims, Janet L. *Marian Anderson: An Annotated Bibliography and Discography.* Westport, CT: Greenwood Press, 1981.

Tedards, Anne. *Marian Anderson.* New York: Chelsea House, 1988.

Maya Angelou

Angelou, Maya. *I Know Why the Caged Bird Sings.* New York: Random House, 1970.

———. *Just Give Me a Cool Drink of Water 'Fore I Diiie.* New York: Random House, 1971.

Shapiro, Miles. *Maya Angelou.* New York: Chelsea House, 1994.

Louis Armstrong

Armstrong, Louis. *My Life in New Orleans.* New York: Da Capo Press, 1986.

Collier, James Lincoln. *Louis Armstrong: An American Genius.* New York: Oxford University Press, 1983.

Tanenhaus, Sam. *Louis Armstrong.* New York: Chelsea House, 1989.

Arthur Ashe

Ashe, Arthur. *A Hard Road to Glory: A History of the African-American Athlete.* 3 vols. New York: Warner Books, 1988.

Ashe, Arthur, with Neil Amdur. *Off the Court.* New York: New American Library, 1981.

Weissberg, Ted. *Arthur Ashe.* New York: Chelsea House, 1991.

Josephine Baker

Papich, Stephen. *Remembering Josephine.* Indianapolis: Bobbs-Merrill, 1976.

Rose, Phyllis. *Jazz Cleopatra: Josephine Baker in Her Time.* New York: Doubleday, 1989.

Schroeder, Alan. *Josephine Baker.* New York: Chelsea House, 1991.

James Baldwin

Baldwin, James. *Go Tell It on the Mountain.* New York: Dell, 1985.

———. *Notes of a Native Son.* New York: Beacon Press, 1984.

Rosset, Lisa. *James Baldwin.* New York: Chelsea House, 1989.

Benjamin Banneker

Bedini, Silvio A. *The Life of Benjamin Banneker.* New York: Scribners, 1971.

Conley, Kevin. *Benjamin Banneker.* New York: Chelsea House, 1989.

Ferris, Jeri. *What Are You Figuring Now? A Story About Benjamin Banneker.* Minneapolis: Carolrhoda, 1988.

Count Basie

Dance, Stanley. *The World of Count Basie.* New York: Da Capo Press, 1980.

Kliment, Bud. *Count Basie.* New York: Chelsea House, 1992.

Morgun, Alun. *Count Basie.* New York: Hippocrene Books, 1984.

James Beckwourth

Beckwourth, James P., and T. D. Bonner. *The Life and Adventures of James P. Beckwourth, Mountaineer, Scout, Pioneer, and Chief of the Crow Nation.* 1856. Reprint. Lincoln: University of Nebraska Press, 1972.

Dolan, Sean. *James Beckwourth.* New York: Chelsea House, 1992.

Wilson, Elinor. *Jim Beckwourth: Black Mountain Man, War Chief of the Crows, Trader, Trapper, Explorer, Frontiersman, Guide, Scout, Interpreter, Adventurer, and Gaudy Liar.* Norman: University of Oklahoma Press, 1972.

Mary McLeod Bethune

Franklin, John H., and August Meier, eds. *Black Leaders of the Twentieth Century.* Urbana: University of Illinois Press, 1982.

Halasa, Malu. *Mary McLeod Bethune.* New York: Chelsea House, 1989.

Meltzer, Milton. *Mary McLeod Bethune: Voice of Black Hope.* New York: Viking, 1987.

Guion Bluford

Haskins, James, and Kathleen Benson. *Space Challenger: The Story of Guion Bluford.* Minneapolis: Carolrhoda Books, 1984.

Gwendolyn Brooks

Brooks, Gwendolyn. *Annie Allen.* 1949. Reprint. Westport, CT: Greenwood, 1972.

———. *Selected Poems.* New York: Harper & Row, 1963.

———. *The World of Gwendolyn Brooks.* New York: Harper & Row, 1971.

Blanche K. Bruce

Christopher, Maurine. *America's Black Congressmen.* New York: Thomas Y. Crowell, 1971.

St. Clair, Sadie Daniel. *The National Career of Blanche Kelso Bruce.* New York: New York University Press, 1947.

Ralph Bunche

Haskins, James. *Ralph Bunche: A Most Reluctant Hero.* New York: Hawthorn Books, 1974.

Mann, Peggy. *Ralph Bunche: U.N. Peacemaker.* New York: Coward, McCann & Geoghegan, 1975.

Rivlin, Benjamin, ed. *Ralph Bunche: The Man and His Times.* New York: Holmes & Meir, 1990.

George Washington Carver

Adair, Gene. *George Washington Carver.* New York: Chelsea House, 1989.

Kremer, Gary R. *George Washington Carver: In His Own Words.* Columbia: University of Missouri Press, 1986.

McMurry, Linda O. *George Washington Carver: Scientist and Symbol.* New York: Oxford University Press, 1981.

Charles Chesnutt

Chesnutt, Charles W. *The Conjure Woman.* Ann Arbor: University of Michigan Press, 1969.

———. *The Wife of His Youth and Other Stories of the Color Line.* Ann Arbor: University of Michigan Press, 1968.

Thompson, Cliff. *Charles Chesnutt.* New York: Chelsea House, 1992.

Shirley Chisholm

Chisholm, Shirley. *The Good Fight.* New York: Harper & Row, 1973.

———. *Unbought and Unbossed.* New York: Houghton Mifflin, 1970.

Scheader, Catherine. *Shirley Chisholm: Teacher and Congresswoman.* Hillside, NJ: Enslow, 1990.

John Coltrane

Selfridge, John. *John Coltrane.* New York: Chelsea House, 1995.

Simpkins, C. O. *Coltrane.* Baltimore: Black Classic Press, 1989.

Thomas, J. C. *Chasin' the Trane.* New York: Da Capo Press, 1976.

Chuck Cooper

George, Nelson. *Elevating the Game: The History and Aesthetics of Black Men in Basketball.* New York: Simon & Schuster, 1992.

Bill Cosby

Adams, Barbara Johnston. *The Picture Life of Bill Cosby.* New York: Watts, 1986.

Cosby, Bill. *Fatherhood.* New York: Doubleday, 1986.

Haskins, Jim. *Bill Cosby: America's Most Famous Father.* Houston: Walker, 1988.

Herbert, Solomon J., and George H. Hill. *Bill Cosby.* New York: Chelsea House, 1992.

Benjamin O. Davis, Sr., and Benjamin O. Davis, Jr.

Davis, Benjamin O., Jr. *Benjamin O. Davis, Jr., American: An Autobiography.* Washington, D.C.: Smithsonian Institution, 1991.

Fletcher, Marvin. *America's First Black General: Benjamin O. Davis, Sr., 1880–1970.* Kansas: University Press of Kansas, 1989.

Frederick Douglass

Quarles, Benjamin. *Frederick Douglass.* New York: Atheneum, 1976.

Russell, Sharman. *Frederick Douglass.* New York: Chelsea House, 1988.

Sundquist, Eric J., ed. *Frederick Douglass: New Literary and Historical Essays.* New York: Cambridge University Press, 1990.

Charles Drew

Lichello, Robert. *Pioneer in Blood Plasma: Dr. Charles Richard Drew.* New York: Simon & Schuster, 1968.

Mahone-Lonesome, Robyn. *Charles Drew.* New York: Chelsea House, 1990.

Wynes, Charles E. *Charles Richard Drew: The Man and the Myth.* Urbana: University of Illinois Press, 1988.

W. E. B. Du Bois

Aptheker, Herbert, ed. *Annotated Bibliography of the Published Writings of W. E. B. Du Bois.* Millwood, NY: Kraus-Thomson, 1973.

Du Bois, W. E. B. *The Souls of Black Folk: Essays and Sketches.* 1903. Reprint. New York: Vintage Books/Library of America, 1990.

Stafford, Mark. *W. E. B. Du Bois.* New York: Chelsea House, 1989.

Paul Laurence Dunbar

Dunbar, Paul Laurence. *The Complete Poems of Paul Laurence Dunbar.* New York: Dodd, Mead, 1980.

———. *The Uncalled.* 1898. Reprint. New York: Irvington, n.d.

Gentry, Tony. *Paul Laurence Dunbar.* New York: Chelsea House, 1989.

Katherine Dunham

Dominy, Jeannine. *Katherine Dunham.* New York: Chelsea House, 1992.

Dunham, Katherine. *Dances of Haiti.* Los Angeles: Center for Afro-American Studies, University of California, Los Angeles, 1983.

———. *A Touch of Innocence.* New York: Books for Libraries, 1980.

Marian Wright Edelman

Edelman, Marian Wright. *The Measure of Our Success: A Letter to My Children and Yours.* Boston: Beacon Press, 1992.

Tomkins, Calvin. "Profiles: A Sense of Urgency." *New Yorker,* March 1989, 48–74.

Duke Ellington

Collier, James Lincoln. *Duke Ellington.* New York: Oxford University Press, 1987.

Ellington, Mercer. *Duke Ellington in Person.* Boston: Houghton Mifflin, 1978.

Frankl, Ron. *Duke Ellington.* New York: Chelsea House, 1988.

Ralph Ellison

Bishop, Jack. *Ralph Ellison*. New York: Chelsea House, 1988.

Ellison, Ralph. *Invisible Man*. New York: Random House, 1952.

Ella Fitzgerald

Colin, Sid. *The Life and Times of Ella Fitzgerald*. London: Elm Tree Books, 1986.

Kliment, Bud. *Ella Fitzgerald*. New York: Chelsea House, 1988.

Marcus Garvey

Garvey, Amy Jacques, ed. *Philosophy and Opinions of Marcus Garvey*. New York: Atheneum, 1986.

Lawler, Mary. *Marcus Garvey*. New York: Chelsea House, 1988.

Nembhard, Len S. *Trials and Triumphs of Marcus Garvey*. New York: Kraus Reprint Co., 1978.

Althea Gibson

Biracree, Tom. *Althea Gibson*. New York: Chelsea House, 1989.

Gibson, Althea. *I Always Wanted To Be Somebody*. New York: Harper & Brothers, 1958.

———. *So Much To Live For*. New York: Putnam, 1968.

Dizzy Gillespie

Gentry, Tony. *Dizzy Gillespie*. New York: Chelsea House, 1991.

Gillespie, Dizzy, with Al Fraser. *To Be or Not To Bop*. New York: Doubleday, 1979.

Horricks, Raymond. *Dizzy Gillespie*. New York: Hippocrene Books, 1984.

Nikki Giovanni

Giovanni, Nikki. *Black Feeling, Black Talk*. New York: Morrow, 1970.

———. *Gemini: An Extended Autobiographical Statement on My First Twenty-five Years of Being a Black Poet*. New York: Penguin Books, 1976.

Alex Haley

Haley, Alex. *The Autobiography of Malcolm X*. New York: Grove Press, 1965.

———. *Roots: The Saga of an American Family*. New York: Doubleday, 1976.

Shirley, David. *Alex Haley*. New York: Chelsea House, 1994.

Lorraine Hansberry

Hansberry, Lorraine. *A Raisin in the Sun*. New York: Random House, 1969.

Nemiroff, Robert, ed. *Lorraine Hansberry: The Collected Last Plays*. New York: Plume, 1983.

William H. Hastie

Ware, Gilbert. *William Hastie: Grace Under Pressure*. New York: Oxford University Press, 1984.

Matthew Henson

Dolan, Edward F. *Matthew Henson, Black Explorer*. New York: Dodd, Mead, 1979.

Gilman, Michael. *Matthew Henson*. New York: Chelsea House, 1988.

Robinson, Bradley, with Matthew Henson. *Dark Companion*. New York: McBride, 1947.

Chester Himes

Himes, Chester. *My Life of Absurdity*. New York: Doubleday, 1972.

———. *A Rage in Harlem*. London: Allison and Busby England, 1985.

Wilson, M. L. *Chester Himes*. New York: Chelsea House, 1988.

Billie Holiday

Holiday, Billie, with William Dufty. *Lady Sings the Blues*. New York: Penguin Books, 1984.

Kliment, Bud. *Billie Holiday*. New York: Chelsea House, 1984.

White, John. *Billie Holiday: Her Life and Times.* New York: Universe, 1987.

Lena Horne

Buckley, Gail Lumet. *The Hornes: An American Family.* New York: Knopf, 1986.

Lanker, Brian. *I Dream a World: Portraits of Black Women Who Changed America.* New York: Stewart, Tabori and Chang, 1989.

Palmer, Leslie. *Lena Horne.* New York: Chelsea House, 1989.

Langston Hughes

Huggins, Nathan. *Voices from the Harlem Renaissance.* New York: Oxford University Press, 1976.

Hughes, Langston. *Selected Poetry of Langston Hughes.* New York: Knopf, 1959.

Rummel, Jack. *Langston Hughes.* New York: Chelsea House, 1988.

Zora Neale Hurston

Hurston, Zora Neale. *Their Eyes Were Watching God.* Urbana: University of Illinois Press, 1978.

Walker, Alice, ed. *I Love Myself When I Am Laughing . . . & Then Again When I Am Looking Mean & Impressive: A Zora Neale Hurston Reader.* New York: Harcourt Brace Jovanovich, 1979.

Witcover, Paul. *Zora Neale Hurston.* New York: Chelsea House, 1991.

Jesse Jackson

Colton, Elizabeth. *The Jackson Phenomenon.* New York: Doubleday, 1989.

Jakoubek, Robert E. *Jesse Jackson.* New York: Chelsea House, 1991.

Landess, Thomas H. *Jesse Jackson and the Politics of Race.* Ottawa, IL: Jameson Books, 1985.

Jack Johnson

Jakoubek, Robert. *Jack Johnson.* New York: Chelsea House, 1990.

Johnson, Jack. *Jack Johnson Is a Dandy.* New York: Chelsea House, 1969.

Roberts, Randy. *Papa Jack: Jack Johnson and the Era of White Hopes.* New York: Free Press, 1983.

James Weldon Johnson

Fleming, Robert E. *James Weldon Johnson & Arna Wendell Bontemps.* Boston: G. K. Hall, 1987.

Johnson, James Weldon. *Negro Americans, What Now?* New York: AMS Press, 1971.

Tolbert-Rochaleau, Jane. *James Weldon Johnson.* New York: Chelsea House, 1988.

Barbara Jordan

Blue, Rose, and Corinne Naden. *Barbara Jordan.* New York: Chelsea House, 1992.

Haskins, James. *Barbara Jordan.* New York: Dial Press, 1977.

Jordan, Barbara, and Shelby Hearon. *Barbara Jordan: A Self-Portrait.* New York: Doubleday, 1979.

Ernest Everett Just

Manning, Kenneth R. *Black Apollo of Science.* New York: Oxford University Press, 1983.

Coretta Scott King

Garrow, David J. *Bearing the Cross: Martin Luther King, Jr., and the Southern Leadership Conference.* New York: Morrow, 1986.

King, Coretta Scott. *My Life with Martin Luther King, Jr.* New York: Holt, Rinehart & Winston, 1969.

Martin Luther King, Jr.

Branch, Taylor. *Parting the Waters: America in the King Years 1954–63.* New York: Simon & Schuster, 1988.

Jakoubek, Robert. *Martin Luther King, Jr.* New York: Chelsea House, 1989.

King, Coretta Scott. *My Life with Martin Luther King, Jr.* New York: Holt, Rinehart & Winston, 1969.

Lewis Latimer

Norman, Winifred Latimer, and Lily Patterson. *Lewis Latimer.* New York: Chelsea House, 1994.

Turner, Glennette Tilley. *Lewis Howard Latimer.* Englewood Cliffs, NJ: Silver Burdett Press, 1991.

Malcolm X

Davies, Mark. *Malcolm X.* Englewood Cliffs, NJ: Silver Burdett Press, 1990.

Gallen, David. *Malcolm X.* New York: Carroll & Graf, 1992.

Rummel, Jack. *Malcolm X.* New York: Chelsea House, 1989.

Thurgood Marshall

Aldred, Lisa. *Thurgood Marshall.* New York: Chelsea House, 1990.

Haskins, James. *Thurgood Marshall: A Life for Justice.* New York: H. H. Holt, 1992.

Hess, Debra. *Thurgood Marshall: The Fight for Equal Justice.* Englewood Cliffs, NJ: Silver Burdett Press, 1992.

Toni Morrison

Century, Douglas. *Toni Morrison.* New York: Chelsea House, 1994.

Morrison, Toni. *Beloved.* New York: Plume, 1987.

————. *Jazz.* Boston: G. K. Hall 1993.

Carol Moseley-Braun

"Braun Pauses for Thanks After a Rocky Campaign." *USA Today,* November 4, 1992, A8.

Clay, William L. *Just Permanent Interests: Black Americans in Congress, 1870–1991.* New York: Penguin, 1992.

Haynes, Karima A. "Will Carol Moseley Braun Be the First Black Woman Senator? *Ebony,* June 1992, 120–22.

Ragsdale, Bruce, and Joel D. Treese, eds. *Black Americans in Congress, 1870–1989.* Washington, D.C.: Government Printing Office, 1990.

Wilkerson, Isabel. "Storming Senate 'Club': Carol Elizabeth Moseley Braun." *New York Times,* March 19, 1992, A20.

Jesse Owens

Gentry, Tony. *Jesse Owens.* New York: Chelsea House, 1990.

Owens, Jesse. *I Have Changed.* New York: Morrow, 1972.

————. *Jesse: A Spiritual Autobiography.* Plainfield, NJ: Logos International, 1978.

Charlie Parker

Frankl, Ron. *Charlie Parker.* New York: Chelsea House, 1993.

Giddins, Gary. *Celebrating Bird: The Triumph of Charlie Parker.* New York: Morrow, 1987.

Priestley, Brian. *Charlie Parker.* New York: Hippocrene Books, 1984.

Rosa Parks

Branch, Taylor. *Parting the Waters: America in the King Years 1954–1963.* New York: Simon & Schuster, 1988.

Parks, Rosa, with Jim Haskins. *Rosa Parks: My Story.* New York: Dial Books, 1992.

Robinson, Jo Ann. *The Montgomery Bus Boycott and the Women Who Started It.* Nashville: University of Tennessee Press, 1987.

Sidney Poitier

Bergman, Carol. *Sidney Poitier.* New York: Chelsea House, 1988.

Keyser, Lester J. *The Cinema of Sidney Poitier.* New York: Barnes, 1980.

Poitier, Sidney. *This Life.* New York: Ballantine/Knopf, 1980.

Adam Clayton Powell, Jr.

Hamilton, Charles V. *Adam Clayton Powell, Jr.* New York: Atheneum, 1991.

Haskins, James. *Adam Clayton Powell: Portrait of a Marching Black*. New York: Dial Press, 1974.

Colin Powell

Adler, Bill. *The Generals: The New American Heroes*. New York: Avon Books, 1991.

Binkin, Martin, and Mark J. Eitelberg. *Blacks in the Military*. Washington, D.C.: Brookins Institution, 1982.

Brown, Warren. *Colin Powell*. New York: Chelsea House, 1992.

Asa Philip Randolph

Anderson, Jervis. *A. Philip Randolph: A Biographical Portrait*. Berkeley: University of California Press, 1986.

Garfinkel, Herbert. *When Negroes March: The March on Washington Movement in the Organizational Politics for FEPC*. New York: Atheneum, 1969.

Hanley, Sally. *A. Philip Randolph*. New York: Chelsea House, 1989.

Paul Robeson

Ehrlich, Scott. *Paul Robeson*. New York: Chelsea House, 1988.

Robeson, Paul. *Here I Stand*. Boston: Beacon Press, 1971.

Robeson, Susan. *The Whole World in His Hands*. Secaucus, NJ: Citadel Press, 1981.

Frank Robinson

Macht, Norman L. *Frank Robinson*. New York: Chelsea House, 1991.

Robinson, Frank, and Dave Anderson. *Frank: The First Year*. New York: Holt, Rinehart & Winston, 1976.

Robinson, Frank, and Berry Stainback. *Extra Innings*. New York: McGraw-Hill, 1988.

Jackie Robinson

Frommer, Harvey. *Jackie Robinson*. New York: Franklin Watts, 1984.

Robinson, Jackie. *I Never Had It Made*. New York: Putnam, 1972.

Scott, Richard. *Jackie Robinson*. New York: Chelsea House, 1987.

Bill Russell

Russell, Bill, and Taylor Branch. *Second Wind: Memoirs of an Opinionated Man*. New York: Random House, 1979.

Sojourner Truth

Corbin, Carole L. *The Right To Vote*. New York: Franklin Watts, 1985.

Dunster, Mark. *Sojourner Truth*. Fresno, CA: Linden Publications, 1983.

Krass, Peter. *Sojourner Truth*. New York: Chelsea House, 1988.

Harriet Tubman

Blockson, Charles L. *The Underground Railroad*. New York: Prentice Hall, 1987.

McPherson, James M. *Battle Cry of Freedom*. New York: Oxford University Press, 1988.

Taylor, M. W. *Harriet Tubman*. New York: Chelsea House, 1991.

Alice Walker

Gentry, Tony. *Alice Walker*. New York: Chelsea House, 1993.

Walker, Alice. *The Color Purple*. New York: Harcourt Brace Jovanovich, 1982.

———. *Possessing the Secret of Joy*. New York: Simon & Schuster, 1992.

Madam C. J. Walker

Bundles, A'Lelia Perry. *Madam C. J. Walker.* New York: Chelsea House, 1991.

Booker T. Washington

Harlan, Louis R. *Booker T. Washington: The Wizard of Tuskegee, 1901–1915.* New York: Oxford University Press, 1983.

Schroeder, Alan. *Booker T. Washington.* New York: Chelsea House, 1992.

Washington, Booker T. *Up from Slavery.* 1901. Reprint. New York: Viking Penguin, 1986.

Ida B. Wells-Barnett

Neverdon-Morton, Cynthia. *Afro-American Women of the South and the Advancement of Race, 1895–1925.* Nashville: University of Tennessee Press, 1989.

Phillis Wheatley

Mason, Julian D., Jr. *The Poems of Phillis Wheatley.* Chapel Hill: The University of North Carolina Press, 1966.

Richmond, Merle. *Phillis Wheatley.* New York: Chelsea House, 1988.

Shields, John, ed. *The Collected Works of Phillis Wheatley.* New York: Oxford University Press, 1988.

Walter White

Fraser, Jane. *Walter White.* New York: Chelsea House, 1991.

Waldron, Edward E. *Walter White and the Harlem Renaissance.* Port Washington, NY: Kennikat Press, 1978.

White, Walter. *How Far the Promised Land?* New York: Viking, 1955.

L. Douglas Wilder

Baker, Donald P. *Wilder: Hold Fast to Dreams.* Cabin John, MD: Seven Locks Press, 1989.

Edds, Margaret. *Claiming the Dream: The Victorious Campaign of Douglas Wilder of Virginia.* Chapel Hill, NC: Algonquin Books of Chapel Hill, 1990.

Yancey, Dwayne. *When Hell Froze Over: The Untold Story of Doug Wilder, a Black Politician's Rise to Power in the South.* Dallas: Taylor Publishing, 1990.

Richard Wright

Urban, Joan. *Richard Wright.* New York: Chelsea House, 1989.

Wright, Richard. *Black Boy.* 1945. Reprint. New York: Harper & Row, 1969.

———. *Native Son.* 1940. Reprint. New York: Harper & Row, 1969.

❧ PICTURE CREDITS ❧

RICHARD RENNERT has edited the nearly 100 volumes in Chelsea House's award-winning BLACK AMERICANS OF ACHIEVEMENT series, which tells the stories of black men and women who have helped shape the course of modern history. He is also the author of several sports biographies, including *Henry Aaron*, *Jesse Owens*, and *Jackie Robinson*. He is a graduate of Haverford College in Haverford, Pennsylvania.